John Gottlieb Morris

ENGRAVED BY JOHN SARTAIN, FROM A DAGUERREOTYPE
BY POLLOCK.

Yours very sincerely

Jno G Morris

John Gottlieb Morris

Man of God, Man of Science

MICHAEL J. KURTZ

MARYLAND HISTORICAL SOCIETY
BALTIMORE

MARYLAND HISTORICAL SOCIETY
201 West Monument Street
Baltimore, Maryland 21201

Founded 1844

First Edition

Manufactured in the United States of America

ISBN 0-938420-58-5

LC Cataloging in Publication Data

Kurtz, Michael J., 1949-
    John Gottlieb Morris : man of God, man of science / Michael J.
Kurtz.
      p.   cm.
    Includes bibliographical references and index.
    ISBN 0-938420-58-5 (alk. paper)
    1. Morris, John G. (John Gottlieb), 1803-1895. 2. Lutheran
Church—Maryland—Baltimore—Clergy—Biography.
3. Baltimore (Md.)—Biography. I. Title.
BX8080.M6K87 1997
284.1'092—dc21
[B]   97-10282
                                     CIP

∞ The paper used in this publication meets the minimum
requirements of the American National Standard for Information Sciences—
Permanence of Paper for Printed Library Materials, ANSI Z39.48-1984.

Cover and frontispiece illustration:
John Gottlieb Morris circa 1850; engraving by John Sartain
from a daguerreotype by Henry Pollack, Baltimore.
(Maryland Historical Society.)

To
Cherie Loustaunau
and
Florence G. Ronquist
without whose support
and encouragement
I could not have
completed this book.

History is the essence
of innumerable biographies.

THOMAS CARLYLE

Contents

Preface

I discovered John Gottlieb Morris almost ten years ago when I was conducting research in preparation for a lecture series on the history of First English Lutheran Church in Baltimore, Maryland. From the outset, I was fascinated with Morris, the congregation's first pastor. The range of his intellectual interests—theology, natural science, history, education, and cultural institution building—had a Renaissance quality.

A deeper look at the man revealed prodigious accomplishments in all of his endeavors, which spanned a life lasting nearly ninety-two years. To truly appreciate this man meant mastering his contributions to the story of nineteenth-century American cultural progress. Here was a life worth remembering. Thus the genesis of this biography.

As Morris's biographer, I found his productivity a somewhat mixed blessing. He left a voluminous amount of letters, articles, pamphlets, and books which revealed the breadth of his professional work, and these took far longer to absorb and analyze than I ever imagined. But, more importantly, Morris's letters, autobiographical writings, and the extant portions of his diaries revealed a driven, passionate, and complex man.

Reconciling John G. Morris's public and private personas proved the most difficult and fascinating of my biographical tasks. Though the source materials reveal much about Pastor Morris and his dealings with colleagues, friends, and foes, we find very little concerning those closest to him, the Morris family. A diary covering the mid-1850s through the mid-1860s, kept by one of the his daughters, Georgianna, has survived. This partially opens the door on the family's life, but the personality of Morris's wife, Eliza Hay, remains obscure and unfocused. A few entries from John G. Morris's unpublished diaries provide some tantalizing hints about the marital relationship, but, unfortunately, there is little else of use.

There are several individuals whose support and assistance have proven invaluable and merit special recognition. Dr. John G. Lynch, former pastor of First English Lutheran Church, first introduced me to Morris and his fascinating life and times. Pastor Lynch also gave much needed encouragement during the long process of preparing this book. Dr. Charles H. Glatfelter, professor emeritus of history at Gettysburg College, guided me to the archival materials and literature critical for an understanding of Morris and his era. I am indebted to him for advice on research strategies, insight into people and events of the period, and judicious suggestions for improving the text. I thank also Dr. Frederick K. Wentz, professor emeritus at the Lutheran Theological Seminary at Gettysburg, for his careful reading of the manuscript, and the thoughtful questions he posed.

With source material on Morris scattered among several repositories, professional assistance was critical. I particularly wish to acknowledge David Hedrick, chief of special collections at the Musselman Library of Gettysburg College; Sara Mummert of the A. R. Wentz Library at the Lutheran Theological Seminary at Gettysburg; Elizabeth Schaaf, archivist at the Peabody Institute in Baltimore, and Karen Stuart, formerly with the Maryland Historical Society.

I owe a special acknowledgement to Cherie Loustaunau for the countless hours she spent preparing and editing each draft of the manuscript. Her care and thoroughness immeasurably improved the text.

Finally, I thank the members of the Publications Committee of the Maryland Historical Society for supporting this biography and Ernest Scott for his wise counsel and assistance as my editor.

M. J. K.

Annapolis, Maryland
January 1997

Introduction

America went through a profound social, economic, and cultural transformation during the course of the nineteenth century. The demands of nation-building brought to the fore innovators and leaders of every variety. Among these leaders, John Gottlieb Morris of Baltimore (1803-1895) played a major role in the arena of cultural transition. Though little known today, the Baltimore pastor and civic leader collaborated intimately in changing the nature of Lutheranism in America, in creating several major cultural institutions, and in materially aiding the rise of professional science.

The America of 1803 remained oriented to the eastern seaboard and the old links to Europe. Westward expansion, which would change the course and destiny of the nation forever, was in its early stages. By the end of Morris's life, the United States spanned the continent and stood poised as the next Great Power. The impact of immigration, the Industrial Revolution, and the Civil War shattered the bonds of European tutelage.

As a young boy, Morris lived in a country that fought two wars with Great Britain to assert its right to existence and freedom. Such a precarious national condition was hard to imagine by 1895. American power and productivity had then reached world-class status. But the America which John G. Morris knew experienced far more than economic and material transformation. Just as profound was the shaping of an American cultural identity. In this arena Morris made his mark.

As one of the early crusaders for an English-language Lutheran church, Morris realized that the church had to adapt to its new-world environment if it hoped to survive and flourish. Mid-century waves of conservative immigrants fed the fierce ideological disputes that tested Morris's mettle and his vision. The struggles of the Lutheran church in many ways paralleled those of that other great immigrant group, the Roman Catholics.

John G. Morris, in many ways the model for the clergyman as the man of letters and civic leader, remained to the end an ardent patriot. As such, he always sought to advance the causes of American science, American history, and American culture. He did pioneering work as an entomologist and labored for decades to nurture and foster the nascent American scientific community. With Joseph Henry, Spencer Baird, Benjamin Silliman, and Louis Agassiz, among many others, Morris's goal was an American science free of its dependence on Europe.

As an historian and bibliophile, John G. Morris made crucial contributions to his adopted hometown, Baltimore, Maryland. The Baltimore of 1827, when Morris arrived in the city, could boast precious little about its cultural life. Robust economically, with both a thriving port and inland trade, Baltimore could not compete as a cultural center with its rivals Philadelphia, New York, and Boston. Morris came to the fore in the struggle to raise the cultural life and standards of Maryland's largest city. To him goes the credit for creating Baltimore's first great library and reference collections at the Maryland Historical Society and the Peabody Institute. At the same time, he sought to raise the level of popular culture through leadership of the lyceum and popular lecture movements. The talented and opinionated Morris always fought for principles which he believed advanced knowledge, culture, and morality.

By the end of his life, the era of the generalist and the men of letters who dominated the cultural scene had passed; the age of the specialist with advanced academic degrees had dawned. Men of letters and leisure gave way to cultural institutions, led by permanent, professional staff. Morris made key contributions to this transition.

Not surprisingly, such a complex era produced a culture equally as complicated. By turns kindly and combative, straightforward and ambivalent, Morris's strong character molded the form and content of his contributions to American culture. This interaction provides the context for the story of a fascinating man in a time of rapid cultural change, the legacy of which is still with us.

Part One

Foreshadowings

1893-1895
&
1803-1827

*Philosophy is perfectly right in saying
that life must be understood backward.
But then one forgets the other clause —
that it must be lived forward.*

Sören Kierkegaard
Journals and Papers, 1843

1

Journey's End

The old man's prodigious physical stamina began at last to fail him during the hot, steamy Maryland summer of 1895. Just a few months away from his ninety-second birthday, John Gottlieb Morris's iron constitution weakened, no longer responsive to the drive of his formidable intellect and will. Yet he worked on.

Daily the Lutheran pastor went to his study at his summer retreat in the small village of Lutherville, north of Baltimore. There he wrote what seemed a never ending stream of articles for church periodicals. The old causes still stirred him: battles over the very nature of Lutheranism in a new world; fidelity to the heritage of the great Reformer of centuries ago.

Occasional breezes filtered through the stately trees which surrounded the two-story frame house atop one of Lutherville's highest points. As the wind moved the sultry air in the study, John G. Morris felt again his almost primal need to be out once more in the woods and fields.

Consumed with a passion for nature, Morris longed to continue his butterfly collecting, his life-long study of all those interlocking mysteries of the natural world. For those "ramblings," above all else, had helped preserve his remarkable physical vigor. But the time for all this was passing. The time for scientific inquiry and path-breaking professional work had almost wound down.

Doggedly, the old man answered the voluminous correspondence which poured in. Letters relating to his work as president of the Maryland Historical Society, the Society for the History of the Germans in Maryland, and the Lutheran Historical Society demanded Morris's attention and response. For decades, he had toiled to build these institutions, to create library collections, to push forward the progress of American culture and civilization. He had so much more to do, but his life forces continued to drain away.

Yet, he could not, would not, stop. He promised two young scientists that he would visit them in the fall and use their microscope to study entomological specimens. He had so much more to learn. The voracious intellectual appetites of a lifetime died hard. As his body and mind warred for control, his soul experienced deep loneliness. Living such a long life was hardly an unmixed blessing. So many of his family, close friends, and antagonists—for this most opinionated of men had his share of foes—had gone before him.

To granddaughter Louise and his pastor Charles Albert, it seemed the old man's decline had really begun two years earlier. The summer of 1893 had devastated the aged Morris. In June, like a lightning bolt, his beloved nephew and ministerial colleague, Charles A. Hay, had suddenly died. The loss of Hay, surrogate for his own sons who had not survived infancy, left the old man inconsolable. With distress, Albert witnessed Morris's collapse at the funeral, where he wept uncontrollably as he gripped Hay's coffin.[1] Worse was to come.

In August, the youngest Morris child, Anna Hay, died on her forty-second birthday. Morris never expected to outlive any of his four daughters, who had survived the perils of infancy and childhood that had taken six of their siblings. The loss of Anna Hay, on top of Charles's death, was more than he could bear. Already a widower for almost eighteen years, Morris sank into a mourning from which he never recovered.

For his family and colleagues, his ninetieth birthday, in the fall of 1893, had provided an opportunity to rally around the old gentleman. Morris was almost overwhelmed at a meeting of the Maryland Historical Society on the eve of his birthday. The members expressed their great respect and fondness for him and voted to send him a basket of ninety roses. For once the man, known for his ready wit and quick repartee, was almost at a loss for words. But the essence of the man comes through in his brief, heartfelt response:

> This is a surprise to me. I have received congratulations, and I expect more in my mail tomorrow. I must tell you that this is exceedingly gratifying. It is difficult for me to believe that I am ninety, and I sometimes believe that recorders of my birth have set the clock ahead of time. I expect I shall be wished many happy returns of the day, as the new bride was, but the clock will soon stop its ticking. The will of the Lord be done.[2]

Scientific colleagues from Washington, D. C., placed Morris's accomplishments and personality in perspective when they wrote:

Your friends and fellow entomologists send heartfelt greetings on your 90th birthday. We connect you with the very beginnings of entomology in this country, and hold you dear, not only for your works, but also for your big heart and jovial manner.[3]

There were times in the months ahead when the John G. Morris of old reasserted himself. His last February 22 was such a moment. The short, stout old clergyman, with the piercing eyes set in a face dominated by his strong, determined chin, embarked on a day which would have exhausted a far younger man. He attended the funeral of an old friend, celebrated Founders' Day at the Johns Hopkins University, and spent the afternoon at his favorite charity, the House of Refuge for delinquent boys. After a brief dinner with his family, he once again went out into the streets of Baltimore, this time to preside over a meeting of the Society for the History of the Germans in Maryland. When he was still out late in the evening, the Morris family sent a grandson to look for him. Returning home after 11:00 PM on his own steam, the proud Morris was irritated by the fuss. He snapped, "Why do you think I can't take care of myself?"[4] He never doubted he could.

Yet family and friends had cause for worry. Morris's decline was slow, steady, and irreversible. But he kept working, finishing his last round of newspaper articles only three weeks before the end. Tenacious as always, he struggled as long as he could. But the end came, painlessly, at his beloved "Oak Grove" in Lutherville, in the presence of his surviving daughters—Maria Louisa, Georgianna, and Mary Hay. On October 10, 1895, at ten minutes past eleven in the evening, John G. Morris breathed his last.

An outpouring of emotion greeted his passing. For his life's work mirrored much of nineteenth-century America. The Maryland Synod of the Lutheran Church attended in a body the funeral held at St. Mark's Church in Baltimore.[5] They realized that the success, even the survival, of Lutheranism in Baltimore and the country had rested in no small measure on the zeal and determination of this man.

Representatives of the Peabody Institute, the Maryland Historical Society, and the Society of the History of the Germans in Maryland accompanied the casket to Pennsylvania Station for the final trip to York, Pennsylvania, Morris's birthplace.[6] All of them knew that Morris's passionate devotion to American culture had made their institutions into models of learning and progress. Serving as honorary pallbearers was a small token of appreciation and esteem.

Eulogies from scientific admirers came to the grieving family. The Brooklyn Entomological Society honored Morris as a "pioneer," whose work "formed a foundation" on which American entomology was built. The Maryland Academy of Sciences remembered with sadness and respect the contributions of a founder and patron.[7] To many, the passing of John G. Morris evoked feelings that his era was also ending.

Slowly, the train pulled out of Baltimore headed toward York. After sixty-nine years, John G. Morris was going home. As he wished, he was buried next to Eliza Hay, his wife of forty-eight years, and their daughter Anna Hay. The native son had returned to where it had all begun so long ago.

2

Early Years

J ohn Gottlieb Morris began life on November 14, 1803, in York, Pennsylvania, the youngest of nine children born to Dr. John Samuel Gottlieb Morris (1754-1808) and his wife Barbara. The last of three sons who survived infancy and grew into adulthood, John Gottlieb entered into a strong-willed and success-ful family.

Dr. John Morris, a native Prussian who immigrated to America in 1776 to fight on the side of the colonists, had a flourishing medical practice as one of the few educated physicians in York County. During the youngest son's first years, his physician father experienced growing debilitation from what the elder Morris de-scribed as "nervous prostration." In October 1808, Dr. Morris died at age 54.[1]

Though John Gottlieb had no memory of him, he "sacredly cherished" until the end of his life all of his father's surviving papers, diaries, and letters. From them, and the stories told by his mother, the younger Morris learned about his father's training in Germany as an apprentice surgeon and his promotions in the American army for conspicuous bravery during the battle of Camden. The young boy discovered that his father had changed the family name from Moritz to Morris lest, as American officers warned, the British execute him as a Hessian deserter if they captured him. At the end of his life, Morris proudly reproduced in his mem-oirs the letter of commendation his father had received from his commander, the Marquis De La Rouerie, at the time his regiment was mustered out of service in York in 1783. Morris also noted that he had his father's membership certificate and diploma for the Society of the Cincinnati, signed by George Washington.[2]

In listening to family stories and reading through his father's papers, John Gottlieb learned about another key aspect of his father's personality and character.

This involved Dr. John Morris's lifelong commitment to his Lutheran faith. Baptized and confirmed as a Lutheran in Prussia, Dr. Morris became an active lay leader in York's German Lutheran church and a close friend of the pastor, the Reverend Jacob Goering. The depth of Dr. Morris's piety and faith emerges from his diary entry on the day his first-born son, William, died.

> October 10, 1788 lamentations of Jeremiah chapter 1:6, "For these things mine eyes runneth down with water because the comforter that should relieve my soul is far from me." This is the lamentation I made when it pleased the Lord to chasten us with his afflicting rod by removing by death our first born, the hope of us both, our dear little son William.[3]

John Gottlieb found in his father's diaries "a truly pious man." The diaries were filled," the son recounted years later, "with prayers, meditations, and Scripture quotations, and among them is a very creditable German poetical eulogy on Rev. Jacob Goering, who baptized me, and who died in 1807."[4] The legacy Dr. John Morris left his sons thus included a patriotic love of America, professional success, and devotion to the Moritz family's historic religious faith. Neighbors and acquaintances fondly remembered the doctor as "a man of independent spirits, genial and kindly heart, much interested in the young, approachable by all classes, a master of books, a lover of man, and possessed of wide information on many subjects."[5] The same sentiments would later apply to the youngest son.

Unintentionally Dr. Morris left another legacy to his youngest son, the one who could not remember him. At key points, we will find that John Gottlieb's dealings with male authority figures he considered distant or aloof (e.g., certain teachers and employers) resulted in contentious and ruptured relationships. The early loss of his father, and the attendant anger and frustration, resulted in a dark side to an otherwise positive "paternal inheritance."

Dr. Morris's legacy included another important component. He left his family financially secure. The success of his practice and the wisdom of his investments in bonds, certificates, and Pennsylvania and Ohio farm lands resulted in a estate, when settled, of over $50,000 in 1815 dollars. Dr. Morris left one-third of the estate to his wife, with his three sons equally dividing the remaining two thirds.[6] The three sons could face the future, from the financial perspective at least, with confidence.

With the death of the father, John Gottlieb's mother and his eldest brother Charles Augustus became the dominant family members in his life. In his memoirs, *Life Reminiscences of an Old Lutheran Minister*, Morris recounted in numerous places the powerful influence of his "beautiful" and "pious" mother. Barbara Morris's deeply held German Lutheran pietism molded her young son's behavior and, ultimately, his life's work. Morris wrote, "I seldom missed Sunday morning church from my earliest days, although I then understood very little of the German sermon. I was taught this duty by my pious mother and made it a matter of conscience, although I felt no special religious interest in the service." Morris remembered that his mother "never purposely neglected public worship, and had daily prayers in the family. . . . Under God her maternal teachings and prayers and blameless example have influenced my whole life."[7]

Throughout his youth, John Gottlieb attended the weekly prayer meetings his mother held in the family home for the ladies of the church. He felt the "profoundest admiration" for the woman who for him came nearest "to the artistic ideal of feminine beauty, and was . . . as good as she was beautiful." His first newspaper article, written as a college student, deplored the time his fellow students "lost in visiting the ladies."[8] This reflected both Morris's admiration for his mother and the pietistic environment in which she raised him.

Several incidents reveal the depth of Barbara Morris's influence on her youngest son. From the distance of old age, Morris remembered a Sunday in his youth when he and a friend skipped church services to go fishing at Louck's dam--not an unheard of event for a young boy. Morris recalled that each chime of the church bells "sent a pang to my heart, for I was consciously neglecting a duty, and acting contrary to my mother's wishes. Even to this day, whenever I pass that place in the cars to Harrisburg, the recollection of that Sunday morning comes up painfully. I do not mean to say that I feared offending God so much as I feared wounding my mother's feelings, if she had known it." Throughout his adolescence, as well as in adulthood, Morris avoided dancing, profanity, liquor, and any moral infractions that transgressed his mother's standards. These standards, reported Morris, later helped him avoid the "temptations" available to college students.[9]

Though not animated by deep religious feelings at this point, the young Morris had developed a highly sensitive conscience which internalized his mother's moral strictures and expectations. All this resulted in a controlled, disciplined young man, a model of decorous conduct poised for professional success and social respectability. Such highly-charged moral sensitivity did have its less appealing aspects. In reminiscing about fellow students at York County Academy, for example, Morris noted with disapproval that "several of them . . . lacked energy and decision, and were satisfied with living a humdrum, indolent sort of life, content with mediocrity in all things."[10] In this revealing passage, Morris exhibited little patience with those he judged deficient in character and diligence. In holding himself and others to high standards, he at times lapsed into censorious self-righteousness. This did not ease his path in managing several critical relationships later in life.

Charles Augustus Morris (1792-1874), the third family member who exerted great influence in John Gottlieb's early years, functioned in effect as the young boy's guardian. An interesting figure in his own right, Charles Morris exhibited some of the same family characteristics identified with John Gottlieb. Foremost among these was a life-long commitment to the cause of evangelical religion, specifically the Lutheran church. No doubt influenced by his pious parents, Charles served briefly as a Lutheran minister under the guidance of the local pastor in York, John George Schmucker. Vaguely described "poor health" brought this interlude to a quick close around 1815. Given that Charles Morris lived until age eighty-two and built a successful business career, he must have had a basically sound physical constitution. Perhaps he found himself not temperamentally suited to the demands of pastoral ministry. Whether or not fueled by his disappointment in his own failure, Charles became an ardent advocate of the ministry as the future career of his brother and ward.

Like his father, Charles Morris became a successful professional in York. First, he began a mercantile business with Jacob Small, his father-in-law. Then he founded the Morris Drug Company, which remained active as one of the oldest pharmaceutical companies in the country until it closed in 1961.[11] Like his father, Charles engaged in numerous local philanthropic activities, educational and religious. In later years, brothers Charles and John Gottlieb worked together on a number of church-related ventures, with Charles often providing the needed financial resources. Charles's role as functional father and confidant would remain a constant factor in the lives of the two men. The older man's continued solicitude for his brother ensured a close and warm relationship. This type of solicitude remained essential for anyone seeking a successful relationship with John Gottlieb.

The middle son in the Morris family, George, played almost no role in John Gottlieb's life. Mentioned only briefly in *Life Reminiscences*, George, a lifelong bachelor, stayed in York as a successful coal merchant and banker. He died at age fifty-eight in 1856.[12] The silence enveloping the relationship between George and John Gottlieb prevents a clear perspective or understanding of what transpired between the two brothers. Though George engaged in some philanthropic activities in York, he seems to have shared few of the common interests that bound Charles and John Gottlieb.

Besides his family, two other individuals had a profound impact on the young John Gottlieb. Both the Morris family's pastor, John George Schmucker (1771-1854), and his minister son, Samuel Simon (1799-1873), had almost lifelong relationships with the youngest Morris son. Pastor Schmucker, an important civic leader in predominantly German-populated York and York County, played a major role in American Lutheranism after the death in 1787 of the patriarch of Lutheranism in America, Henry Melchior Muhlenberg, and up to the ascent to leadership of his son Samuel Simon in the 1820s.

An ardent Lutheran proponent of the revivalist goals and techniques dominant in evangelical American Protestantism in the first decades of the nineteenth century, the elder Schmucker worked ceaselessly for the conversion of sinners, with the consequent moral reform of society. A powerful preacher, he urged on his listeners the need to repent and convert to a lifetime of "piety to God and charity to man." John Gottlieb felt great respect for his "revered" pastor, who strongly reinforced the moral and religious values instilled in the Morris family. John George Schmucker's dedication to the revival of "experimental Christianity" in America helped mold the religious worldview of his son, Samuel Simon, John Gottlieb, and countless others.[13] Later, during the early years of his ministry, Morris worked closely with the elder Schmucker to further the evangelical cause. Always he remembered his former pastor as a warmhearted and sincere man.

Samuel Simon Schmucker and John Gottlieb Morris, on the other hand, had a complex relationship, one that ultimately affected, in part, the course of American Lutheranism. In a letter written in the last months of his life, however, Morris claimed that he and the younger Schmucker, the premier Lutheran churchman in the second quarter of the nineteenth century, were neither boyhood friends nor schoolmates. That seems unlikely given the fact that Schmucker was less than five years older than Morris and, when the Schmucker family moved to York in 1809, the two young men attended Christ Church, the city's only Lutheran church. In any event, the two came together as student and teacher in 1816 when Schmucker became the head of the classical department at the York County Academy.[14]

Schmucker, by that point, had completed two years of study at the University of Pennsylvania and would within a few years emulate his father by entering the Lutheran ministry. Many years later, Morris remembered Schmucker during his two years at the academy as "a promising young man," who "did not go into the company of the young people of the town, and hence was not a favorite. He was studious, and loved his books more than society."[15] Ironically, in a span of ten years Schmucker and Morris would enter into the sensitive mentor-student relationship three times. This relationship, distasteful to at least one of the parties from the beginning, laid the foundation for much of Morris's later success and tribulation.

Next to close family relationships and the ties he had with the Schmuckers, young John Gottlieb was strongly influenced by the city in which he spent his early, formative years. York, located in the southeastern section of Pennsylvania near the Maryland border, had some 2,500 inhabitants in 1803, most of them German immigrants. Surrounded by well-cultivated farms sustained by the rich limestone and fertile soil of the region, York was a busy and prosperous town. Founded in 1749, and the seat of the Continental Congress from September 1777 through June 1778, York was no backwater.

Exciting things had happened at York. Here Congress approved the Articles of Confederation, received news that the French would grant aid, and stopped the Conway cabal against George Washington. Located only fifty-six miles north of Baltimore, the city's and the region's trade was already focused on the burgeoning port on the Patapsco River. John Gottlieb's later deep involvement with Baltimore, almost lifelong, reflected close ties between the two cities.

Predominantly German-speaking, York boasted of prosperous merchants, skilled artisans, and a growing professional class of lawyers and educators. Dr. John Morris and his sons fitted in well with this milieu and contributed to it in very substantive ways.

Lutheran roots in York even predated the city's founding. Christ Church was organized in late 1741; for almost a century this German-speaking church was the only Lutheran congregation in the city, and the largest of any denomination. A large two-story stone building, the church was packed on Sunday mornings to hear Pastor John George Schmucker deliver one of his powerful German-language exhortations to repentance and faith in Christ. Throughout John Gottlieb's youth his family faithfully attended church services and Sunday school, becoming one of the mainstays of the congregation.

As an active young member of the congregation, John Gottlieb formed some close friendships which lasted a lifetime. Foremost among these were with the Hay children, and daughter Eliza in particular. The Hays lived across the street from the Morrises and the young people saw each other daily. John Gottlieb and Eliza probably little envisioned the lifelong ties they would ultimately share.

In this German-oriented yet proudly American environment the curious and lively youngster began to grow up. Though by no means a metropolis, York was a bustling town with numerous shops and stores, many of them made of brick and stone. Merchants and artisans selling their services and farmers bringing produce to market made for an energetic and entertaining scene.

York was of course caught up in the excitement generated by the War of 1812 and the British attack on nearby Baltimore. One of John Gottlieb's strongest boyhood recollections involved the day the York Volunteers marched south to aid their fellow citizens in Baltimore. From the perspective of old age, Morris wrote: "I distinctly remember how the mothers, wives, sisters and lady friends of these men wept as the company marched out of town to the tune of 'The Girl I Left Behind.' I also remember the day of their return, a few months after, when there was great joy in York."[16]

Inspired by such martial scenes, many of the boys of York, including John Gottlieb, formed a military company. Marching at first with pikes of tin attached to the ends of a staff, the boys eventually obtained guns for their drills. Enthralled, John Gottlieb later wrote he "became quite an expert in the manual exercise and in company drill, and have not forgotten it to this day. I also practiced sword exercise thoroughly, and was strongly inspired with youthful military ardor."[17]

Into the mix of pietist sensibility was added the stern stuff of military discipline, weapons, and, potentially, combat. From this mixture evolved a strong-willed young man, disciplined in his work, and ready to fight when necessary. These traits would serve John Gottlieb well in the personal and professional battles which lay ahead.

Only sketchy information exists about John Gottlieb's earliest schooling. Apparently, he began his formal education around the age of eight at the small parochial school operated by the German Lutheran Church in York. Morris remembered the education at the parochial school, and much of what he received when he first transferred to the York County Academy, as woefully inadequate.[18]

From the beginning, brother Charles played a key role in his ward's educational development. He gave John Gottlieb his first arithmetic lessons and placed his youngest brother in the only reputable secondary school in the area, the York County Academy. Though sons of the "first families" in York attended the school, the level of education remained uneven until the return to York of Samuel Simon Schmucker as an instructor in 1816.

Despite deficiencies in formal schooling, John Gottlieb at an "early age" became a voracious reader of plays and books. By his mid-teens, the young man was reading Shakespeare, Addison, Swift, Boswell and the German playwright Kotzebue. He also began a life-long practice of memorizing and reciting prose and poetry, discovering that he loved to participate in debates and developing what he later called, "education and voice culture."[19] An abiding love of the English language and literature remained with him for life. Interestingly, even though brother Charles helped him with arithmetic, he never mastered the subject and later lamented his problems in handling "numbers."

The academy did provide John Gottlieb with one major benefit—stimulating his precocious ability with languages. He studied Latin and Greek, the first of several languages for which the young man showed a marked aptitude. Later, he learned Hebrew, French, and developed his German language skills, first acquired at home, at church, and in the streets of York. The combination of language skills, broad reading interests, and an inquisitive mind laid the framework for John Gottlieb's later professional and scholarly success.

Other interests and skills came to the fore during Morris's youth and adolescence. A budding interest in music fortified his outgoing disposition. He enjoyed singing at church, school, and with his friends. He found that he had a "fair voice for singing as well as learning musical notes after a fashion." He mastered the lute so that he could join the York County Band.[20] In later life, he found his musical skills quite useful when as a minister he had to "raise the tune." Perhaps just as important, he always enjoyed getting together with friends and spending the evening listening to music and singing.

Obviously a young man of promise, John Gottlieb, with his family, had to decide on his next educational step. With his intellectual abilities becoming clearer, and with the financial and professional legacy of his father as a model, a college education seemed in order. The advent of the highly intelligent and disciplined Samuel Simon Schmucker at York County Academy provided John Gottlieb with a needed two-year period of academic preparation for college.

In September 1820, the youngest Morris son took the next major step forward—gaining acceptance into the sophomore class at Princeton College in New Jersey. Why Princeton? Though John Gottlieb did not explain the choice in later life, his guardian and brother Charles probably determined the course of action. That Charles accompanied his brother on the two-day trip to Princeton certainly indicated his approbation and interest in the outcome. Perhaps the fact that Samuel Simon Schmucker went from teaching at York County Academy to studying at Princeton's Theological Seminary influenced the Morris family decision. John Gottlieb's guardian certainly realized that the college, the fourth oldest in the United States, offered one of the best educations available at that time.

The seventeen-year-old young man found the entrance examination surprisingly easy. Years later, he recalled "my trepidation in the presence of the Faculty, in the examination room, and also my exultation when informed of my admission. I leapt down three or four steps from the door to the campus in one joyous bound, and rushed across the street to the hotel where my brother was waiting in painful anxiety for the result. I heard several students who were standing around, and who observed my exuberant delight say, 'That fellow has got through, surely.' I was wild with joy."[21] In noting his brother's intense feelings, John Gottlieb revealed his sensitivity to Charles's high level of emotional involvement in his youngest brother's life and success. Young John Gottlieb's exultation at leaving York and his boyhood behind fairly leaps off the pages of *Life Reminiscences*. Though he sincerely loved his family and the friends of childhood, the promise of freedom and independence irresistibly beckoned to the intellectually gifted and restless young man. He had outgrown York.

Though delighted to begin his college life at Princeton, John Gottlieb did feel, perhaps for the first time in his life, intimidated. He became painfully aware of his so-called country roots, which he claimed, "made me feel awkward, and exposed my rusticity to a ridiculous degree." Despite his awkward feelings, John Gottlieb made an, important discovery during his year and a half at Princeton—that he had excellent leadership and "companionable" qualities. He stood well in his classes, won a prize for declamation, and began exhibiting a shrewd understanding of human nature. When he won the $30 declamation prize offered by the American Whig Society, he "returned it to the society, as some others had done before me. This was considered liberal and honorable, and the act secured me additional respect."[22]

John Gottlieb's outgoing nature made him numerous friends as he joined various college clubs and societies. For the first time, the young student lived with men from different parts of the country and diverse social and economic backgrounds. This broadening period in John Gottlieb's life helped set the stage for his openness as an adult to a variety of experiences and people. In good measure, this openness softened somewhat his judgmental side and revealed many of the personable traits attributed to his father.

Nonetheless, his mother's influence maintained a powerful hold. Despite numerous opportunities for participation in the usual college pranks, John Gottlieb manifested an already well-developed sense of moral rectitude, propriety, and inhibition. He remembered: "I indulged in no vulgar college mischief and no dissipation, both of which I considered ungentlemanly, irrespective of their immorality; but I do not think I was deterred from them by any religious motive. I remembered my mother."[23] Though he later rejected the "exceeding rigid morality of the presbyterian puritanic type," his time at Princeton initially reinforced the strongly ethical and moralistic worldview and behavior common to Calvinism and to the German Lutheran pietism he learned in his family home and church.[24]

While studying at Princeton John Gottlieb expanded his reading to include novels and plays by Scott, Cooper, and Irving, among others. He also developed two habits which would hold him in good stead. He began for the first time keeping a diary, and he started a copybook of poetry and prose quotes which struck his fancy.[25] Over the years his copybooks provided timely quotations for an unending stream of books, articles, and lectures.

Exposure to the philosophical theory taught at Princeton—Scottish Common Sense Realism—had long-term implications for John Gottlieb's theological and intellectual development. The tenets of Common Sense Realism undergirded the mature Morris's understanding of theology, nature, and science. Common Sense Realism, originally a reaction to the skepticism of the Scottish Enlightenment, used the empirical and inductive method of the seventeenth-century philosopher-statesman Francis Bacon to achieve a union of belief and knowledge—of God's Word (the Bible) and Work (nature).[26]

The Common Sense Realists argued that the mind connected bits of empirical data collected by the senses through "self-evident principles," unverifiable but rooted in "common-sense." These philosophers argued that "whatever begins to exist, must have a cause." This unverifiable "fact" gained acceptance because of its roots in obvious, commonsense experience. For the Common Sense Realists, their philosophy led to understanding truth, knowledge, and God.[27]

Despite his intellectual and social flowering, John Gottlieb was highly critical of Princeton, particularly of the faculty. He found the teaching "fairly perfunctory," and complained about the "cold distance" maintained between faculty and students. Morris resented these authority figures whom he found, like Samuel Simon Schmucker, "aloof" and "unsocial." With the hindsight of years, he also faulted the college for not including several branches of learning in the curriculum and for poor textbooks.[28]

In view of his successful transition to life at Princeton, the Morris family's decision to transfer John Gottlieb to Dickinson College in Carlisle, Pennsylvania, for his senior year seems odd. Why should the young student transfer from such a prominent school to one that had recently teetered on the brink of failure? The answer again mainly rests with Charles Morris. John Gottlieb recalled that Charles, "who controlled my movements, thought that all Pennsylvanians should patronize colleges in their own State, and besides, Carlisle being much nearer home, he concluded to transfer me to that institution."[29] With the end of college in sight, John Gottlieb faced important life decisions. Strong personalities like Barbara Morris and Charles Morris wanted the youngest son, a fellow of great potential, close at hand. They had their own hopes and plans.

Whatever the feelings of other family members, John Gottlieb himself found the change to Dickinson "salutary." Though Presbyterian-affiliated, as was Princeton, the students at Dickinson had more privileges and warmer faculty-student relationships than did their peers at Princeton. John Gottlieb flourished during his brief stay. He reorganized the Belles-Lettres Society, had his first newspaper article published, and continued his involvement with debating clubs and societies, which led to a prize as the college's "best declaimer."[30] Handsome, slender, with reddish-brown hair and piercing, dark eyes, John Gottlieb dressed fashionably and mixed well with his fellow students.

But, for young Morris, the real significance of Dickinson College lies in the fact that here his "mind was fully made up to be a practical Christian." Though circumspect in his memories about the precise reasons for this decision, the influence of his mother remained paramount. John Gottlieb wrote:

> As far back as I can remember, I had what may be called the religious sentiment deeply implanted in me. My mother's teaching, prayers and example impressed me strongly, and even in the gayety of youthful life God was not altogether absent from my mind. I was a conscientious church-goer all my life, but I never until this time made what is ecclesiastically called a profession of religion.[31]

What transpired between mother and son at this time to influence John Gottlieb's religious conversion we do not know. We do know that he and the other students at Dickinson felt great shock at the sudden death of the college president's young son, James Mason. Morris vividly recalled the words of the grieving father as the student pallbearers carried his son's coffin, "Tread softly, young men, tread softly, for you bear the body of the Holy Ghost." According to his own testimony, Morris often used these words when he presided at funerals of young men.[32] The death of James Mason must have focused John Gottlieb's attention on religion and the future in a way no other single event had done.

Also, during his year at Dickinson, John Gottlieb heard for the first time the fiery preaching of Benjamin Kurtz (1795-1865). A fervent Lutheran minister dedicated to the "revival of religion," Kurtz preached on the need for repentance and public conversion. Kurtz's preaching may have influenced John Gottlieb, who found the minister "a strong man."[33] Whatever the case, this marked the beginning of a long relationship between the two men that spanned the most turbulent decades in American Lutheranism. As one immediate effect of his religious profession, John Gottlieb joined in student prayer meetings where "most of us there made our maiden effort in leading public prayer."[34]

By the end of his college career in 1823, John Gottlieb faced his first major dilemma. Should he study for the Lutheran ministry or pursue some other path? "After graduation I went home," he wrote, "and now came the struggle."[35] His father and brothers provided models of success in medicine, business, and civic pursuits. Yet, John Gottlieb's parents and oldest brother also provided a legacy of strong attachment to the church. Basically, the young graduate's choices boiled down to either following his father's example, or completing the pastoral career once begun by Charles Morris.

Beneath the dilemma over career path, though, lay a more complex, personal dilemma. By age twenty, John had developed all of its major contours. Outgoing, gregarious, with a broad range of interests, he had a keen intellect that indicated the potential for great success. On the other hand, the early loss of his father left him susceptible to the need for support and approval from older men. His reliance on his brother Charles and his frustrations with Samuel Simon Schmucker and the faculty at Princeton provide early indications of the depth of this need. When frustrated on this score, John Gottlieb had already demonstrated a capacity for anger and resentment. This latent anger, coupled with a tendency to judge others harshly, loomed as potential obstacles to his future success and happiness. Resolving these conflicts would fully test, often painfully so, the ambitious young graduate.

3

Call to Ministry

Graduation from college and the return to his family home brought Morris's struggles to a head. He wrote, "I had not fully decided to study for the ministry, and my conflict of mind was painful."[1] Fundamentally, the conflict involved what career the young man would pursue and where he would pursue it. Both facets of the conflict revolved around issues of independence and identity. We saw Morris's great joy at going to Princeton, his first foray as a young adult into the wider world. If he remained in York, he faced a life as a successful professional or business man, actively involved in civic affairs, and tied closely to his family. This meant remaining in the shadow of his dominant mother and elder brother. No matter how much he loved them, Morris wanted more. Having tasted personal and academic success at college, the ambitious young man craved independence and recognition.

The issue of what career path to follow brought these threads together. Morris acknowledged that "the way to success in several other pursuits was open to me."[2] Medicine, law, or business meant, in all probability, staying in York and remaining in relative obscurity. The ministry offered the potential for broader vistas. To understand Morris's final decision, we need to view it from his perspective.

> There was nothing supernatural or even extraordinary in the circumstances of this, my "call to ministry." I thought I had the religious qualifications—that is, I was a sincere believer, and wished to do good in the best way I could. I was in perfect health and constitution. I had some of the attributes of a good speaker, and I thought that by culture I might make a fair preacher. I had means of my own, so that I need not be a burden on the church; my brother was very anxious that I

should study for the ministry, but neither he nor my mother ever urged it upon me. The Lutheran Church had less than 300 ministers at that time, and her sphere of activity was constantly enlarging, whilst the ministry was not multiplying in proportion. Providence had cast my lot within her limits, and I concluded that this was the field for me to work in, and I entered. This is the only "call to the ministry" I know anything of. The Church needed my services, I thought, and I cheerfully offered them. I regarded her need as equivalent to a call from her, and hence I concluded it was the divine will.[3]

The rational, objective tone of Morris's words stand in sharp contrast to the dramatic, personal "conversion" experiences expected from evangelical Protestant ministers of the day. The fact that the church had far fewer ministers than needed meant that a pastoral career required leaving York. Evaluating his physical, intellectual, and social assets, Morris realized that the future prospects of a college graduate such as himself in the Lutheran ministry seemed fair indeed.

On a more personal level, a decision for the ministry ensured the ardent approval of Barbara Morris and Charles Morris. With this decision, young Morris could gain distance and freedom and yet retain the love and support he needed. A perfect compromise. Yet a compromise ultimately doomed to failure without one essential ingredient: Morris's belief that he had a call to the ministry. Though never emotional or mystical about religion, from boyhood onward, Morris remained a sincere, orthodox believer. He never rebelled against his family's piety or the church's teaching. For Morris, divine providence ruled all human affairs. The coincidence of the church's lack of talented ministers, his heritage as a Lutheran, his family's desires, and his own personal needs meant to Morris that God's will lay in the path to ministry.

The soundness of the decision immediately became apparent. As Morris put it, "I finally determined for the pulpit and then my mind was at rest." He turned to the task at hand and never looked back. "From that time," he wrote, "I gave myself entirely to the work, and made preparations accordingly. The question was, where should I study theology?"[4] This question posed serious difficulties for a Lutheran in the 1820s. With the exception of a small seminary in upstate New York, Lutherans had no Andover, Harvard, or Princeton to train their ministers. Lutherans had to attend the seminaries of other denominations or find Lutheran ministers willing to tutor theology students. At this point, Morris and his brother Charles decided he would not attend the most likely seminary, Presbyterian Princeton. Instead, the Morrises felt the need for a Lutheran introduction to theology, and thus sought a tutor from among the qualified ministers of the denomination.

Charles Morris's high degree of control and involvement in his youngest brother's life continued. He wrote to Dr. Charles R. Demme, a prominent German

Lutheran pastor in Philadelphia, requesting that he accept John Gottlieb as a theology student. For whatever reason, Demme declined the request.[5] Interestingly, Morris did not ask his pastor, John George Schmucker, to serve as his theological mentor. This would have left him in York for several more years and violated his need to get away. With some reluctance, the Morris family decided to send the aspiring theologian "all the way" to New Market, Virginia, in the Shenandoah Valley to study with Samuel Simon Schmucker. Recently ordained, the younger Schmucker had charge of a small country congregation. With his eventual goal of opening a Lutheran seminary in mind, Schmucker accepted Morris and several other men as students in an informal "preparatory school."[6] For the second time, John G. Morris entered into Samuel Simon Schmucker's orbit. This proved fateful for both men.

Schmucker and Morris began their careers at a particularly turbulent point in American religious life. In the decades after the American Revolution the various Protestant denominations struggled with the spiritual torpor that resulted from the war and with the inroads made by English deism and French rationalism in undermining traditional Christian dogma and practices. Dismissed scornfully by evangelical Protestants as "infidelity," deism and rationalism substituted reason for faith and revelation. Deists and rationalists reinterpreted Christian doctrines, such as the divine nature of Christ and the inspired nature of the scriptures. They stripped away supernatural explanations and reduced Jesus and the scriptures to only a model and guide for a moral human life.[7]

Beginning in the 1790s, a gradual, but powerful, reaction began. Religious revivals, first among college students at Hampden-Sydney College and Yale and then along the western frontier of Kentucky and Ohio, grew into what became known as the Second Great Awakening. This revival followed by some fifty years the mid-century fervor, known as the Great Awakening, which had swept the colonies. The Second Awakening—a cultural, as well as religious, phenomenon—sought to counteract philosophical rationalism and restore the moral tone of a society which had just experienced almost three decades of political turmoil and war. Most particularly, church people feared that the thousands of settlers flocking to the untamed, uncivilized western frontier would succumb to an almost pagan "barbarism."

The frontier revivals featured lengthy "camp meetings" with fiery preaching designed to provoke among participants a personal conversion and commitment to Christ. The techniques used, eventually codified under the term "new measures," were always controversial and eventually became the focus of a conservative reaction. The "new measures" featured "protracted meetings"; animated, fiery, "heart-searching" preaching; calling out "sinners" for private prayer; "anxious" or "inquiry" meetings; and the "mourner's bench." Revivalist fervor, for the most part, swept Protestant denominations weakened by war and rationalism.

Among Lutherans, Benjamin Kurtz, the contemporary of Samuel Simon Schmucker and Morris, preached a total commitment to revivalism and the "new measures." Lutherans steeped in the German pietist tradition, such as John George Schmucker, accepted the basic revivalist tenet of personal commitment and conversion. Not surprisingly, Schmucker, Morris, and many of their peers were swept up in the evangelical, revivalist spirit.

By the 1820s, evangelical Protestants, regardless of denomination, felt themselves bound together as individuals "converted" to Christ and committed to the conversion of the nation and the world. Between 1816 and the 1830s, these Protestants formed a series of voluntary, interdenominational societies designed to achieve the religious and social goals of the Second Awakening. Organizations such as the American Bible Society, the American Tract Society, and the American Sunday School Union became the vehicles for the conversion of the world and the moral reform of society.[8]

Lutherans, like other Protestants, faced the challenges of rationalism and the potential loss of adherents in the great western migration, but they confronted several issues particularly their own. The language question was the foremost problem. Lutheran immigrants in colonial America had worshiped and received religious instruction in German, the language of Luther. But, in the first decades of the nineteenth century, pressure to use English in the life and work of the church mounted. In New York, Maryland, and the Carolinas, bilingual preaching and separate English-speaking congregations began to appear. However, in Pennsylvania, Virginia, and Ohio, adherents of German strongly resisted the trend.

The traditionalists argued that the preservation of Lutheran identity and orthodoxy depended on perpetuating the use of German. They viewed English as shallow, frivolous, and the vehicle for the insidious ideas of Enlightenment rationalism.[9] The German-use advocates had only to point to the New York Ministerium to substantiate their argument.[10] By 1807, the ministerium had switched to English to conduct its business and, with the ascent of Frederick H. Quitman to its presidency, rationalism spread quickly among local congregations. In his 1814 catechism, Quitman, like others imbued with rationalist ideas, rejected "outworn creeds" by denying the validity of the Apostles' Creed and the Lutheran confessional documents of the sixteenth century.

Those who fought to introduce English into Lutheran church life argued the issue from the demographic perspective. Many German-Americans had, by and large, lost facility in using the German language. Surrounded by an English-speaking cultural environment, their continued adherence to a German-speaking Lutheranism became increasingly dubious. Advocates of the use of English denied that language bore responsibility for doctrinal falsehoods associated with rationalism.[11] In fact, association with other English-speaking evangelicals in a great Protestant crusade beckoned as the best antidote to rationalism and the only hope for saving those migrating to the "barbarous" west.

In many ways the language issue boiled down to the question of whether preserving the unique or "peculiar" doctrines of Lutheranism had a greater urgency than joining in the Pan-Protestant crusade sweeping America. This question touched on the larger issue of denominational identity and unity.

Both rationalism and the revivalist Second Awakening, in differing ways, threatened continued Lutheran cohesiveness. The Pennsylvania Ministerium, the oldest and largest Lutheran synod, from the 1790s onward reacted to the rationalist threat by de-emphasizing Lutheran confessional particularity and drawing closer to the Moravian and Reformed churches, both rooted in the heritage of German pietism and culture. Pennsylvania Lutherans and the German Reformed Church in 1818 actively discussed opening a joint seminary at Franklin College in Lancaster, Pennsylvania. Similar unionist tendencies occurred among the German-speaking churches of North Carolina, and in New York Episcopalians and English-speaking Lutherans pursued a possible merger.[12]

Some Lutherans, however, remained skeptical of the theological basis and methods pursued by the revivalists, even though leaders such as John George Schmucker and Benjamin Kurtz urged them to adopt the goals and many of the methods of an all-encompassing evangelical and revivalist Protestant crusade to combat the forces of rationalism and "infidelity." Moved by the ardent pietist belief in personal conversion and missionary fervor, these Lutheran supporters of revivalism felt that a joint crusade provided the only hope for defeating the foes of religion. Benjamin Kurtz, for example, argued for complete acceptance of revivalist methods, and advocated a total alliance with evangelical Protestantism.[13] Lutheran denominational identity seemed fast eroding.

In fact, though, the situation began to stabilize and improve toward the end of the century's second decade. Prominent leaders in the Pennsylvania Ministerium, including J. H. C. Helmuth, George Lochmann, and John George Schmucker, though they differed in varying degrees on how Lutherans should relate to other Protestants, agreed that Lutheran identity urgently required strengthening. Between 1818 and 1820, these men, as well as leaders in other Lutheran synods, formed an umbrella advisory body, known as the General Synod, designed to serve as a forum where synods could cooperate on issues of common concern. Though at no time did all synods belong to the General Synod, its creation served as a major institutional step in preserving a distinct Lutheran confessional identity.[14]

From the early 1820s onward, Samuel Simon Schmucker, the theological and professional mentor for Morris and his generation, played an increasingly dominant role in the affairs of the General Synod. Indeed, Schmucker's goals and vision would dominate Morris and the church for the next twenty-five years. By the end of the 1820s, he had, almost singlehandedly, saved the General Synod from disintegration, founded the first major Lutheran seminary in the United States at Gettysburg, Pennsylvania, and translated a German theological handbook for use in seminary training.[15] To strengthen Lutheran identity and maintain needed flexibility, Schmucker insisted that the acceptance of only one of the Lutheran confessions or "symbols," the Augsburg Confession* of 1530, was necessary. Even at that, Schmucker, in the licensure and ordination oaths he wrote for use by the district synods of the General Synod, required only acceptance of the "fundamental doctrines of the Word of God . . . taught in a manner substantially correct in the doctrinal articles of the Augsburg Confession."[16] For Schmucker this formulation preserved ancient Christian dogma and allowed for the evolution of theological knowledge, which he felt had taken place since the Reformation. From Schmucker's point of view, this compromise preserved the essential uniqueness of Lutheranism and permitted Lutherans to join with other Protestants in the great evangelical crusade to "save" America and reform society.

By 1830, the Lutheran church in America had stabilized from the twin shocks of Enlightenment rationalism and the aftermath of the Revolutionary War. A general sense of order prevailed with the growth of new synods and the survival of the national body, the General Synod. The inauguration of Gettysburg Seminary in 1826 promised to provide an adequate supply of pastors. The need for a seminary was absolutely desperate. Few Lutheran congregations had the exclusive use of a Lutheran pastor, and the needs of the western settlements were almost completely unmet. The increasing use of English in most synods, as well as the broad, generic basis for Lutheran confessional conformity, presaged the time when American Lutheranism would find itself in closer communion, both religiously and culturally, with other Protestants. Though some conservative, mostly German-speaking, Lutherans opposed this trend, they remained a distinct minor-

---

*The Augsburg Confession is the declaration of faith prepared by the reformer Philipp Melanchthon and presented by the Lutheran princes to Emperor Charles V at the Diet of Augsburg in 1530. The confession became the basic credal statement for Lutherans.

ity. Nothing on the horizon foretold the dramatic cultural transformation that would change the face of Lutheranism in the 1840s.

The urbane young Morris found himself thoroughly disconcerted upon arriving in rural New Market, Virginia: "Behold me now installed in a struggling obscure Shenandoah county village of 400 inhabitants, who were exceedingly plain and uncultivated for the most part, but the majority were good specimens of American German thrift and frugality. . . . I had never before lived in a place where there was no first class school, no reading room, no newspaper printed, no debating society, no band of music, no musical parties, no picnics or excursions, no public lectures, not even a show or exhibition of jugglers." Though Morris credited the Lutherans of New Market, and most others as well, with "thrift and frugality," he also viewed them as "behind other communities in intelligence, enterprize and education."[17] Raising the cultural level of American Lutherans would, as time went on, become one of Morris's great passions.

Morris complained about Schmucker: his aloof manner, his immersion in translating a German theology text, and his absences for "four or five weeks" at a stretch. This does not necessarily provide a fair portrait of Schmucker.[18] The studious and zealous young Pastor Schmucker wrote in his diary on December 9, 1823, "This day in reliance on the gracious will of my heavenly father, I commenced a course of theological instruction after having matriculated the following young men as students: John G. Morris of York, Pennsylvania; John Reck of Winchester, Virginia; and George Schmucker, son of my uncle Nicholas Schmucker."[19] Hardly the words of a disinterested teacher. Yet Morris's antipathy, begun at York County Academy, continued to smolder. Furthermore, Morris, the only college graduate, found himself back to "reciting Greek grammar and the elements of natural philosophy."

Despite his inauspicious surroundings, Morris's twenty months in New Market formed the basis for his theological perspective for years to come. Schmucker had Morris and the others read Mosheim's church history, Bible history, Jahn's archeology, and philosophy.[20] Schmucker brought erudition to his teaching of Lutheran orthodoxy and the piety of his father and his mentor, J. H. C. Helmuth, as well as the Calvinist and Puritan views of his professors at Princeton Seminary. Schmucker instructed his students in the elements of the German school of theology known as biblical supernaturalism. This tradition held to the absolute authority of the scriptures, with scientific and historical methods used to prove authenticity. Morris never wavered in accepting the essential link between revelation and science.

From Pietist and Puritan traditions, Schmucker differentiated between fundamental and non-fundamental beliefs found in the Bible and theology. While accepting the basic doctrines in the Apostles' Creed and the Augsburg Confession, Schmucker viewed certain articles, such as the virgin birth, Christ's descent into hell, and the presence of Christ in the Lord's Supper, as nonfundamental or not essential for a Christian to believe. For Schmucker, acceptance of biblical doctrines as proclaimed in the primary Lutheran confessional document of the Reformation era, the Augsburg Confession, remained the only valid test for denominational orthodoxy and membership. He never embraced the theological details elaborated in the other Lutheran confessional writings of the era. For over two decades, Morris too adhered to this point of view, retaining always evangelical Protestantism's intense sense of mission and strong anti-Roman Catholicism.[21]

An evangelical fervor that emphasized personal conversion, commitment to Christ, and the importance of the Christian enterprise informed Schmucker's discussions with his students. "After some months of study," Schmucker allowed his pupils to begin preaching, teaching Sunday school, and leading prayer meetings. Though Morris later discounted these ventures as nothing more than following the Methodist system, "with the same unstable results," he benefited from the experience. The elitist Morris learned how to communicate with people of little education and less sophistication. He experienced first hand the level of culture and morality outside urban centers. All this broadened his understanding of people and the great need for, among other things, an educated and competent clergy. Significantly, Schmucker confirmed Morris as a communicant member of the church.[22]

In later reminiscences about this critical period in his life, Morris clearly distinguished between the influence of John George Schmucker and that of his son. Morris recalled that when he was a student his pastor, the elder Schmucker, gave him the first "clear oral illustration of the Lutheran doctrine of the Lord's Supper," in "language never forgotten." On the other hand, Samuel Simon Schmucker, according to Morris, later abandoned his father's teaching, and led Morris and others to false "New England Zwinglian views."[23]

Do Morris's charges against S. S. Schmucker of indifference to his students and unorthodox teaching ring true? Certainly Schmucker's extensive efforts to save the fledgling General Synod and his deep involvement in church work must have restricted the time he spent with his students. Clearly Morris wanted and felt he needed more attention from his mentor. Yet Schmucker's deep commitment to theological education and his innate seriousness of purpose make it highly unlikely that the picture of almost careless indifference which Morris painted is accurate.

In the matter of orthodox religious belief and teaching, Morris provides contradictory testimony. On the one hand, he gave credit to John George Schmucker for teaching him the orthodox Lutheran understanding of the sacraments. Yet Morris also wrote, "The peculiarities of the Lutheran faith, especially on the sacraments, were not taught me when I was young, and when I first came under the influence of teachers in later years [i.e., S. S. Schmucker] I was led to the opposite direction, and I said and wrote and printed some things which I have regretted a thousand times."[24] Did the Schmuckers, father and son, hold differing beliefs? Did Samuel Simon Schmucker seduce Morris and others away from "true Lutheranism?"

While treasuring their religious heritage, neither Schmucker placed an undue emphasis on confessional subscription. Both supported a generic Lutheranism closely allied with other American Protestants in the great evangelical crusade spawned by the Second Great Awakening. The elder Schmucker wrote little or nothing on the sacraments, and the younger man's views remained consistent. S. S. Schmucker understood baptism and the Lord's Supper as symbols of God's grace and love and no more. He did not view Luther's teaching of "the Real Presence in the Lord's Supper" as an essential or fundamental article of faith required of all Christians. In this he never wavered. J. G. Schmucker's intense interest in revivals and the millennial coming of the Kingdom of God left him little time or concern for creeds, confessions, and sacramental nuances.[25] What Samuel Simon Schmucker taught Morris in the 1820s represented the "true Lutheranism" of the day—adherence to basic Christian articles of faith as expressed in the Apostles' Creed and the Augsburg Confession, though with reservations in the case of the latter.

What lies behind the selectivity and inaccuracy of Morris's reminiscences? Later confessional battles certainly influenced his memory, though perhaps another unrecognized factor entered into the equation during the months at New Market. Despite painting his teacher as aloof and unsociable, Morris had to acknowledge that "the settlement of the young minister was quite an event in the vicinity. He was the only really educated minister for twenty five miles around; his style of preaching was so fresh and interesting; he was so gentlemanly and neat in his appearance and withal so good looking, and unmarried besides, that he attracted general attention."[26] Was Morris jealous?

Young Schmucker, the favored son of one of the Lutheran church's most respected leaders, had already drawn favorable attention from the church at large. Obviously, he had a bright future as a major denominational figure. John G. Morris, though talented and gifted, lacked Schmucker's visibility, prominence, and, above all, the benefits of a strong paternal relationship. No matter how much his mother and eldest brother supported him, Morris lacked a father. The intimate and personal working relationship between the Schmuckers simply highlighted all that Morris had lost at age five. When John George Schmucker retired from the fray of church politics, Morris's anger toward his son began to emerge into public view. Though it was not consciously articulated, Morris never forgave Samuel Simon Schmucker his good fortune in having an enduring relationship with his father. Despite undeniable talents, Morris never quite achieved Schmucker's stature in the Lutheran firmament.

Another factor, incipient during the New Market period but more significant in later years, affected the Morris-Schmucker relationship. This was a fundamentally different view on the nature of religious experience. Morris remembered attending, along with his colleagues, a Methodist prayer meeting where "I stopped in the middle of a prayer because I was dreadfully annoyed by the holy groanings of a Methodist brother. . . . They denounced us as cold and dead."[27] Though he never shared Samuel Simon Schmucker's dedication to the causes of evangelical religious and social reform, Morris did remain for the next several decades in the camp of those Lutherans, led by Schmucker, who were supportive of the evangelical and revivalist movement. Personal and theological differences were heightened by Morris's far-ranging intellectual, social, and cultural interests and eventually led to an almost complete estrangement between the one-time mentor and pupil.

In early 1825, Schmucker resigned his pastoral charge at New Market, and began preparing for his life's work, the opening of a Lutheran theological seminary at Gettysburg, Pennsylvania. With the closing of the "pro-seminary" imminent, Morris again faced the issue of where to pursue his theological studies. Not feeling confident enough of his theological knowledge and pastoral skills, the young student rejected overtures to accept a pastoral call. Again he turned to brother Charles and his mother for direction. After much discussion, the Morrises decided that John would not go to Princeton, at least not "just then." Rather, they decided he would spend the winter with the German Moravian community in Nazareth, Pennsylvania.

With the Moravians, Morris felt he could advance in German and Hebrew, and experience the "piety" which so animated his mother. Though he did not find "heaven on earth" or even greater proficiency in German, young Morris did improve his Hebrew and enjoyed "a very happy and profitable winter."[28]

Reluctant to accept a call and with the seminary at Gettysburg not yet opened, Morris next decided to continue his studies at Princeton Seminary. The seven months of his second sojourn at Princeton critically influenced his theological and intellectual development. Though he still rejected what he termed "Puritanic" opinions concerning predestination and sabbath observance, he began developing an appreciation for church history and the virtues of a rather conservative confessionalism with a respect for creeds and tradition. All of this stimulated Morris's interest in history and, eventually, in the historical traditions of Lutheranism.[29]

Morris's three professors at Princeton influenced him in different ways. Two were strongly confessionalist. Though aloof and formal, the professor of church history, Samuel Miller, instilled in his students respect for the tenets of confessionalism, particularly the Presbyterian proclamation of faith, the Westminster Confession. Charles Hodge, the youngest professor, taught Hebrew and scripture and eventually became known as one of the staunchest confessionalists in American Presbyterianism. Morris's scholarly aptitude earned him admission as a senior in the seminary and placement in Hodge's private class on advanced Hebrew. This began a five-decade friendship between Morris and Hodge.

Morris's third professor, on the other hand, reinforced much of what he had learned from Schmucker. Archibald Alexander, originally from the Shenandoah Valley and intensely evangelistic, taught systematic theology and pastoral care. He stressed the importance of personal conversion to Christ as the only method of grace and religious revivals as the ultimate tool in spreading the kingdom of God. Most importantly, Alexander stressed the symbolic nature of the sacraments and his belief that all Protestants were united on the basis of a few, "fundamental" doctrines found in the Apostles' Creed.[30] Though Morris practiced what Alexander taught for many years, eventually the intellectual and theological perspective he absorbed from Miller and Hodge helped lead him in new directions.

Once again, Princeton offered young Morris more than formal education. Invited to join the Round Table Club, Morris discussed "high theology" with this group of "intellectual aristocrats." Further, seminary authorities selected Morris as one of four men to make Bible Society speeches in the chapel. He also taught Sunday school and preached in nearby communities.[31] As with his earlier experiences in college, Morris's personality and natural ability earned him stature and respect from his peers.

While still at Princeton, Morris faced another important decision. A Lutheran church in Philadelphia, St. Matthew's, invited him to preach. Despite Samuel Schmucker's written entreaties, Morris declined the invitation, knowing in all likelihood it would lead to a pastoral call. "I was afraid," he wrote, "that perhaps I might be tempted by the flattering prospect of things to rush into the ministry before I had finished my seminary course. I was urged to accept the call, for it really amounted to that, by S. S. Schmucker, who had heard of it, which perhaps was well meant, but which displeased me much, for I was still writhing under some unhappy reminiscences."[32] Whether Morris really lacked confidence in his training or did not want a call to a Philadelphia church remains unclear. In any event, Morris once more decided to try the teacher-pupil role with Schmucker the younger at Gettysburg.

Just before beginning classes at the new seminary in the fall of 1826, Morris attended the annual session of the Maryland-Virginia Synod in Winchester, Virginia.[33] There he took an examination for a license to perform ministerial functions, under the general restrictions set by the Synod for this last step prior to ordination. The well-educated Morris had no trouble with reading and analyzing the first few verses of Genesis in Hebrew.[34] Taking this examination and his refusal to preach at St. Matthew's plainly indicated that Morris intended to work outside Pennsylvania. Indeed, his days as a seminary student seemed numbered.

The 1826 Maryland-Virginia Synod convention proved momentous for Morris in another way. On the way back to York, he spent a few days with Charles Philip Krauth (1797-1867), one of his examiners. While at the Martinsburg, Virginia, parsonage "an intimacy grew between us," Morris recalled years later. A close personal and professional friendship began that lasted until Krauth's death in 1867. A scholarly and affectionate man, six years Morris's senior, Krauth always remained supportive of the younger man during the many travails of the ensuing decades. From the perspective of a lifetime of friendship, Morris wrote that he "admired and loved" Krauth "more dearly than any other man, except my own brothers." Krauth clearly felt the same, naming one of his sons for Morris.[35]

Briefly stopping in York before reporting to the new seminary, John G. Morris underwent a severe family trial. For the first time, John George Schmucker asked Morris to preach to his home congregation. Years later, Morris could vividly recall the drama of the occasion.

> This was a trial; all my old companions and other persons among whom I had been reared were there; my mother was there, but not a word did she say before or after. I knew, however, she was praying for me. The only person besides myself who was at all apprehensive was my brother, Charles A. Morris, whose sensitively nervous nature was so excited by fear of my utter failure that it was with difficulty that he could force himself to church, and when there he took a seat near the door so that he might escape in a hurry in the event of my coming to a dead halt and being compelled to leave the pulpit in disgrace. It was the severest trial of his nervous system that he ever encountered. I do not think he slept a wink that night, and I am sure he ate nothing during the preceding day.[36]

Understandably, Morris found preaching in his home church for the first time a bit unsettling. But, given his already successful public speaking experiences at Princeton, Dickinson, and New Market, his high level of anxiety is noteworthy. He must have found his brother Charles's emotional investment in his success unnerving on this occasion. The reasons for Charles Morris's agitation are unclear. Perhaps his own unhappy experiences in the pulpit haunted him. But it is clear that in the years ahead Charles supported his youngest brother's church work in every way possible. Charles's financial support would prove particularly helpful in sustaining brother John's long pastoral career.

With relief, no doubt, Morris left York and went to Gettysburg. Morris, the only student in the first class with formal, synod-granted licensure, stayed for all of one month. During that time, he attended a few classes and mostly occupied himself with writing and reading in the room he rented from a Mrs. Hutchinson on South Baltimore Street. Again, he groused over the younger Schmucker's lack of "pastoral supervision" or "pastoral" care.[37] That he continued to find Schmucker unacceptable should not have surprised Morris.

Perhaps returning to a rural ambience was also unsettling for Morris. Gettysburg in 1826, though a county seat, was small, isolated, and self-sustaining. Dairy farming, stock-raising, and cultivating fruit orchards were the main occupations for most of the area's inhabitants. Though not as rustic as the Shenandoah Valley, Gettysburg had little of the culture on which Morris thrived.

Finally realizing that he must accept his "eclectic" theological training as the best he could expect to receive, Morris began seriously considering job opportunities. He did not have long to wait. Within a few weeks of arriving in Gettysburg, he accepted an invitation from a struggling congregation in Baltimore, First English Lutheran Church, to preach. Morris did so several times, and soon received a call to serve as the congregation's first, permanent pastor. "After consultations with my brothers and others," Morris wrote, "and proper religious consideration, I agreed to go."[38]

After rejecting several calls, why did Morris accept this one? It is especially surprising in view of the fact that Schmucker had recommended Morris to the congregation. Such support had certainly ended the earlier possibility of his taking the church in Philadelphia. Given Morris's awareness of Schmucker's putative role in the call to St. Matthew's in Philadelphia, his assertion that "I do not know who mentioned my name" to First English sounds improbable.[39]

Several factors contributed to Morris's decision and to overcoming his aversion to Schmucker's advice. He realized that the end had come for his period of study and training. More important, relatives of Barbara Morris lived in Baltimore and surrounding areas. This greatly increased the merits of Baltimore in young Morris's eyes. He could leave York and establish his own identity while retaining his mother's approval and receiving some support from the extended family near at hand. The fifty-six miles separating York from Baltimore seemed just the right distance.Another important factor was the reason for the new congregation's existence. The founders of First English left German-speaking Zion Church so that their children, growing up in an American, English-speaking cultural environment, would remain Lutherans. To this cause, in Baltimore and the country at large, Morris dedicated his pastoral career.

Part Two

The Young Professional
1827-1839

*In youth men are apt to write more
wisely than they really know or feel; and
the remainder of life may not be idly
spent in realizing and convincing
themselves of the wisdom which they
uttered long ago.*

NATHANIEL HAWTHORNE
Preface to The Snow Image

4

Emerging Church Leader

After John G. Morris settled in his newly adopted city in 1827, he laid the foundations for his emergence, during the next twelve years, as a significant leader in the life of the Lutheran church. In this critical period, the talented and ambitious young pastor immersed himself in the primary issue facing Lutheranism, the transition from a German-based cultural focus to an English-speaking, American one. From the beginning, Morris dedicated himself to the cause of a Lutheranism rooted in the environment of the New World and capable of retaining the allegiance of future generations. He never wavered from this commitment. It was as a dedicated churchman that Morris began to make his mark as an American cultural leader.

The character of Morris's new home, Baltimore, helped shape the nature and tone of his work. In the midst of booming growth, Baltimore in 1827 boasted a population of almost 80,000 and a reputation as a prosperous, attractive city. Mrs. Frances Trollope, mother of the English novelist Anthony Trollope, visited the city a few years after Morris arrived and reported:

> Baltimore is in many respects a beautiful city; it has several handsome buildings, and even the private dwelling houses have a look of magnificence, from the abundance of white marble with which many of them are adorned. The ample flight of steps and the lofty doorframes, are in the best houses formed of this beautiful material.[1]

Economically, the development of steam-generated power accelerated the growth of textile manufacturing, iron works, and milling. The creation of the Baltimore & Ohio Railroad beginning in the late 1820s stimulated the shipment of wheat from western Maryland to Baltimore for milling, and then abroad as part of Baltimore's expanding foreign trade. Baltimore's bankers, manufacturers and merchants, such as George Peabody of Riggs and Peabody, ardently supported the railroad's westward development, as well as canal building and other improvements, to meet the fierce competition of New York City and Philadelphia for control of the lucrative Ohio valley trade. Although, for a variety of reasons, Baltimore did not ultimately defeat its northeast urban rivals, the city's mood in the late 1820s remained sanguine. Home building boomed, for example, with the construction of five hundred new homes between 1824 and 1829.

Increased economic activity stimulated an influx of poor, rural whites, free blacks, and, by the mid-1830s, a growing number of foreign-born immigrants, who filled the menial jobs fueling the transportation and manufacturing boom. The closing of the Second Bank of the United States in 1836, however, caused numerous bank failures in Baltimore and began a period of economic and social turmoil. Bank failures, compounded by the Panic of 1837, brought Baltimore's economic boom to a halt and led to a sharp rise in poverty and violence. The ensuing social distress caused growing labor agitation, street riots, and violent hostility toward free blacks and immigrants, as the competition for scarce jobs waxed. For the rest of the ante-bellum period, Baltimore became known for its violence-prone, volatile population.

The cultural scene reflected a similar pattern of advance and retreat. A surge in literary and poetic creativity after the war of 1812 began to ebb by the 1830s. A group of young lawyers, physicians, and journalists formed the Delphinian Club which, for a time, was the center of literary activity in Baltimore. Poets and writers, such as Edward Coote Pinkney, John Neal, John Pendleton Kennedy and, for a brief period, Edgar Alan Poe, produced a stream of materials for the city's newspapers and journals.

Though the founding of the Maryland Academy of Science and Literature and the Maryland Institute for the Promotion of the Mechanical Arts in 1825 had raised hopes for a cultural ascent, these expectations proved barren. This reflected the city's preoccupation with economic concerns and the social rigidity resulting from a city and state that tolerated slavery. The social controls needed to enforce the slave codes stifled free expression and cultural experimentation.

The burning of the Baltimore Lyceum during a wave of arson in the winter of 1835 symbolized the turmoil which filled the civic arena for most of John G. Morris's first dozen years in Baltimore. The attack on the Lyceum destroyed the focus of Baltimore's cultural life, and represented working class anger toward the social élite they held responsible for the city's economic failures.[2]

Morris's first year at First English Lutheran Church marked his transition from seminary student to full-time pastor. He also made another, more personal transition. On November 1, 1827, he married Eliza Hay (1808-1875), his child-hood friend from York. The ninth child and third daughter of Jacob Hay and Mary Rudisill Hay, Eliza came from a prominent Pennsylvania German family. Eliza's father, a merchant, bank director, and local jurist, had a long and close relation-ship with the Morris family as a friend and neighbor. Jacob Hay, in fact, served as one of the executors for Dr. John Morris's estate. John Gottlieb and Eliza knew each other well. With the two families living across the street from one another and both devout German Lutherans, the two young people, separated in age by only two and a half years, had shared many activities.[3]

Despite his long relationship with Eliza, Morris delayed marriage until after he had received a full-time pastoral call and ordination as a minister (October 1827). The timing reflected one of Morris's strongly held beliefs. Seminary stu-dents of his time and later entered into what Morris termed "premature and often inconsiderate engagements." The practical churchman observed that "not a few young men, as their education advances and experience is extended, discover that their choice of juvenile years was not judicious, and they change their minds to their own discredit and the disappointment and wretchedness of the lady in ques-tion. Some, in mingling with society, find ladies more refined, intelligent, hand-some and perhaps better endowed with worldly goods, and reject their first love, and thus occasion scandal."[4] By waiting until he was professionally established, and then marrying a woman he had known for years, from his own social and economic background, Morris took every prudent step to ensure a happy union. The Morris family's approval of the union strengthened the ties between the two young people.

We know little about Eliza Hay Morris. Though scarcely mentioned in *Life Reminiscences*, the few references to the person John G. Morris found "dearer to me than my life," hint at the depth of his feelings for her. At key points in his life, such as the decision to leave First English in 1860, Morris acknowledged consulting his wife. For Eliza, the lack of a public persona reflected the almost exclusively domes-tic role expected of middle- and upper middle-class women in nineteenth-century America.[5]

Certainly Eliza Morris's seven pregnancies between 1828 and 1838 focused her time and energy on domestic matters. Losing five of her first seven children before their first birthday assuredly took a heavy emotional toll. From a family portrait of the 1840s, we find a thin-lipped serious woman fully enmeshed in her responsibilities as mother and pastor's wife. The Morrises' losses, though high, reflected a normal death rate for children in their first year of life in northern and mid-Atlantic cities during the ante-bellum era.[6] With motherhood the most respected domestic function for women, the loss of so many children must have made Eliza Hay Morris's first years in Baltimore particularly difficult.

Though reticent in his memoirs about his wife and family, Morris expressed deep feelings in his personal diary and in the private family register which recorded births and the all too common early deaths. "I never wrote a chapter," stated Morris the father, "with more mingled emotions of joy and grief and while I now write, my heart beats strongly with gratitude to my Heavenly Father for the children He has given me and at the same time I am bowed down with grief that they were not all spared to me, but His heavenly will be done and I do not murmur." Pain, resignation, and subtle recriminations mingled together. In stark terms, Morris recorded that his son John, their first-born," had "lived but seven hours." He felt that "my dear Eliza was prematurely delivered . . . owing to some indiscretions on her part—some long walks in the hot sun and lifting a heavy table." This anger never again appeared in any of Morris's extant diaries and papers.. Any breach Morris's attitude may have caused in the marital relationship remains unknown though distinctly possible given his judgmental streak.

The loss of a second child, again within a few hours of birth, brought the Baltimore pastor almost to the brink of despair. Morris wrote, "God has again been pleased to visit me with affliction and I am again a mourning parent. My dear wife was delivered of a well formed female infant, but 8 hours after it was no more. This being the second child we have lost, renders it particularly hard, but I am glad Eliza endures it so nobly—I have nearly abandoned all hope of ever raising any children, for they tell me, that abortions are more frequent with those women who have suffered them in first pregnancy."[7] This time, Pastor Morris's grief did not result in lashing out at his wife. Rather, a deep pessimism had set in.

With evident relief, and probably a touch of amazement, Morris could finally record, on May 25, 1830, that "last evening at ten minutes after 8:00 Eliza delivered of a female child," and that twenty-six hours later, "both are doing extremely well."[8] The successful birth of Maria Louisa Morris helped assuage the pain of the earlier losses and restored a sense of confidence and hope to the young couple. In all, John and Eliza Morris would have ten children, with four daughters living to adulthood. The loss of two sons, and the fact that his brothers had no children, meant the eventual end of the direct Morris line. In the later years of his life, this would again resurrect painful feelings for Morris.

Joy again found a place in the Morris household. After daughters Maria Louisa (1830-1907) and Georgianna (1838-1918) survived the critical first years of life, both gave promise of becoming lively and intelligent young women. Perhaps as significant, Eliza's nephew, Charles A. Hay (1821-1893), joined the family

38

circle in 1835. Sensitive to the fourteen-year-old boy's early loss of his father, the young pastor tutored his wife's nephew for a year and helped him enter the sophomore class at Pennsylvania College, the new Lutheran college in Gettysburg. Morris always remembered young Hay's stay in his home with "great fondness." He confided to Charles P. Krauth about his nephew: "What a fine temper he has. I never had the occasion to scold him once all the while he was with me."[9] Quite a statement from the critical and demanding Morris. He took a life-long interest in Charles Hay, helping him to enter the ministry and embark on a notable career. A close personal and professional relationship endured between the two men until Charles's death in 1893. Charles Hay replaced the sons Morris lost.

During these early years in Baltimore, Barbara Morris and brother Charles continued to provide support and advice to the youngest member of the family. Morris's prodigiously active professional life demanded a stable and supportive family network. As his career became increasingly complex and public, this need only increased. Fortunately for Morris, he found what he needed.

Morris's congregation exemplified the change and struggle going on in Lutheranism, and proved a good training ground for the new pastor. Organized by a small group of dissidents from German-speaking Zion Lutheran Church, the founders of First English believed that the future of Lutheranism depended on the introduction of English into church worship and life. They feared that their children would drop away from a church which remained aloof from the evangelicalism dominant in American Protestantism. First English represented part of a trend growing in Lutheranism since the early part of the century that sought closer contact with other Protestants, yet maintained a basic commitment to a separate identity as Lutheran Christians. Samuel Simon Schmucker and the General Synod symbolized this course of action. Low levels of new German immigration seemed to ensure the eventual triumph of assimilation.

Though the cause of English-speaking Lutheranism would eventually triumph, Morris faced some immediate problems in Baltimore. From the beginning, he proceeded "amid hard work and many difficulties" to build up his church. The pastors of Zion Lutheran Church, J. Daniel Kurtz and John Uhlhorn, received the new pastor with "cold politeness" when he called on them, and did nothing to aid the new congregation. To Morris's great disappointment, many former members of Zion, who had left the German church and joined other Protestant denominations, failed to rally to the English Lutheran church. Morris experienced little success in attracting the former members of German churches, whether they had ceased attending any church or joined other denominations. This he attributed to the hostility of German Lutheran ministers who seemed to dislike English Lutherans even more than other denominations.[10]

Whatever the reason, Morris's congregation had to depend on other sources to grow. The new pastor "spent much time upon my sermons" and visited his congregation "often." He also followed up with strangers who visited his church and had no denominational affiliation. Since many Baltimoreans, like most Americans, had no formal church membership, he had a large pool of potential members. Always careful not to interfere with those already enrolled in other churches, Morris's persistent visits to people attending one of his Sunday sermons (he preached morning and evening) or his Wednesday evening lectures gradually added new members to First English's rolls. Morris's zeal emerges from his daily study of Hebrew so that his sermons and Wednesday lectures on difficult biblical passages would both strengthen the current members and appeal to those looking for a church home.[11]

Despite his evident zealousness, and indications that his work would meet with success, the young pastor harshly criticized his own motivation and ability. Though his "congregation has increased far beyond my expectations," Morris reported in his diary that "my spirits are often depressed, and I sometimes fear that I have not done as should have done in choosing the ministerial profession." He worried that "my heart is cold" and that he needed the courage to confront his "people as impenitent sinners hurrying to the bar of judgment." As time passed, Morris's early anxieties and doubts about his vocation eased, and hard work and continuing success absorbed his energies and emotions. Inner fears that he had merely followed the promptings of his mother and brother were replaced by solid proof of his own motivation and competence, and the certainty he had received a call. A certainty that would never desert him in the tumultuous decades ahead.[12]

The public perception of Lutherans in Baltimore posed another major obstacle to Morris's efforts to increase his congregation. He at first encountered hostility or indifference from other Protestants who viewed Lutherans, whether German or English-speaking, as "not demonstrative in their piety," with "no interest in the religious activities of the day."[13] In other words, Presbyterians, Baptists, and Methodists did not see Lutherans as full participants in the great evangelical crusade.

Morris confronted this problem soon after his arrival. Within a month, he began a Sunday school for forty-eight young people, and by 1832 had a formal, flourishing program with 236 students, with a library of some 250 volumes. In combining the Lutheran respect for catechetical instruction with the American zeal for the Sunday school movement, Morris in effect announced his adherence to the "American Lutheranism" championed by Schmucker. Throughout his career, Morris saw the Sunday school as one of the essential tools in strengthening allegiance to the church, in serving as a starting point in building new congregations, and in linking Lutherans with other Protestants. Morris also took great personal satisfaction in his Sunday school work. As he tartly noted in his diary, his Sunday school success "shows what can be done for the Lutheran church here by proper management." In July 1832, Morris proudly told Krauth that five young men, all teachers in his Sunday school, had "come out" for Christ in public prayer. In all, the delighted pastor noted, twenty men had gone through a public conversion experience.[14]

Other steps Morris took to integrate English Lutheranism into Baltimore's religious mainstream included holding weekly public prayer meetings; establishing a temperance society in his congregation; and preaching a series of temperance sermons.[15] All this, in addition to his successful Sunday school, built bridges to other Protestants through the establishment and use of commonly accepted evangelical institutions and symbols.

As part of his effort to break down the suspicion of other Protestants, and to capitalize on his intellectual and social interests, Morris soon became acquainted with the most prominent and active ministers and laymen in other churches. For example, he studied Hebrew with the Reverend John Breckinridge, a former tutor of Morris at Princeton, and an "Old School" Presbyterian, "all soul and liberality." Other prominent ministers with whom Morris formed close relationships included Albert Helfenstein of the German Reformed Church and John M. Duncan of the Reformed Presbyterian Church.[16]

Morris also became active in several of the interdenominational religious societies of the period, particularly the American Bible Society. In respect for his abilities, the Maryland Bible Society sent Morris to Frederick and Hagerstown to stimulate the zeal of local societies for distributing Bibles to every home. Morris's successful efforts so angered the pastor of a Roman Catholic church in the area that he roundly attacked Morris for facilitating the distribution of Protestant translations of the Bible. By December 1830, Morris had enrolled as a life member of the American Bible Society.[17]

As a result of all his efforts, John G. Morris's congregation grew. In 1827, the church had thirty-seven communicants; in 1837, there were 152. Much change and progress also occurred in the "brick and mortar" aspect of church life. In 1830, the congregation purchased its first organ and built a parsonage for Morris and his family. Other additions included a new 36 by 50-foot lecture room, twenty-eight new pews, the renovation of the old lecture room to rent it as a day school, and the introduction of gas lighting in 1838.[18]

For Morris and First English Lutheran Church the decade of the 1830s climaxed in a large-scale revival, which saw eighty people join the congregation.[19] Though Morris later discounted the efficacy of revivals and lamented the fact that few of the new adherents remained over the long-term as church members, the immediate success of the revival and the steady growth of the 1830s left the pastor and congregation with a sense of momentum.

In addition to his extensive work in Baltimore, Morris began early in his career to play an active role in the regional and national life of the Lutheran church. As an advocate of progressive, English-speaking Lutheranism, he secured election within a year of his ordination (1827) as the corresponding secretary of the Maryland Synod's newly constituted Domestic Missionary and Parent Education Society, an organization dedicated to obtaining financial assistance for needy students interested in studying for the ministry. Morris and the other members of the society understood that a well-educated clergy remained the best hope for the church's future in America. Morris lamented the "superficial training" that many of his fellow-ministers received. At all costs this problem cried out for correction.

Other signs of success for Morris soon followed. The Maryland Synod elected him secretary three times (1833-1835), and he twice served as president (1836 and 1837). He was regularly appointed a delegate to sessions of the General Synod and served as treasurer (1833) and secretary (1839).[20] In all his posts, Morris supported the missionary and educational endeavors on which he felt the success of the church depended. In the small circle of Lutheran church leaders, the ambitious Morris quickly gained recognition for his competence and personal drive. From recognition flowed respect and, eventually, leadership in the life and politics of the Lutheran church.

The Baltimore pastor's contributions as a Lutheran confessional leader, Lutheran educator, and evangelical reformer formed the three pillars on which he built his denominational career. Over the decades, in all three areas, Morris fought to assimilate Lutheranism into the mainstream of American Protestantism, while retaining the crucial elements of its religious heritage. The obstacles he encountered from the beginning—the resistance of German-American traditionalists, the indifference of "fallen away" Lutherans, and the ignorance of many Protestants about Lutherans—never deterred him. Morris's vision of Lutheranism in America, nascent in 1827 but more firmly developed by 1839, never let him rest.

His concern from the beginning focused on the question of confessional identity. On the resolution of this issue, more than any other, the ultimate fate of the Lutheran church in America depended. As a follower of the younger Schmucker,

Morris supported the concept of Lutheran unity based on adherence to the religious principles of the Reformation as "substantially taught" in the Augsburg Confession. In keeping with this stance, and with his ardent desire for the cultural transformation of the church in America as a constant spur, Morris in 1831 became the first editor of a new English-language church paper, *The Lutheran Observer*. Though somewhat reluctant to take on additional duties, Morris succumbed to the enthusiastic urging of his General Synod colleagues. In the inaugural edition, the twenty-seven-year-old clergyman wrote:

> Though the paper bears the distinctive name of our church, yet we do not wish it to be regarded as an exclusively partisan publication. We desire to hold communion with all who love the Lord Jesus in sincerity; — and though the largest portion of our paper may be occupied by the affairs of our own church, yet it will not be because we think that of all the others, 'the temple of the Lord are we.'[21]

In arguing for conditional acceptance of the Augsburg Confession, "communion" with other believers, and reliance on the Scriptures as "the only rule of our conscience," Morris sought to clear away barriers dividing Lutherans from other American Protestants. By rejecting certain doctrines in the Augsburg Confession then unacceptable to many Protestants, and embracing a spirit of fervent piety, editor Morris stressed the ties that united evangelical Protestants.[22] Along these lines, in the *Observer* and in a catechism he completed in 1831 at the request of the General Synod, he joined with other evangelical Protestants in rejecting a particularly controversial aspect of Lutheran doctrine, the nature of the sacraments.

Morris objected to what he considered the "long exploded doctrine of baptismal regeneration." He saw baptism as an "ordinance" by which an individual "is solemnly initiated into society of Christians," and thus made a "partaker of all the privileges of the church." He interpreted infant baptism as the receipt of a "promise from the heavenly father," not the washing away of original sin and the gift of sanctification as traditionally taught.[23]

Like other evangelicals, Morris emphasized that only when sinners experienced a conversion, repented, and led godly lives would they experience the full results of regeneration and sanctification. This ability of the sinner to aid in his or her own salvation separated American evangelicals from those who adhered to traditional Protestant teachings on man's depravity and inability to contribute to his own sanctification. Most American Protestants of the era, with the exception of strict Calvinists, conservative Lutherans, and a few other groups, adopted the evangelical position.[24]

Though Morris claimed "that he thought it best to say nothing respecting the controverted point of Christ's presence in the sacrament of the Supper," he in fact made his position perfectly clear. He viewed the Lord's Supper "as a memorial of his [Christ's] suffering and death," in which those who were "really qualified" (i.e., "converted" Christians) partook "of the emblems of the broken body and shed blood of my beloved Saviour." Not so many years later, Morris would castigate such views as "Zwinglian" and bitterly accuse Samuel Simon Schmucker of leading him and many other young ministers away from the true Lutheran teaching of Christ's Real Presence in the Lord's Supper.[25]

Morris's editorial support for a "generic" Lutheranism focused solely on those "fundamental" doctrines essential for a Christian's salvation, avoided doctrinal battles, accepted the idea of theological evolution and progress since the Reformation, and helped lay the groundwork for a new crusade, the cause of Protestant union. He strongly backed Schmucker's 1838 call in the *Fraternal Appeal* for a great Protestant confederation of denominations. Joined, in Schmucker's view, by a common acceptance of "fundamental" doctrines enunciated in the scriptures and the early creeds of the church, Protestants could retain their organizational distinctions yet unite in a great crusade of evangelical reform. Morris described the *Fraternal Appeal* for his readers as an "elaborate, well-written paper," showing "much research and ingenuity."[26]

In addition to supporting a general Protestant confederation, Morris also urged a union between Lutherans and the German Reformed. At the 1833 sessions of the Maryland Synod and the General Synod, Morris led the forces advocating a merger. He chaired the General Synod committee charged with exploring the "specific basis" for a union and evaluating the advantages and disadvantages of any merger. Despite the committee's failure to reach a "definite" conclusion on the issue, Morris's interest in the German Reformed remained constant.[27] He believed that both denominations shared a great bond because of their common German heritage, and both faced a similar struggle in adapting to the American cultural environment. No doubt Morris's Pennsylvania background, where many Lutheran and Reformed congregations shared buildings and even, at times, pastors, also stimulated his interest. In any event, he often served as an official observer at German Reformed church conventions.

Besides advocating closer denominational ties, Morris urged readers of the *Observer* to adopt the basic tools of evangelical Protestantism, prayer meetings and revivals. He encouraged Lutherans who were doubtful about the effects of protracted religious meetings to have confidence that "extraordinary times" required "extraordinary efforts." Morris denied that "these extraordinary efforts" reflected "religious fanaticism." On the contrary, he believed that Lutheran ministers, grounded in traditional "ecclesiastical usages" and a program of catechetical instruction, could prevent any emotional "excess." At the heart of all this remained the essential prerequisite: Lutheran use of English in church worship and life. Passionately, Morris hailed the "incalculable benefit" for Lutherans of the introduction of English into the church and lamented the "miserable infatuation of our fathers" for whom the German language "must be maintained even if the church is dispersed."[28]

By minimizing doctrinal differences, emphasizing "practical" Christianity, and stressing the need for English, Morris clearly hoped to align Lutherans with the great evangelical crusade of American Protestantism. Yet, even at this early point in his career, the first hints of an ideological change began to appear. Unlike Schmucker and many other Protestant leaders, Morris's theological perspective became increasingly animated by an appreciation for and interest in history. During the 1830s, he developed a particular interest in Martin Luther and the Reformation era.

Morris's historical interests manifested themselves in several different ways. He successfully advocated that the Maryland Synod designate the Sunday nearest October 31 as Reformation Sunday, and he urged similarly successful action on the General Synod. In addition, he translated, for publication in the *Lutheran Observer*, extensive passages from Merle d'Aubigne's *History of the Reformation*. Interested in relating information about Luther's early years, particularly facts about his parents and home life, he labored for over six months translating d'Aubigne's work. Though excessively partisan by the standards of modern scholarship on the Reformation, he viewed d'Aubigne's work as "excellent" in both style and facts.[29]

Morris's fascination with Luther had several sources. From boyhood, he had absorbed biographies, beginning with Plutarch's *Lives*. This fit in with the culture of the age, which put great stock in heroic character, and the moral purposes that an informed appreciation for history and biography revealed. Inclined to history and biography, and proud of his German Lutheran heritage, Morris felt a natural attraction to Luther. Convinced of the reformer's divinely-inspired contributions to Western civilization's spiritual and civic progress, Morris believed Lutherans and other American Protestants lacked a full appreciation for the importance of Luther and the Reformation. To his way of thinking, this imperiled a Protestantism besieged by a resurgent Roman Catholicism. While many evangelical Protestants, such as S. S. Schmucker, shared this fear, few had Morris's growing respect for the historical perspective.

Morris also had a developing appreciation for German theology, which experienced a renaissance among German Lutheran scholars in the 1830s and 1840s. He noted with pleasure a visit to Princeton, during which he stayed with Charles Hodge and discussed at length German theological and philosophical developments. Morris urged his friend Krauth to join him in getting American publishers to print translations of the best new theological literature for the "English-reading public." Morris attempted to further this project by seeking support from several prominent Lutheran church leaders, including Henry L. Baugher, Michael Jacobs, and Martin Luther Stoever.[30] His interest in expanding theological knowledge seems particularly striking since many considered Schmucker's most original doctrinal work, *Popular Theology* (published in 1834), as more than adequate for the theological needs of American Lutherans.

Morris's awareness of Lutheran historical traditions also stimulated his involvement in liturgical development and renewal. During the 1830s, he served on various Maryland Synod and General Synod liturgy commissions. The work of these commissions reflected the general need in the church to develop an English liturgy, as well as to make available hymn books, catechisms, and other devotional books in English.

Early in his career, Morris advocated more than merely translating German liturgies or maintaining what he termed the "plain Presbyterian style" (under which pastors were free to devise their own modes of worship) then in fashion with the relatively few English-worshipping Lutheran congregations. Rather, he favored the adoption and use of "an entire new or at least greatly improved liturgy," that would be standard throughout the church. His ideas on what a complete liturgy should contain evolved as his knowledge of the traditional, historic Lutheran liturgy developed. He advocated for a time that the General Synod adopt the liturgy of the East Pennsylvania Synod, one of the more conservative district synods, and proposed it as a model to the other district synods.

The young minister wanted a liturgy that contained several forms of confession, prayers for the sick and "other conditions of life," and forms for administering the sacraments and for marriage, burial, and ordination. All this was far more elaborated and prescribed than Schmucker, acknowledged to have a modest interest at most in liturgical issues, and others could support. Morris, Krauth, Philadelphia pastor Charles R. Demme, and their confederates had to wait decades for their ideas to come to fruition. As Morris summarized, "For a long time there was a desire expressed to reform our bald and spiritless mode of worship and several liturgies were prepared by committees, but none met with general acceptance."[31]

Strengthening Lutheran identity by promoting the cause of denomina-
tional-based higher education became the second pillar of Morris's career as a
Lutheran pastor. Throughout his long career Morris devoted great energy to the
development of two fledgling church institutions at Gettysburg, the Theological
Seminary and Pennsylvania College (present-day Gettysburg College). Both the
seminary, founded in 1826, and the college, chartered by the state in 1832, sought
to rectify the continuing desperate shortage of trained Lutheran clergy. Samuel
Simon Schmucker, the principle motivating force behind both schools, planned
that men interested in the ministry and needing college-level instruction would
first go to Pennsylvania College and then on to the seminary. Though the
College's educational goals always extended beyond preparing men for the seminary, the close ties forged between the two institutions remained. Many of the
College's students would go on to theological training as Schmucker had hoped.

The ties in great part resulted from the fact that both schools, usually in dire
financial straits, often shared faculty, and had men who served on the boards of
directors of both institutions. John G. Morris exemplified this phenomenon. Traveling by horse and coach until the railroad reached Gettysburg in the 1850s, Morris gave annual lectures at the seminary on "Pulpit Elocution" and the "Relations
of Physical Science to Revealed Religion" from 1869 to 1894, while he pioneered
the teaching of natural history at the college during the 1840s. From the beginning, he occupied a position of leadership in directing the destinies of both the
seminary and the college. In 1828, the Maryland Synod appointed the recently
ordained minister to the seminary's board of directors, on which he served until
1836, functioning as secretary. Morris resumed his seat in 1840, remaining for the
rest of his life and serving several terms as president during a crucial period in the
seminary's history (1844-1846, 1847-1851, 1857-1861). Playing a similarly important role in the life of the college, Morris joined twenty-six other men as original
trustees at the school's founding. He served on its board as secretary from 1832
until 1835, and rejoined the board in 1844, remaining until the end of his life.[32]

Morris's zeal for education and his commitment to a strong American
Lutheran church fueled his work. With the other directors, he helped select faculty members and set academic standards and curricula. Important to the future of
both schools, Morris and his colleagues recruited students and sought financial
assistance for the needy. His hard work helped sustain the seminary and the college during their trying first decade.

Morris focused his energy on creating libraries, a critical need for schools with
hopes of developing into recognized centers of higher education. He gave a great

deal of attention to raising funds for book purchases and, most significantly, to cataloguing the new acquisitions. As demonstrated in his personal life and with First English's Sunday school library, Morris appreciated the role libraries could play in raising the general level of knowledge and culture. All of his work as a cultural leader featured libraries, and other types of collections, as the cornerstone of the enterprise.

While the indefatigable Morris enjoyed his work at Gettysburg as a welcome intellectual complement to his pastoral duties, he encountered one major problem. It boiled down to the need to work closely once again with Samuel Simon Schmucker, who dominated both Gettysburg institutions. His vision and driving will set the framework for all major decisions and initiatives. With his father serving as president of the board of directors until the end of the 1830s, the younger Schmucker had virtually unchallenged control of the seminary.

An early critical issue for the financially precarious theology school was Schmucker's desire to create a second professor's position to assist him. With the seminary barely solvent, this posed obvious difficulties. Also, church leaders debated the most likely source for a new professor, with many favoring a candidate from Germany. This reflected the still overwhelming German ethos of American Lutheranism, as well as the theological renaissance underway in Germany.

Morris did not share his misgivings with fellow seminary directors, but wrote to Charles Philip Krauth: "The Prof. [Schmucker] complains of his extensive correspondence and I am beginning to think that if he would curtail that and attend to his own special business, we might perhaps do without an additional teacher." Morris was unimpressed with Schmucker's complaint that the growth of the student body from eight to twenty-three necessitated a second faculty member. In addition to skepticism about the need for a second position, Morris seriously doubted the seminary's ability to raise the $10,000 required to fund the position. Despite his critical stance, Morris could still acknowledge that Schmucker was "a faithful servant of the Lord, and an ardent friend of the Seminary."[33]

Difficulties with fundraising and the lack of interest among German professors in journeying to far away Gettysburg ended any hope of obtaining a scholar from Europe. Instead, Schmucker and the board turned to a German already in America, Ernst L. Hazelius, then teaching at Hartwick Seminary in upstate New York. Morris followed Schmucker's lead and supported the Hazelius appointment as the best solution under the circumstances.

During Hazelius's brief tenure at Gettysburg, he and Morris developed a close relationship. Visiting Morris in his Baltimore home, the German professor reminisced fondly of the kindness he had received from Dr. John Morris when he stopped in York in 1800. This sealed the friendship, despite a twenty-eight-year age difference. He sympathized with Hazelius's almost immediate discomfort at living in Schmucker's shadow, a feeling the younger man knew all too well. When a member of the South Carolina Synod asked Morris to recommend someone with the professorial qualifications appropriate for the new seminary the Synod intended to open, Morris recommended Hazelius for the post. When the South Carolinians approached Hazelius, he leapt at the opportunity and soon left Gettysburg.[34] Morris actively encouraged the board to fill the second professor's post next with his friend Krauth. Though appointed, Krauth declined when Pennsylvania College selected him first for a professorship and then the presidency.

In 1838, the seminary board turned to former member Morris and appointed him professor of biblical and Hebrew literature. Schmucker's preeminent position at the seminary meant he would have had a voice in all the appointments and would have approved of Morris. This continued a series of gestures going back to Morris's acceptance at the "pro-seminary" in New Market, which signaled Schmucker's high regard for his student.

In a long, anguished letter to Krauth, the thirty-five-year-old Morris poured out his dismay about his election. Morris expressed concern about the Lutheran identity of his congregation, and expressed fervent belief in his calling to urban pastoral work. Further, Morris, as a General Synod advocate, doubted that conservative Pennsylvania Ministerium pastors, who distrusted "centralizing" tendencies in the church, would welcome his selection. As Morris put it, "My theological and political sentiments differ in some respects from those of most of your men, and that might produce unpleasant collision."[35]

No doubt these factors influenced Morris. On a deeper level, though, he feared he might lose the personal and professional freedom he had worked so hard to achieve. He had no intention of living permanently in the shadow of Samuel Simon Schmucker. Life at Gettysburg would bring him into regular contact with Schmucker *pere* and *fils*, and thus remind him of an inner loss he continued to feel. Despite a cry from the heart, "Oh that I could be in both places at the same time," Morris declined the board's appointment and opted to remain in Baltimore.[36]

While declining to join the seminary faculty, Morris faced an identical situation, also in the turbulent year of 1838, at Pennsylvania College. In April, the board elected him professor of rhetoric, German literature, and French. Schmucker also played a role in this effort. Chosen as one of three board members to advise Morris of his election, Schmucker traveled to Baltimore to gain the young pastor's acceptance. He obviously wanted his former student at Gettysburg and seemed unaware of Morris's antipathy, or at least discounted its seriousness. With

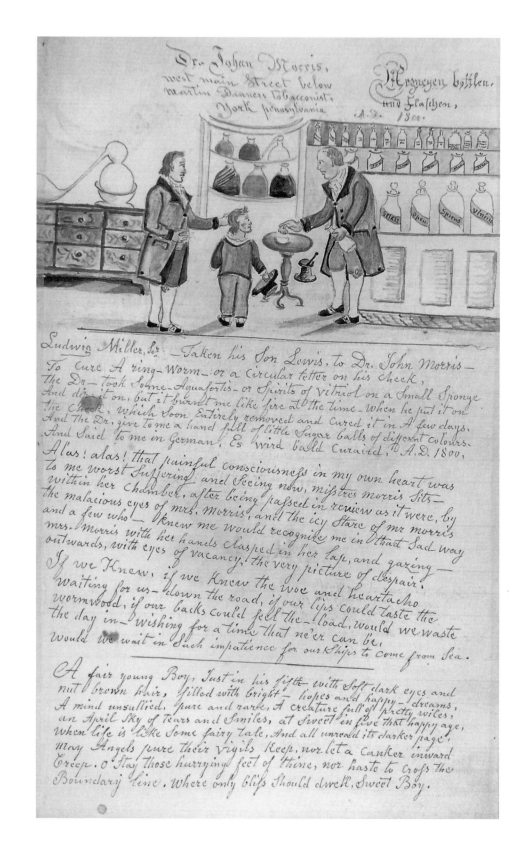

Dr. Johan Morris,
west main Street below
martin Danners tobacconist.
York pensylvania

Arzneyen bottlen.
und Flaschen,
A.D. 1800.

Ludwig Miller, Sr. — Taken his Son Lewis, to Dr. John Morris —
To cure A ring-worm — or a Circular tetter on his cheek,
The Dr — took Some — Aquafortis — or Spirits of Vitriol on a Small Sponge
And dip't it on, but it burnt me like fire at the time — When he put it on
the cheek, which Soon Entirely removed and cured it in A few days.
And the Dr. give to me a hand full of little Sugar balls of different colours.
And Said to me in German, Es wird bald Curaied, A.D. 1800,

Alas! alas! that painful consciousness in my own heart was
to me worst Suffering, and Seeing now, mistress morris Sits —
within her Chamber, after being passed in review as it were, by
the malacious eyes of mrs. Morris, and the icy Stare of mr morris
and a few who — Knew me would recognise me in that Sad way
mrs. Morris with her hands clasped in her lap, and gazing —
outwards, with eyes of vacancy. the very picture of despair.
If we Knew, if we Knew the woe and heartache
waiting for us — down the road, if our lips could taste the
wormwood, if our backs could feel the — load, would we waste
the day in — wishing for a time that ne'er can be.
Would we wait in Such impatience for our Ships to come from Sea.

_____

A fair young Boy, Just in his fifth — with Soft dark eyes and
nut brown hair, filled with bright — hopes and happy — dreams,
A mind unsullied, pure and rare, A creature full of pretty wiles,
an April Sky of Tears and Smiles, at Sweet in five that happy age,
When life is like Some fairy tale, And all unreald its darker page,
May Angels pure their vigils keep, nor let a canker inward
Creep. O Stay those hurrying feet of thine, nor haste to Cross the
Boundary line. Where only bliss Should dwell, Sweet Boy.

Opposite page:
Drawing by Lewis Miller of
Dr. John (Johan) Morris at work
in 1800.
(*York County Historical Society.*)

Portrait of JGM as a young man.
(*Courtesy Helen Berry.*)

Below:
The German Lutheran Church
in York (Christ Church), 1799.
(*York County Historical Society.*)

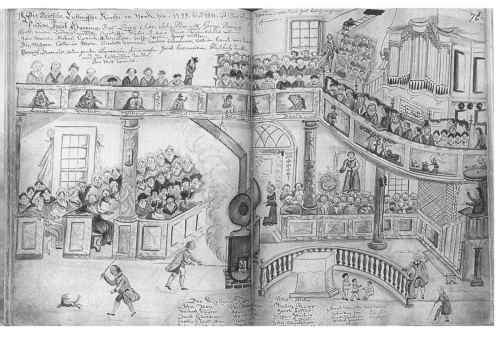

The College of New Jersey (Princeton College). (*Princeton University Libraries.*)

Theological Seminary of the Presbyterian Church, Princeton, New Jersey, 1843. (*Princeton Theological Seminary.*)

Battle Monument, Baltimore, ca. 1838. (*Still Pictures Branch/American Cities List No. 2, National Archives.*)

Athenaeum, St. Paul and Saratoga Streets, Baltimore. (*Maryland Historical Society.*)

First English Lutheran Church, Lexington Street, Baltimore. (*Maryland Historical Society.*)

JGM, his wife Eliza, and daughters
(from left) Maria Louisa, Anna Hay,
and Georgianna in the 1840s.
(*Courtesy Helen Berry.*)

Eliza Hay Morris and daughter.
(*Courtesy Helen Berry.*)

Samuel Simon Schmucker.
(*Still Picture Branch/79-T-2041A,
National Archives.*)

Pennsylvania College.
(*Still Picture Branch/79-TM-12,
National Archives.*)

JGM's long friendship with Charles Philip Krauth dated to seminary days. (*Still Picture Branch 79/T-2035A, National Archives.*)

Lutheran Theological Seminary at Gettysburg, ca. 1860. (*Still Picture Branch/79-T-2047, National Archives.*)

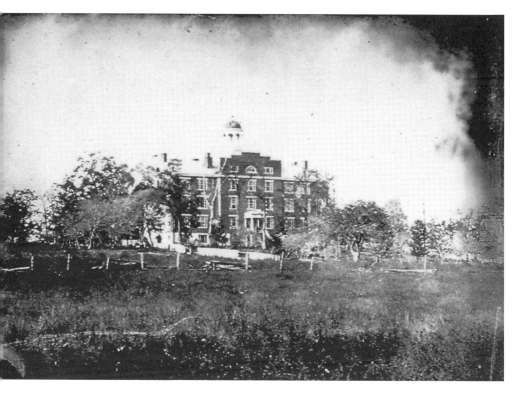

less distress than with the seminary's offer, Morris informed the college board that he declined their offer because "I cannot . . . find it consistent with my view of duty."[37]

Another proffered honor caused John G. Morris infinitely more problems. In September 1839, at the instigation of Schmucker and Thaddeus Stevens, the noted Pennsylvania politician, the board suspended its rule for awarding honorary degrees. They conferred a doctor of divinity degree on Morris immediately, and did not follow their usual practice of making the nomination at one semiannual session and approving or disapproving it at a subsequent session. The reasons for the board's suspension of procedure remain unclear, but in any case Morris would have none of it.[38] He immediately wrote asking probing questions about why the board had suspended its rule for him, the role of the faculty, if any, in the process, and if the board had rejected another potential honoree because the time frame for submitting nominations was not followed.

Eventually Morris's concern about the board's process found its way into the *Lutheran Observer* and an irate Thaddeus Stevens wanted to revoke the honor. After some further correspondence, Morris formally declined the degree, but he assured the board he no longer questioned the legality of its action. Morris explained to the board that "with the elevated standards of education which you have raised, you ought to make the qualifications for your collegiate distinctions correspond, and none but eminently distinguished men should in my view, be honored with your doctoral diploma." The board accepted Morris's communication "as satisfactory."[39] Once again we find Schmucker proposing an honor for him and Morris rejecting it. Though college records do not indicate the board ever awarded Morris a doctor of divinity degree, within a few years the clergyman was generally referred to as Reverend Doctor John G. Morris, D.D. In 1875, the college awarded Morris an honorary doctor of laws degree. Morris also refused to accept this honor.

Morris's defensiveness about the whole issue of honorary degrees is clear from passages in *Life Reminiscences*, which he intended for publication:

> I opposed most of those nominations in the College Board, and it was because I did not want to aid in cheapening the title; and, secondly, because most of the nominees did not come up to my standard; and, thirdly, there were so many others equally entitled to it on the basis assumed by their friends, and why discriminate? But, some may ask, "How was it in relation to yourself?" It was just so. I challenge anyone to say that I ever, by letter or in any other way, accepted any of the college titular honors bestowed upon me. No such letter will be found noticed upon the Secretary's record nor anywhere else; and if my name sometimes appears in print with these suffixes, I have never authorized the use of them.[40]

While Morris's notions of modesty and the need to raise academic standards deserve some credence, there is more to the issue. For decades, letters were addressed to "Dr. John G. Morris" or "John G. Morris, D.D., L.L.D.," with no word of correction from the addressee. Most of Morris's publications appeared with the honorary titles listed, a matter that Morris surely could have controlled. Morris's stubborn refusal in 1839 was, at heart, an angry response to the offerer, Samuel Simon Schmucker. Once in this bind, Morris had to maintain the position he expressed to the Gettysburg board. And he did so as the passages in *Life Reminiscences* illustrate. But the proud John G. Morris enjoyed, and certainly never rejected, recognition of his accomplishments.

The third pillar of Morris's cultural contribution to the development of Lutheranism in America involved the great crusade of evangelical reform. As already noted, he worked assiduously in the national and state Bible societies, the Sunday school movement, and with church efforts to support financially needy seminary students. He also helped organize the temperance movement in the Maryland Synod, decrying rum as a "harder master" than even slavery.[41]

Morris also became known as an ardent proponent of the domestic missionary movement. Like others animated by a fervent religious spirit, he felt that settlers moving into sparsely settled parts of Maryland and points in the "far west" needed missionaries, armed with Bibles and other religious supplies. At Morris's instigation, the General Synod sponsored a missionary conference in 1835. Though not much happened as a result of the conference, Morris did help organize a missionary society for the General Synod and for years served as its corresponding secretary.[42] Slowly a regularized process for selecting missionaries and supporting them evolved. Morris, for his part, spent countless hours writing reports, letters, and newspaper articles keeping the cause of mission work front and center before the church. In all these reform efforts, Morris sought to raise the spiritual and cultural level of society in general and Lutherans in particular. Morris believed the results of "pure religion" (Protestantism) and moral reform strengthened American institutions for a never-ending battle against the forces of disorder and unbelief.

On the great reform issue of the pre-1860 period, the abolition of slavery, Morris adopted a basically conservative position. Though never a supporter of slavery as an institution, the practical Morris realized that the growing controversy over abolition threatened the unity of the Maryland and General Synods. He supported an 1834 resolution adopted by the Maryland Synod which stated "that we highly approve of the views and operations of the Maryland Colonization Society, and cordially recommend its claims to all our ministers and churches." The way to avoid "future internal wars and bloodshed" involved the gradual emancipation of slaves and their relocation to Africa.[43] This process, admittedly slow, would eventually end slavery and eliminate the potential for racial conflict. Though highly unrealistic in retrospect, the colonization scheme attracted the support of many prominent Americans.

Morris gave numerous addresses in support of the Maryland Colonization Society, and backed its activities in the pages of the *Lutheran Observer*.[44] He supported the efforts of Benjamin Kurtz and others to keep the slavery issue off the agenda of the General Synod, lest it too split, like the Baptists and Presbyterians, along sectional lines. From Morris's point of view, those who advocated more active abolitionist efforts posed a threat to civic and church unity. Members of the Franckean Synod, in fact, felt that their staunch support for abolitionism doomed their efforts to join the General Synod, and that Morris, as General Synod secretary, had deliberately lied about the real issue at hand.[45] Though innovative in much of his church work, in this area Morris showed little vision. Eventually the slavery crisis forced hard choices and decisions. For the time being though, denial and unrealistic alternatives could still carry the day.

By 1839, Morris was thoroughly engaged in the struggle over the evolving cultural identity of the Lutheran church. Yet this was not the only venue for his multifaceted interests and prodigious energy.

5

A Passion for Scholarship

The fervent nationalism, strong personal convictions, and pioneering zest for innovation that formed the basis for John G. Morris's success as a church leader likewise fueled his ambitions in two other areas of the cultural arena: the maturing of American scholarship, especially in science, and the development of American cultural institutions. Morris laid the foundations for his success by first establishing a reputation for sound scholarship. This he had accomplished by 1839, after only twelve years in Baltimore. From the beginning of his professional life, he developed a passion for scientific knowledge and pursuits, first in geology and then entomology. At the same time, the young minister's historical interests, particularly in Luther and the Reformation, became manifest. All of this eventually made him a model of that nineteenth-century phenomenon, the educated clergyman as theologian, scientist, and man of letters. From his scholarship, pursued decade after decade, flowed some of Morris's greatest contributions as a cultural leader.

The foundations of Morris's scholarly perspective rested on the philosophy of Common Sense Realism, its religious expression, natural theology, and the spirit of romanticism which permeated the age. The young churchman's intellectual development blossomed in a cultural milieu that sought to integrate new perspectives on the universe, man, society, and history into the tenets of Christian revelation as commonly understood by orthodox Protestants. Throughout his life, Morris's framework for interpreting science and history remained the philosophy and theology he learned at Princeton College and Seminary.

The dominant school of theological thought in the English-speaking world during the first half of the nineteenth century, natural theology sought to unite, or "harmonize," nature and revelation. Morris and other advocates of natural theology believed nature contained clear evidence of God's existence, and that nature proved the truth of divine revelation. Theologians of this school used the tools of science (the Baconian inductive method) and religion (biblical philology) to explore God's creation and revelation. As one historian of nineteenth-century science and religion has noted, "natural theology was a discipline in which Christian philosophy and empirical science merged."[1]

Morris studied the phenomena of nature to comprehend the union of God's work and word. He supplemented study of scriptural texts using the archeological and philological tools that constituted biblical "lower criticism." His scientific work rested on the fundamental premise that divine providence directed an orderly, stable, and purposeful universe reflective of a beneficent creator.

The spirit of romanticism, though not particularly Christian in its worldview, also influenced Morris's scholarly development. Like the romantics, he viewed the universe as a living, cosmic, organism which grew and changed, not as the clock- like mechanism of the rationalist Enlightenment. History represented a slow but steady march toward progress and a natural state based on overriding, general "principles."[2] If nature informed revelation, then history held the key to understanding man and society. Whether in art, literature, or history, Morris and his era in general found fascination in the mysterious, the remote, and the individual.[3]

Morris's scholarly interests brought him into contact with both élite and popular culture. Given his background and education, the élite Conversational Club, as a signal mark of recognition, inducted Morris into membership. Consisting of only twelve members—"four doctors of medicine, four doctors of divinity, and four gentlemen distinguished for literary attainments"[4]—the club featured sparkling discussions on the political, social, and intellectual topics of the day. Morris fondly recalled that "a subject was started and it was talked out, or a member would relate an incident or tell a story, on which the rest of us would make remarks, and thus the evening would pass enlivened by wit, brilliant talk and social intercourse."[5] This fitted perfectly with Morris's college experiences in debating societies. As a member of the club, he formed close ties with John Pendleton Kennedy, Brantz Mayer, and J. H. B. Latrobe, all of whom contributed mightily to Baltimore's cultural life, and to Morris's ascent to civic and cultural leadership.

The 1830s witnessed the flowering of the lyceum movement, dedicated to spreading the benefits of knowledge and culture and to raising the cultural level of the general public. Within two decades, lyceums sprang up in hundreds of American cities and towns, using a system of public lectures as the primary vehicle for education and instruction. Designed as a forum free from the partisan and sectarian disputes of the day, the public lecture focused on scientific and educational topics that would hopefully succeed in raising the level of popular culture. Free and open to the public, these lectures provided a golden opportunity for ambitious young professionals, such as Morris, to gain recognition.[6]

Such public lectures, first organized in Baltimore in 1830, proved a perfect forum for the well-educated and witty Morris. He gave his first lecture in 1833, when he "held forth" on the topic of "The Honey Bee." The ardent speaker recalled that, "this lecture, with various additions, has been repeated by me more than twenty times in various places, and frequently by special request. It interested people everywhere, for it is wonderful how few persons know anything about the extraordinary habits of that little insect. I had large painted illustrations (as I have for all my lectures), which add much to the understanding of the subject and to the relief of the lecturer."[7] Through the years, he would give hundreds of lectures in Baltimore and other cities, most of which resulted from his scientific research and literary interests. His success as a lecturer, among other things, led to his election as president of the Baltimore Lyceum.

Along with his work as a public lecturer, he also began to give public readings. Usually drawn from the texts of Shakespeare and other dramatists, the readings exposed many people to the literary classics for the first time. When well done, they also provided lively entertainment. Morris, from his youth a "spouter" of Shakespeare and others, adapted easily to the public reading stage. "Determined to pay attention to Belles Lettres studies," he read to hundreds of audiences, and eventually began to teach elocution.[8]

Morris also went to hear all the public readers appearing in Baltimore. His avid interest in speech aided him immensely in his work as a preacher and lecturer. By the end of the 1830s, between his sermons, Wednesday evening lectures at First English, and public lectures and readings, Pastor Morris had earned a solid position in the small circle of Baltimore's cultural leaders. His scientific research and historical writings only added to his luster.

Morris's scientific work sprang from his love of nature, ardent belief in natural theology, and his desire to raise the level of "respectability" of the Lutheran clergy in the eyes of others. His first scientific article, "Geology and Revelation," illustrated both his fascination with one of the century's expanding frontiers of knowledge, and the depth of his religious commitment. Like other natural theologians and scriptural theologians, he sought to reconcile scientific evidence with Genesis, demonstrating that Nature "proved" the validity of scripture.

In the article, Morris specifically focused on the first several verses in Genesis I and the Mosaic chronology for the creation of the world. The Mosaic theory of the origins of the world became the focal point of dispute among scientists and theologians during the 1830s as geological evidence about the origins of the universe increased. Morris's scientific interpretation of geological evidence reflected that of French naturalist Georges Cuvier and his theory of "catastrophism," which argued that fossil remains in various layers of geologic strata showed the world much older than the Mosaic account, and that the earth had developed as a result of a series of cosmic catastrophes. Cuvier argued that two universal floods had occurred. The first took place after a first creation event and had destroyed all existing life. According to Cuvier, fossil remains (including human bones) proved that God created new life about six thousand years ago, thus preserving the integrity of the Mosaic story. Cuvier argued that after the second great flood, the one recounted in Genesis, God preserved man and all animals living at that time through Noah and the Ark.[9]

The other school of geological interpretation, propounded by Sir Charles Lyell, a Scottish geologist, argued that the same biological, physical, and chemical forces that currently worked on the earth's surface were the same forces, and at the same intensity, which had over geologic time formed the earth's surface. Lyell discounted "catastrophism" and the idea of two creations. Lyell's concept, known as "uniformitarianism," helped lay the foundation for evolutionary biology and a new way of understanding the earth's development.[10] To Morris, Lyell and his followers represented the "advocates of the doctrine of chance, and . . . the absurd idea of the eternity of matter."[11] This debate raged more than twenty years before Charles Darwin's *On the Origin of Species*.

Morris in his article accepted Cuvier's scientific arguments concerning the ancient history of the world, the two great floods, and the creation of man and all currently living organisms about six thousand years ago. This acceptance of "catastrophism" reflected Morris's education at Princeton, his avid reading in natural science, and his own growing involvement in collecting and identifying animal fossil remains, as well as living creatures, particularly butterflies and moths (*Lepidoptera*).

In arguing against the "infidel" or unbeliever, Morris relied on more than scientific evidence. As a good natural theologian, he used the tools of biblical philology. He saw the first two verses of chapter I of Genesis as recounting two creation events. In his view, the Hebrew in verse 1, "In the beginning God created the heaven and the earth," did not specify any particular time period, hence the geologists had room for interpretations about the origins of the earth. The Bible does not explain science, he asserted; rather the language expressed religious truth. Focusing on the Hebrew text, he explained that Moses did not write "on the day the heaven and earth were created," but instead used the expression "in the beginning"—an indefinite construction allowing geologic explanations about earth history between the creation of the universe and the appearance of man.[12]

Morris argued that verse 2 described environmental conditions immediately prior to the works of creation described in the following verses. His textual analysis of the Hebrew led him to assert that the word for "create" appeared only in verse 1 and that this referred to God's creation of the universe—earth, sun, moon, and stars. When Moses used the Hebrew word for "made," for example, when referring to God's actions on the fourth day of the second creation account, he referred to God's constituting or appointing the sun, moon, and stars in relationship to the earth, not to the original time of creation. Thus geology did not contradict scripture.[13]

For Morris, geologic evidence about the earth's history and human history (i.e., fossil remains, topographical features) supported the scriptural text in Genesis, with the proper understanding of the Hebrew language. He concluded:

> These are a few of the facts in which geology and the scriptures illustrate and establish each other. There are others which are only probable, but which need not now be mentioned. Enough has been said to show that the unbeliever gains no advantage by calling on geology to aid him in his attacks on revealed religion. That science is triumphantly marshalled against him. Its discoveries demonstrate the God of nature to be the God of the bible."[14]

The Baltimore pastor's views on geology and revelation quickly came under attack, reflecting the complex intellectual ferment of the era. Jonathan Horwitz, a Baltimore physician, wrote a spirited *Defense of the Cosmogony of Moses*. He attacked Morris for passing off the views of other scientists as his own, for misinterpreting the Hebrew text of Genesis 1, and for making the common error of trying to make the scriptures accord with geology.[15]

Horwitz's charge of plagiarism, often hurled at nineteenth-century scholars by later generations, did not hold up. Though, like many scholars of the period, Morris did not use quotation marks, he clearly stated that his scientific and religious ideas reflected those of Cuvier and William Buckland. In accusing Morris of ignorance of the original Hebrew, Horwitz showed his own linguistic deficiencies. The physician argued that the phrase, "In the beginning," did not signify an indefinite period, but the first of a regular series of events.[16] In fact, Horwitz did not understand the Hebrew language. The phrase does connote an indefinite period of creation with God as the originator of the process.

Horwitz rejected the scientific idea of the earth's creation over millions of years. Though the "catastrophist" school eventually succumbed to the "uniformitarian" interpretation, Morris did have a basically accurate perspective on the ancient nature of earth history and the significance of fossils as evidence. Also, his use of biblical "lower criticism"—analyzing scriptural texts using archeological and philological tools—led him to a correct understanding of the Bible as the source of revealed religious truth, not literal scientific fact.

Morris's article and the resulting attack illustrated that the debates of the era did not simply involve "science versus religion." Rather, scientists and theologians often found themselves allies in differing camps. The pre-Darwin era saw "catastrophists" and "uniformitarians" squaring off with scientists and theologians on both sides. In addition, some like Horwitz argued for the literal interpretation of scriptures and rejected the notion of nature or science informing the Genesis text. After Darwin's *On the Origin of Species* was published in 1859, the "harmonizers" of "catastrophism" (older geologists, natural theologians) faded into amateur status. Biblical fundamentalists now fought both with advocates of a non-theologically grounded, positivist science, and those (younger professional geologists and Old Testament German scholars) who argued that nature did indeed interpret Genesis, though with different scientific and religious tenets than advocated by the natural theologians of an earlier era.[17]

Morris's harmonizing of geology and revelation showed his intellectual strengths and weaknesses. He had a sound grasp of Hebrew and the fact that Genesis did not describe scientific history, but rather expressed religious beliefs and values. Like all natural theologians, though, he believed in the harmony of science and revelation because the providence of God ordained a purposeful, beneficent universe. Though Morris accepted the ancient nature of earth's history, he firmly rejected any hint of evolutionary change, the notion that the earth had in some fashion or other always existed, and claims that "higher criticism" of biblical texts revealed their historically-contexted meaning. He remained true to the principles of natural theology, and the epistemology embedded in Common Sense Realism, throughout his scholarly career.

During these early professional years, Morris became involved in what ultimately grew into one of his great passions, the scientific study of insects or entomology. His primary entomological interest focused on butterflies and moths, which attracted a "cult of worshippers" that far exceeded the number of collectors of other orders of insects.[18] His lecture on the honey bee represented an early manifestation of his interest. In another example, in 1835, Morris had nephew Charles Hay carry into the parsonage at First English the minerals, insects, and natural history library he had purchased from J. Daniel Kurtz, the former pastor of Zion Church.[19] Other testimonials of interest came from Morris himself.

In *Life Reminiscences*, he remembered that

> It was not until after I had entered the ministry that I really began to study science, and I here desire to record my sincere conviction that, under God, my uninterrupted good health for many years is owing, in a great measure, to my pursuits of this character. My frequent rambling in the fields and woods in search of objects, my researches upon the banks of streams and in the water, my exertions in climbing trees, ascending hills, beating bushes, sweeping the grass with the insect net, turning stones and logs, all contributing to the exercise of the muscles, the expansion of the chest, and to mental and bodily recreation, the agreeable interchange of lighter and severer studies, all aided in giving me a physical constitution which to this day has never been assailed by severe sickness of twenty-four hours duration.[20]

In his solitary "ramblings," the driven and intense clergyman found release and renewal. Emotionally high-strung, like his father and brother Charles, the physical exertions of entomology provided the sense of balance which Morris, often involved in battles and conflicts of various kinds, sorely needed.

In keeping with his belief in the importance of science, Morris also encouraged Charles Philip Krauth, now president of Gettysburg College, to support the study of natural science at the college. For Morris, a truly liberal education included natural science. In writing about God and creation, he asked, "If he has systematized it so perfectly, should man close his eyes and his heart?" As the decades went on he collected thousands of animal and plant specimens (mostly butterflies and moths), "systematically arranged and labeled by the help of my books or by fellow naturalists," and preserved them in large folio volumes. He also studied botany so that he could understand the food supply of insects.[21] The quality of Morris's work and his growing reputation led to correspondence with other scientists and exchanges of specimens.

An early example of this correspondence involved Thaddeus W. Harris, the librarian at Harvard College who also served as professor of natural history and had a notable collection of insects. Morris wrote in the summer of 1839 informing Harris, whom he had never met, that "for several years I have paid as much attention to Entomology as my parochial engagements would allow." He shared information about a species he believed was unknown to Harris. He encouraged Harris and other "masters in the science" to organize a meeting that might lead to an "American Association of Naturalists." He also strongly urged Harris to press for publication and wide distribution of the writings of Thomas Say and other early American entomologists.[22]

Harris's response indicated that he accepted Morris as a serious student of science. He acknowledged that he had not known of the species Morris described to him. He assured the young pastor that he gave credit to all those around the country who sent him word of new discoveries. Harris expressed frustration and regret that his efforts heretofore in convening a "congress of naturalists" had failed.[23] Morris's future direction and activities in the cause of science became clear by the end of the decade of the 1830s: stimulating research and publication, sharing information about scientific specimens, and creating an institutional framework to foster awareness of the importance of science to American culture.

Besides his scientific pursuits, Morris also had a lifelong interest in history. Like his scientific work, his historical endeavors bore fruit over the next several decades. As noted previously, Morris had initiated in the Lutheran church formal observance of October 31 (or the nearest Sunday) as the commemoration of the Reformation. Also, in the pages of the *Observer*, he had translated long passages from Merle D'Aubigne's *History of the Reformation*. His interest in the Reformation later blossomed into an intense and productive focus on the life of Martin Luther.

He revealed his views on the nature of history, and the role of the Reformation in it, in a sermon in 1834, later published as "Necessities and Blessings of the Reformation." For Morris, the Reformation resulted from God's choice of Luther to cleanse the church of its corruption and renew moral life. Morris saw the Reformation as a "revolution" which changed the character of the religious and political world and led to new modes of thought and action. He also felt the Reformation was necessary because the corruption of the Roman Catholic Church had interfered with the historical purity of the Christian faith. With the triumph of the Reformation, the path toward civil and personal liberty and freedom of conscience could begin anew.[24]

Like other historians in "romantic" nineteenth-century America, Morris believed that in Europe, and later in America, the liberal or "natural" principles of religious freedom (Protestantism), political liberty, free thought, and the spirit of commerce had triumphed. The principles and laws of the moral world reflected a dynamic providence at work in the affairs of men. Morris's sense of the inevitability of progress over medieval Catholic decay and the triumph of "natural" principles over corruption and darkness reflected not only traditional Protestant attitudes, but also American romanticism's emphasis on the nation's divinely appointed role in the world's evolution toward the "natural" state. For Morris, the "natural" principles flowed from the Reformation and culminated in nineteenth-century America, which had an evangelical mission to spread its political and religious system around the globe.[25]

Morris's sermon contained several other themes common to the Romantic era. The stress on the progress of America and Protestant northern Europe, in contrast to Catholic southern Europe, Ireland, and South America, reflected the racially based (Teutonic versus Latin) theory of national character prevalent in Romantic thought. He also sought to awaken in his fellow Protestants an appreciation of the blessings of the Reformation and the need to safeguard them from the Roman Catholic Church. Though he urged promotion of the Reformation's principles through "truth in argumentation," and not by "fire or sword," he represented that part of the Protestant spectrum of opinion that was alarmed over the growing flow of Catholic immigrants.[26]

Morris's methodology reflected the conventions of his time. Though he used secondary sources, these had a serious scholarly character. For example, in reviewing the biographies of Renaissance and Reformation popes, he used the work of Johann Mosheim, a respected, eighteenth-century church historian. For the most part, Morris weeded out hoary myths about the popes, and accurately portrayed Leo X as a "civil debounaire gentleman uninterested in religion" and Clement VII as "adept at dissimulation."[27] He showed a serious attitude toward historical chronology and causation by noting the roles of pre-Reformation reformers and church councils.

All of this reflected the didactic and artistic duty of the Romantic historian to understand what really happened, accurately portray historical characters, and, through good writing, bring alive the "Spirit" of the age. Morris, like his fellow historians, combined the Renaissance respect for history as philosophical teaching by example and the Romantic notion that God's providence determined the course of history and the moral world through the action of general laws in harmony with one another.[28] This paralleled the "harmony" natural theologians saw between nature and revelation, and the cause and effect that the natural scientists studied.

Though Morris exhibited a great concern for truth in writing history, he viewed the world with the definite bias of the "Whig" school of interpretation, which saw history from a progressive Protestant perspective based on the theory of dominant "natural principles." Throughout his professional life, he adhered to this school of historical interpretation, which mirrored his stance toward natural theology.

Another work of Morris's, "German Literature," showed other concerns and interests. This article, published in 1838, attempted to show "exalted" German achievements in literature and intellectual arts, and thus to counter the unfortunate impression recent German immigrants had made on Baltimoreans. Arguing by analogy, the classic approach used in natural theology, he claimed that the sound of dialects had more to do with the education or ignorance of those speaking them (e.g., comparing German and Yorkshire dialects) than with any inherent deficiency of the language. He went on to stress the German contribution to philosophy, philology, poetry, drama, and education.[29]

In all this, he deflected criticism of the new immigrants by stressing the superiority of German culture and its contributions to intellectual progress. He sought to still the criticism of his English-speaking compatriots by reminding them of the common Anglo-Teutonic cultural heritage. In this he reflected the Romantic period's racially-based method of evaluating societies and cultures. In the coming years, he would place ever-increasing emphasis on integrating German immigrants into the Lutheran church and American society and explaining to his countrymen the worth of German culture and its relationship to American culture.

By 1840, John G. Morris had emerged as a significant figure in the cultural life of Baltimore and the Lutheran Church. In the ensuing two decades, he earned a national reputation.

Part Three

Turning Points
1840 - 1860

*It's a long lane that knows
no turnings.*

ROBERT BROWNING
The Flight of the Duchess

6

Denominational Warrior

In the mid-years of John G. Morris's life and career, several dramatic turning points occurred which transformed him into a cultural leader of major importance. As sectional and sectarian animosities darkened the country's horizon, Morris joined with others in seeking to build an inclusive, national-oriented culture. His early promise as a cultural pioneer reached fulfillment through his work as a denominational leader, scientist and scholar, and institution-builder. From all this activity emerged his overriding commitment to fostering and spreading an American culture reflective of the nation's religious, intellectual, and natural environment.

The personal turning points in Morris's career intersected with momentous changes in American life. After 1840, increasingly large waves of German and Irish immigrants began to change radically the urban centers of the northeast and led to a marked quickening in westward expansion. These immigrants affected the cultural ethos of the nation by gradually expanding the religious and social framework beyond the predominantly British influence of the colonial and early national periods.

At this point, the United States was well into the initial phase of its industrial revolution. Changes in manufacturing, transportation, and communications, particularly in New England and the midwest, fostered a growing sense of separation and isolation in the southern states of the Union.

The increasingly bitter debate over slavery accentuated sectional antagonisms already aggravated by the social and economic transformation occurring in the north and midwest. These tensions during the 1840s and 1850s led to splits in several major religious denominations, serious dissension over the war with Mexico, and a growing intolerance that threatened the Union itself.

In the midst of these centrifugal forces, many individuals and groups sought to stem the sectarian and sectional bitterness. Efforts at fostering American education and scholarship, particularly in science, typified this approach. Other efforts focused on maintaining unified national church bodies and creating cultural institutions which could channel hostile passions into more positive outlets. All such efforts revolved around building *American* religious institutions, *American* scholarship, and *American* culture. In this great crusade Morris labored mightily and produced much of enduring value.

Throughout this period, Morris's earlier commitment to the development of English-speaking Lutheranism rooted in American soil remained the focal point of his work as pastor and church leader. Yet, the Baltimore churchman's understanding of what constituted Lutheran identity and its relationship to the contemporary American scene dramatically changed during the 1840s. By 1850, a combination of external factors and Morris's continuing personal evolution formed the framework for his transformation.

The stunning impact of German migration through Baltimore and other ports to the north radically altered the nature of the Lutheran church. In Baltimore alone, almost 200,000 Germans landed between 1830 and 1860.[1] Though many moved farther west, thousands remained in the city and had a dramatic effect on the city's religious life. The number of churches and chapels grew from fifty in 1837 to one hundred in 1845 and 150 by 1860.[2]

Morris, as Baltimore's leading English-Lutheran pastor, faced a daunting task. How would the church retain the allegiance of new Lutheran immigrants, regain the adherence of German-American Lutherans lost earlier to other Protestant denominations, and reach the large number of "unchurched" Baltimoreans who formed a majority of the city's society? Morris struggled with these problems first at the local and state level, and then at the national level. These efforts brought him, over time, to an understanding of the deeper issues at stake.

As early as 1839, Morris obtained the support of the Maryland Synod for devising "suitable means for supplying the religious wants of the German emigrants now residing on the Point at Baltimore." He and his colleagues were able to get all unappropriated Synod funds to support missionary work in the teeming Point area. Further, the Synod directed Morris and Benjamin Kurtz to work with the various synods in Pennsylvania "to promote the Redeemer's Kingdom among the German population of the west."[3]

Among Lutherans emigrating for religious reasons, conservative Saxons fleeing the coercion of the Prussian state Union Church [Lutheran and Reformed] formed the largest component. Morris quickly realized that the Saxons feared that losing their German language would threaten their orthodox faith. To these Germans, true orthodoxy meant use of the German language in a church life built around acceptance of Lutheran doctrinal and liturgical practices formulated in the sixteenth century. In this they reflected the revival of Lutheran religious tradition in Germany, and a language-conscious nationalism typical of the era. The formation of conservative synods—Missouri (1847), Buffalo (1845), Wisconsin (1850), and Iowa (1854)—that rejected the General Synod because of its doctrinal positions and American orientation, alarmed Morris and other Lutheran leaders.[4]

Morris helped organize a multifaceted response. He led fund-raising in the Maryland Synod to create German-language chapels and churches in the city and to support urgently needed missionaries. He realized that, at least in the short term, the Maryland Synod, and the General Synod, had to minister to the immigrants in their native language to forge some ties between the newcomers and American Lutherans. Without such ties, and the resolution of budding doctrinal animosities, Morris's goal of a united, English-speaking Lutheranism would prove unobtainable.

In addition to supporting German-speaking missionaries for the immigrants, Morris understood the need for a long-term strategy to reach the American-born descendants of earlier German immigrants and the many "unchurched," non-German Baltimoreans. He and the other advocates of English-language Lutheranism adopted the great evangelizing tool of American Protestantism—the Sunday school. Morris realized that the Sunday school provided not only a forum for religious education, but also a vehicle for developing American civic virtue and culture. Also, the English-speaking Sunday schools would eventually reach the children and grandchildren of the immigrants then flooding American shores.

As a leading figure in Baltimore's religious life, Pastor Morris had the active support of his parishioners at First English in establishing Sunday school chapels in newly developed sections of Baltimore at a distance from the old downtown port area. In his pastor's report for 1841 he noted that his congregation had "contributed upwards of $3,000 to erect a second English Lutheran church in this city, the basement story of which will be finished this fall. An additional Sunday School has been begun in the eastern section of the city by members of our church."[5] Within a few years, Second and Third English Lutheran Churches had organized as flourishing new establishments, with two young pastors, Charles Porterfield Krauth and William A. Passavant, as Morris protégés.

Morris understood the limitations involved in relying only on local initiative. His earlier efforts to organize home missionary activities had borne modest results at best; only a change toward a coordinated national program with strong support from the district synods could have a lasting impact. Societies relying only on support from individual members stood little chance of success in coping with the enormous evangelical task facing the Lutheran church.

Morris's opportunity to push the home mission effort toward a more centralized focus came during the General Synod session of 1843, held at his church in Baltimore. The convention began on a momentous personal note for the forty-year-old pastor. Elected by his fellow delegates to a two-year term as president, Morris experienced his greatest recognition to date as a leader in the national church. Prodded by Morris and the Maryland delegation, other delegates recognized that the mission situation facing the church had reached crisis proportions. As a first step in combating the apathy and inertia plaguing the home mission effort, the General Synod adopted the Maryland proposal that ministers collect a "cent a week" from each parishioner to support missionary activity.[6] Originating in a paper Morris presented to the Maryland Synod a year earlier, this plan generated more money than the efforts of the 1830s had ever achieved.[7]

At the next General Synod convention in 1845, Morris, Kurtz, and other Marylanders led the way in championing a companion measure to the "cent a week" plan, organization of the "Home Missionary Society of the General Synod." Serving as the society's president *pro tempore* and then for years as corresponding secretary, Morris and the other founders sought to organize chapters in each of the General Synod's district synods.[8] They hoped that synodical chapters would generate support for an effort that would be more effective and on a national scale. Two problems troubled the new venture—lack of suitable missionaries and the reluctance of many district synods to surrender funds or control to a central body.[9] The old fear of central, "dictatorial" control that had almost destroyed the General Synod itself in the early 1820s remained a potent force.

By the early 1850s, Morris fully realized that the Home Missionary Society faced a bleak future, with little synodical interest or support for its work. Even his efforts to get the Maryland Synod to function as a mission society had met with limited success.[10] In an attempt to sustain the society, he organized a convention for representatives of the various synodical chapters to meet for a "free exchange" of opinions on the best methods for church extension. Representatives from nine synods met on April 21, 1852, at Morris's church. Participants wrestled with how to generate support for the Society when most synods and the General Synod itself had no official involvement. Morris and the other participants viewed the lack of support for missions among the many Germans settling in the west as cause for great concern. How else to assimilate these Germans into American Lutheranism?

Though the convention produced no dramatic results, it began a series of debates and discussions on the need for a "central authority" for home missionary efforts that bore fruit in the post-Civil War period, when the General Synod itself assumed responsibility for all home missionary activities.[11] Morris's work in this area convinced him that other obstacles—doctrinal, linguistic, and political— must not add to the already overwhelming problems of assimilation.

Rejection of worship practices common among American Protestants featured prominently in the reaction of German Lutheran immigrants to the New World environment. These immigrants intended to retain the German sixteenth-century liturgy they had brought from Europe. Churchman Morris realized this posed another barrier to long-term prospects for Lutheran unity. Further, his deepening appreciation for German Lutheran theology, and consequently for historic Lutheranism, grew as he studied German theological journals and monographs.

Because of his interest and concern, and in spite of the limited success of his earlier efforts, Morris served on the General Synod's standing committee on the liturgy during the 1840s and 1850s, often functioning as the committee's chairman. He and his group faced a formidable set of problems. These included the use of divergent worship practices in different parts of the church and, most importantly, the rejection by the "American Lutherans" of German worship practices they regarded as doctrinally corrupt remnants of Roman Catholicism. The fear that adopting a common liturgy might vest too much power in the General Synod only compounded the difficulties.[12]

In the face of such opposition, Morris and his committee made only slow, fitful progress. In 1843, for example, they convinced the General Synod to recommend that its German-language churches use the Pennsylvania Ministerium's German liturgy.[13] This move opened another line of communication to the ministerium, which had withdrawn support from the General Synod in the early 1820s and had since developed along more conservative confessional and liturgical lines. In the short term, conservative Saxon immigrants probably would not accept the ministerium's liturgy, but adoption of this liturgy might prevent German-language General Synod congregations from leaving and joining the Missouri Synod.

Morris and the Liturgy Committee urged the General Synod in 1845 to recommend the ministerium's English-language liturgy.[14] This went too far for most General Synod delegates. Fear of a uniform liturgy, and one too conservative for much of the General Synod's English-language congregations, loomed large. With many congregations still accepting, in part at least, revivalist practices, a common liturgical service lay decades in the future.

Morris made a final effort at the General Synod session of 1850 at Charleston, South Carolina. He presented a Maryland Synod plan that proposed numerous improvements to the liturgy. Ideas such as recitation of the Ten Commandments prior to the order for public confession and proclamation of the Apostles' Creed met with little favor.[15] Other issues soon captured the attention of the delegates.

Morris's concern about assimilating the German immigrants and his developing appreciation for German theology and historic Lutheran traditions drew him into what historian Sydney Ahlstrom has referred to as the "indigenous" opposition to "American Lutheranism."[16] The doctrinal wars that engulfed Lutherans in the 1840s and 1850s clarified Morris's position and status as a major church leader.

Many of the early battles over doctrine took place in the Maryland Synod, one of the senior and most prestigious of the district synods in the General Synod. In synod meetings between 1843 and 1845, a series of conflicts indicated the depth of developing antagonisms and the direction of shifting opinion. Efforts by "American Lutheran" advocates Benjamin Kurtz and Simeon Harkey, publicly supported by Morris, to gain the synod's approval for a new journal entitled *The Revivalist*, and to elicit clear synodical support for "New Measures" and "American Lutheran" principles failed to obtain majority support.[17] Morris, enmeshed in local and national mission work, observed events and refrained from participating in open debates on doctrinal disputes.

At the General Synod meeting of 1845 Morris for the last time stood publicly with Samuel Simon Schmucker and the "American Lutherans." Morris led the successful effort to achieve closer ties with Presbyterians through the fraternal exchange of delegates at conventions, reciprocal communion rights for members of both denominations, and the exchange of church members in good standing upon request. This complemented a more ambitious move toward Schmucker's dream of a pan-Protestant federation. Morris obtained the General Synod's acceptance of a Schmucker memorial on "Christian Union." Last, but not least, the General Synod set up a committee, led by Schmucker, Morris, and Kurtz, to elucidate and defend publicly the General Synod's doctrinal position and practices.[18] All of this marked Schmucker's final successes within the General Synod.

Schmucker himself, at the end of the 1845 session, clearly defined the issues at stake. In a paper presented to the just organized Lutheran Historical Society, Schmucker expressed his concern about the drift from what he considered "spiritual religion" to an unhealthy emphasis on "voluminous creeds and detailed confessions." To Schmucker, a clear spiritual line from the pietism of Francke and Spener through the labors of Henry Melchior Muhlenberg formed the basis for the religious practices of "American Lutherans." Schmucker insisted that

> the efforts of some ultra Lutherans in our Fatherland [Germany] to roll back the wheels of time about three hundred years and to bring the Lutheran church to the standpoint of the sixteenth century, is no less unphilosophical than antagonistic, and like similar efforts of a few European brethren in our American church, necessarily must and ought to meet with signal defeat.[19]

But soon Schmucker and his allies experienced a powerful backlash from the "ultra Lutherans" in Germany and America.

At this point a series of events unfolded which ultimately led, in Morris's opinion, to disaster. Preparatory to a European tour planned by Schmucker for 1846, the General Synod's committee on foreign correspondence, on which Schmucker and Morris served, issued a circular to "various ecclesiastical bodies of our church in Europe" defending the "American Lutheran" doctrinal stance. Dismissing the "old Lutherans" in Germany and America as a "small party," the circular maintained that the General Synod stood on common ground with the Prussian Union church. The circular expressed the belief of "American Lutherans" that the "last three centuries . . . have . . . produced men . . . equal to the sixteenth century," and that they viewed Luther's "doctrinal construction as essentially correct." They asserted, however, that "the peculiar view of Luther on the bodily presence of the Lord in the Lord's Supper has been abandoned long ago by the great majority of our preachers."[20]

Morris decided to join Schmucker and Kurtz on the European tour, designed to end in London with the founding of the World Evangelical Alliance. Despite his personal antipathy toward Schmucker, he had always intended, as brother Charles put it, to "at some convenient season visit Europe."[21] With Kurtz along, the traveling arrangements seemed tolerable, and Morris planned to take some side trips in any event.

By the time the trip came to an end, Morris viewed the circular as a "senseless blunder" which guaranteed a cool reception from both Union and German Lutheran church leaders. In his opinion, the circular "may have been in conformity to the theological opinions of some in the United Church of Prussia, yet there were thousands of Lutherans who would not sanction it theologically. The United could not understand how men professing such doctrines or denying the fundamental principles of Lutheranism could honestly call themselves Lutheran . . . and the old Lutherans could not recognize men as such who had given up the distinctive points." The reaction, Morris claimed, was that not one of the three visitors received an invitation to preach in a German pulpit, and that the noted German theologian, August Tholuck, rewrote Schmucker's circular into "pure and classic German."[22]

Schmucker partisans, such as his wife Mary Catherine Steenbergen and biographer Peter Anstadt, disputed Morris's point of view. They argued that Schmucker received a cordial welcome during the tour and experienced a great personal triumph, as author of the *Fraternal Appeal*, at the World Evangelical Alliance congress.[23] Yet Morris obviously felt concerned about the trip. His conversations with "old Lutheran" theologians reinforced his developing understanding of historical Lutheranism and the ways in which "American Lutheranism" differed from it. The fact that he never again supported a major Schmucker endeavor lends credence to his claim that the 1846 trip marked his break with Samuel Simon Schmucker.

The public emergence of Morris as a foe of Schmucker came in 1849 with the publication of a new theological journal in Gettysburg, *The Evangelical Review*. Edited by Lutheran minister and Pennsylvania College professor William Reynolds, assisted by Morris and Charles Philip Krauth, the new journal had a decidedly conservative and denominational cast to it. Morris, as early as September 1848, had successfully urged the Gettysburg Seminary's alumni association to adopt his resolution encouraging Reynolds to push forward with a new journal. Morris applauded the proposed publication "of a Quarterly Review . . . devoted to . . . subjects relating to our church, to the defense of her doctrines and elucidation of her history."[24] In a series of articles that appeared in the new journal on "Luther's Larger and Smaller Catechisms," "Catechization," and "Paul Gerhard," Morris proclaimed his conservative allegiance.

In contrast to his earlier non-denominational stance, advocated in the *Observer*, and his strong support for at least some of the "New Measures," Morris now saw Luther's *Small Catechism* as "a book which if sincerely believed in *all* [Morris's emphasis] its teachings will sufficiently distinguish from us our christian neighbors." He at this point clearly opted for Lutheran doctrinal particularity based on Martin Luther's teaching on the sacraments, i.e. baptismal regeneration and Christ's Real Presence in the Lord's Supper. He separated himself from the mainstream of evangelical Protestantism, and from "American Lutheranism," with his conviction that Luther's sacramental stance "embraces views which are not universally adopted even by those who call themselves after his name, but which we honestly believe will be more highly appreciated the more carefully they are studied and the more thoroughly they are understood." No longer the advocate of revivalist "extraordinary manifestations" of grace, Morris now called for reliance on the old Lutheran "catechical system."[25]

In his essay on "Paul Gerhard," Morris, for the first time, used historical characters, real or fictional, to comment on the contemporary theological scene. While avoiding theological controversy in his publications, Morris used this technique during the ensuing decade in an attempt to gain some insulation from the increasingly bitter doctrinal warfare. In "Gerhard," Morris praised the German theologian and preacher of the Thirty Years' War for heroic resistance to the Elector of Brandenberg's efforts to unite Lutheran and Reformed in one church. In praising Gerhard for fidelity to his ordination oath of 1651, which included the validity of the traditional documents and symbols, Morris definitively broke with the "American Lutherans."[26]

Schmucker and his allies refused to accept the Symbols—the Augsburg Confession, the Apology for the Augsburg Confession, the Schmalkald Articles, Luther's Catechisms, and the Formula of Concord—as normative in any sense. They placed total primacy on the Word of God contained in the scriptures, accepting the Augsburg Confession as only a "substantially correct interpretation" with lingering Roman Catholic doctrinal impurities. Morris and others of the "indigenous opposition" believed that the Confession and Luther's Catechism, at the least, did not conflict with scriptural or doctrinal purity.

Morris's private correspondence with Charles Philip Krauth revealed the increasing bitterness. He told Krauth that Benjamin Kurtz viewed *The Evangelical Review* as sectarian, rather than denominational. Morris discounted Kurtz's position as the hostility of one who did not want "a respectable antagonist" to his "low views." Morris's combativeness comes across clearly in his suggestion that William Reynolds not respond to Schmucker's "too long" articles in the *Review* with overly lengthy essays of his own. Morris doubted many people ever read Schmucker's articles.[27] A chasm yawned.

In these critical years in the late 1840s and early 1850s, ideological conflict enveloped the Lutheran institutions at Gettysburg, particularly the seminary. After Morris returned from Europe, he resumed the presidency of the seminary's board of directors, a post he first held from 1844 until 1846. The major problem he faced concerned the Pennsylvania Ministerium's continuing dissatisfaction with the "American Lutheran" theology taught at the seminary. The ministerium seemed intent on establishing its own seminary in a more centrally located section of the state.

The resignation of Morris's nephew, Charles A. Hay, as the seminary's second professor in 1848 presented the board president with an opportunity. Pleased that his nephew had followed his advice to leave the fractious theological scene for the safe harbor of a pastorate, Morris knew that only calling a German theology professor could prevent a second, rival seminary in Pennsylvania. With Schmucker accompanying him, President Morris attended the 1848 session of the ministerium and initiated negotiations which led to the ministerium's pledge of financial support if the seminary called a German professor. Schmucker, by this point, clearly understood Morris's stance. As he wrote his son, Beale, Morris "doubtless encouraged" the seminary's board to call a German professor. But Schmucker believed the board "would not send off to Germany on an uncertainty."[28]

Though, as Schmucker predicted, efforts to attract a German scholar proved fruitless, Morris and the board did convince Charles Philip Krauth to resign as president of the college and to become the full-time second professor. Though "a theologian inclined to the old Lutheran system," Krauth's appointment did not satisfy the ministerium.[29] With the confessional debate waxing hotter, and with the ministerium's rejoining of the General Synod in 1853, the question of German theological instruction came to the fore yet again.

By the early 1850s, the ministerium had extended its interest in German-language education to include Pennsylvania College. The ministerium, with the active encouragement of the Pennsylvania College board of trustees (including Morris), transferred its one-third interest in Franklin College, located in Lancaster, Pennsylvania, to endow a newly created Franklin Professorship of Ancient Languages. In addition, the ministerium intended to establish a professorship of German language and literature at the college. Further, the ministerium now insisted on a third professor at the seminary to teach theology in German.[30] The process of Lutheran assimilation into American Protestantism, seemingly so inevitable in the 1830s, proved a very different matter in the 1850s. The increasingly ethnic and conservative nature of pastors and people required accommodation if the goal of a united, English-speaking Lutheranism had any hope of eventual achievement.

Morris understood this and viewed Schmucker as a definite hindrance. He warned Schmucker that if the seminary did not hire a German theology professor this time, pastors in the ministerium would indeed open a new seminary. Morris pointedly reminded Schmucker that the board had voted for a third professor, and Schmucker had voiced no opposition. Doubtless, Morris caustically wrote to his former mentor, Schmucker's opposition now could only result from the fact that his original position was "misapprehended."[31]

With tensions at a boiling point, Morris sought a resolution. The advent of *The Evangelical Review*, the selection of Krauth as second professor, and the establishment of the Franklin professorship created a favorable environment in the ministerium for a compromise. Morris and the seminary board proposed that the new German language professor at the college also teach theology at the seminary. After the seminary assented to treating the proposed new third professor on an equal par with other faculty, a change obviously aimed at Schmucker, the ministerium accepted the proposed compromise.[32]

By the spring of 1856, Dr. C. F. Schaeffer, nominated by the ministerium and accepted by the seminary board, began his joint appointment to the faculties of the seminary and college. The arrangement never ran smoothly, requiring Morris and others desperately to seek ways to keep the situation in some form of equilibrium. The conservative Schaeffer continually complained that he could not teach all branches of theology in the German language. Schmucker argued that this would divide the institution into two separate seminaries—German and English, confessional and "American Lutheran." Despite several efforts at compromise, the situation was never really resolved to the satisfaction of Schaeffer and the ministerium.[33]

As at the seminary, Schaeffer had his complaints about the college. He reminded the directors that the founders of the college had intended to feature German in the curriculum and this had not occurred. In September 1857 he requested that all students study German as an obligatory course. On the other hand, the ministerium also requested that Schaeffer work full-time at the seminary, and sought to alter its financial commitment to supporting the German professorship.[34]

The board requested that Morris study the complicated situation and propose a solution. He urged his fellow directors to make the study of German obligatory for all students. The board accepted the proposal with slight modifications as the best strategy to resolve the conflict.[35] For the time being, Morris's compromise worked and C. F. Schaeffer remained on the college faculty.

The bitter struggle between the "American Lutherans" and the conservatives in the General Synod, festering since the late 1840s, broke into a final, bitter rupture in early September of 1855. As part of this, the Schmucker-Morris estrangement became complete, irrevocable, and very public. The events of September 1855 turned Morris into a denominational warrior.

Appropriately enough, the struggle commenced in Morris's quiet, dark, book-lined study at 106 North Greene Street in Baltimore. Coincidentally, at least

83

as Morris reported it, Samuel Simon Schmucker was with him in his study when an anonymously-authored, forty-two page pamphlet was delivered. Morris recalled, "The pamphlet had a mysterious air about it. It was a child thrown upon the Church of whom nobody was willing to acknowledge the parentage." This was the "Definite Platform," a proposed "American Rescension of the Augsburg Confession," which purported to modify or omit what the authors felt were "unscriptural and Roman Catholic errors" retained in the Confession.[36]

Immediately recognizing the momentous impact of the document, Morris pointedly inquired of Schmucker about its origin, "and, in evident confusion, he replied, 'Oh! you know well enough where in all probability any attempt to change the Confession would come from.' Of course I did. To the credit of this gentleman, I will here add, that he was the first of the triumvirate of its authors, who had candor enough to admit the fact after the lapse of several weeks. He felt humbled at the idea of fighting behind a tree and openly avowed that he took part in preparing it. The other two never made a public avowal, though they were well known."[37] Morris's contempt was complete.

Quickly leaving the Morris residence, Schmucker had little doubt that his former student would lead the confessional charge against him and his co-authors, Samuel Sprecher, who had married one of Schmucker's daughters, and Benjamin Kurtz. Morris thoroughly rejected Schmucker's position that the Augsburg Confession retained Catholic doctrinal features, such as the ritual of the mass, private confession and absolution, baptismal regeneration, and Christ's Real Presence in the Lord's Supper, and that these must be purged from the venerable Lutheran creed.

Morris at once set to work to engineer rejection of the Definite Platform and Schmucker's effort to force all ministers to accept its provisions. Morris and his allies sought to retain the unaltered Augsburg Confession as the doctrinal basis for General Synod Lutheranism, leaving acceptance of the other Lutheran symbolical books up to the individual.

At the October session of the Maryland Synod, Schmucker and Kurtz, both in attendance, furiously lobbied for the platform. The equally determined Morris fought back. He persuaded the synod president to appoint him chair of a committee to report on a resolution received from the East Pennsylvania Synod rejecting the platform. Kurtz, a vocal member of the committee, sensing the tide against him, at first sought to evade the issue by stating that the platform was not officially before it. At Morris's instigation, the synod soundly rejected this approach. Then the committee, at Morris's insistence, reported out a resolution stressing continued adherence to the oath contained in the ordination service. Though the oath accepted the Confession as only "substantially correct," the resolution was a vindication of the status quo and an implied rebuke of the Platform and its authors. After two days of fierce debate, the Synod passed the resolution.[38] Morris had triumphed over his teacher and, at least in his own mind, his nemesis.

Morris's permanent estrangement from Schmucker and other "American Lutherans" incited a bitter assault in the *Observer*. In an article entitled "Inconsistency—Then and Now," Morris, William Reynolds, and Charles Philip Krauth were assailed for changing their doctrinal positions. The author, using the *nom de plume* "Scrutator," was probably editor Benjamin Kurtz. He quoted Morris's position on the sacraments from his *Catechism* of 1832 and *Popular Exposition*, published in 1840, to prove that the Baltimore clergyman at one time had also advocated positions that modified the Augsburg Confession.

"Scrutator" also quoted from Morris's introduction to Kurtz's 1843 work, *Why Are You a Lutheran?* Morris had written that "this book will be profitable to our people, and they can loan it to their neighbors of other denominations, not with a view of winning them over to the church of the Reformation, but of informing them accurately as to our doctrines and usages."[39] Though Reynolds and Krauth defended themselves in subsequent editions of the *Observer*, Morris refrained from public comment, claiming he did not engage in serious theological discussions in the paper.

Pastor Morris's claim was somewhat disingenuous. Throughout the 1850s, he produced numerous works on Luther, the Reformation and prominent seventeenth- and eighteenth-century German Lutherans, such as pietist pastors Paul Gerhard and John Arndt. In all these works, Morris sought not only to present Germans and Lutherans in a positive light to his countrymen but also to support subtly the confessional movement. In his life of John Arndt, for example, Morris emphasized how much Arndt suffered for adhering to the Lutheran Formula of Concord and resisting efforts to impose the Calvinist Reformed faith. Morris's point was that acceptance of Lutheran symbols and rejection of union with other Protestants were fundamental to true orthodoxy and Lutheran identity.[40] He had come a long way from advocating the ideal of a great evangelical confederation envisioned in the *Fraternal Appeal*.

During these years of denominational strife, the other passionate interests of his life, science and the irresistible pull of scholarship, kept Morris from becoming a bitter and hardened partisan. His scientific pursuits, in fact, were about to bring him unprecedented renown.

7

National Recognition

During these years of development as a leading figure in the life of the American Lutheran church, John G. Morris also blossomed as a pioneer in the arena of American natural science. By the end of this phase in his life, Morris made significant, lasting contributions in his chosen field of entomology. His allegiance to one overarching goal—increasing knowledge of and interest in American science, which he viewed to be of utmost national importance—infused the myriad of Morris's scientific works. His goal reflected the period, which was one of increasing industrialization and rapid improvements in communication and transportation. It led Americans to a deeper appreciation of the importance of science for the country's material and cultural progress, and fostered a desire to emulate, if not exceed, European achievements.

Morris's contributions evolved in three related areas: teaching and lectures, creating important natural history collections, and publishing several major scientific works. In pursuing all these areas of activity, he realized the basic need for a broad, professional American science network. Therefore he also played a role in establishing several important institutions and societies that helped lay the foundation for scientific advancement in the post-Civil War period.

Already recognized as a talented entomologist by the 1840s, Morris began teaching at Pennsylvania College as a part-time instructor in zoology. He worked to obtain the needed scientific apparatus and, most significantly, the specimens he needed for his lectures. He wrote to Spencer F. Baird, a friend and, at that time, professor of natural history at Morris's alma mater, Dickinson College, about his efforts and the reason for them. "I arrived here [Gettysburg] last Monday," Morris told Baird, "and have ever since been laboriously engaged in arranging minerals,

86

shells, and *diversaria* of the cabinet. . . . I lecture one hour each day in zoology and have succeeded thus far in interesting the youngsters very much."[1]

Morris's commitment to awakening student interest in natural science never faltered during his four years of teaching at the college (1844-48) nor in later years as he gave a series of annual lectures at the college and the seminary. He sought to integrate natural science into the curriculum of both institutions because he believed that this branch of science must become a basic component in the liberal arts education provided by American colleges. He frequently urged establishing chairs of zoology at colleges "with good reputations," and that these colleges encourage the collection of "American specimens."[2] In the post-Civil War era, Morris and others in the scientific community achieved their goal—science, including natural history, became an increasingly significant component of the curriculum in America's colleges and universities.

In support of his work as a teacher of science, Morris sought to create a network of American scientists, primarily through correspondence and participation in professional meetings. He and his colleagues collected and exchanged specimens, books, and the latest news about events in the still small scientific community. Among his many correspondents, Morris formed close working and personal relationships with Harvard professors Thaddeus Harris and Hermann August Hagen, the Bavarian naturalist Gottlieb August Wilhelm Herrich-Schaeffer, and Joseph Henry and Spencer F. Baird, academics who became, respectively, the first secretary and assistant secretary of the Smithsonian Institution. Other close colleagues included fellow clergymen and entomologists Daniel Ziegler and E. F. Melsheimer, and professors S. S. Haldeman and J. L. LeConte.

The sociable and intellectually curious Morris formed fast friendships with men in the world of science which lasted a lifetime. These relationships broadened his horizons and gave him respite and perspective, enabling him to get beyond the strife and conflict which enveloped his clerical pursuits. Let us listen to the avid scientist as he describes one of his friendships.

> I became acquainted with that singularly gifted man, S. S. Haldeman, very early in my scientific pursuits. Entomology and conchology were his chief subjects when I first knew him, and his contributions to both these branches are invaluable. Our mutual visits and letters were numerous. He was a genial spirit, inexhaustible in his fund of information on all subjects, without the least display of pedantry or affectation. I learned much from his very instructive conversation, and he was ever ready to communicate by letter whatever he was asked.[3]

In published writings, personal correspondence, and at scientific gatherings, Morris encouraged the collecting of American specimens and the publication of scientific works by his fellow countrymen. He humorously, yet pointedly, promised Baird a statue in his honor if only he completed a still-unfinished manuscript.[4] Morris's zest for spreading scientific knowledge only increased after his election in 1848 as a founding member of the American Association for the Advancement of Science (AAAS). His love of travel made these expeditions all the more pleasurable, whether he went by coach, train, or ship. Morris thoroughly enjoyed meeting people from all walks of life and, of course, observing the natural environment around him. He always remembered with pride and pleasure meeting famed European naturalist and Harvard professor Louis Agassiz at an AAAS session held in August 1860 in Newport, Rhode Island. Both men, as Morris remembered it, immediately "took to each other," and, "I met him frequently afterwards and I visited him at Cambridge. We usually spoke German, and that perhaps may have contributed to drawing us nearer together Sometimes he imperceptibly glided into French, but I did not venture on French with him, and drew back to the language of the Vaterland, in which I could get along more fluently and correctly. He is a world-known man, and I need say nothing more of him here. His letters, which I have preserved, are highly valued by me."[5]

Morris also brought the cause of American science to the general public. Using the public lecture circuit, he combined his ready wit and erudition in explaining to his listeners the utility of natural history when applied to farming, gardening, and other practical matters. He did this most effectively in a series of popular lectures at the recently-created Smithsonian Institution during the 1850s. He argued for the necessity of understanding the nature of soil, plants, and trees, as well as the anatomical structure of animals, to combat diseases injurious to crops and animals.[6]

He especially wanted to increase popular understanding of invertebrate animals and their effect on field crops, garden plants, flowering plants, and fruit and forest trees. During his lectures, he discussed in detail insect transformations, habits, and the impact on the natural order of completely eliminating particular species. His sensitivity to the environment expressed itself when he lamented the lack of care and attention paid to the nation's vast forests. He was not far off the mark when he predicted that perhaps a century would pass before the government appointed a "public officer" responsible for "woods and forests."[7] Meanwhile, there was much to be done: understanding, through a rigorous process of scientific classification, the physical characteristics and habits of all flora and fauna would preserve the essential links of nature so critical for a prosperous economy.

A talented teacher and lecturer, Morris knew that the scope of scientific knowledge had to expand for a truly successful incorporation of science into American life.

In the field of natural history and entomology, this meant, first of all, creating collections of specimens for classification, research and study. He thus set about creating several important collections: at Pennsylvania College, the Maryland Historical Society (MHS), and an impressive personal accumulation of his own.

At Gettysburg, Morris's collecting efforts revolved around the Linnaean Association. In 1844, he inspired thirty students from the college and the seminary to form the association, the third college natural history society organized in the nation. The students elected the part-time instructor first president of the association, and Morris worked zealously for the next six years to create a collection that would further his own knowledge of comparative anatomy, improve his teaching, and inspire students to explore the mysteries of the natural world.[8]

In creating Pennsylvania College's natural history collection, Morris devoted countless hours in acquiring and classifying numerous specimens. Within a year, he had acquired sixty-five bird specimens, ninety-two reptiles, ninety-seven fish and crustacea, 900 shells, and 1,100 insects.[9] As he worked on the collection, which he obtained through exchanges, purchases, and the timely donation of specimens from the recently dissolved Maryland Academy of Art and Science, his understanding of invertebrate animal anatomy rapidly grew. His collecting also provided excellent illustrations for his lectures.

As the collection grew, Morris obtained funds for cabinets to house the specimens. Even more important, he led the students in spearheading the construction of a building on the College's campus devoted to the study of natural history. At the dedication of Linnaean Hall in 1847, he hailed the first building ever "conceived, designed, erected, and completed through the agency of the students."[10]

Elected a member of the seven-year-old Maryland Historical Society in 1851, Morris contributed substantially to the creation of yet another natural history collection. Alarmed by what some viewed as the society's neglect in collecting, preserving, and diffusing information on the natural, as well as the civic and literary, history of the state, members took action in May 1857. The society created a natural history committee, and voted to pursue collecting specimens of Maryland flora and fauna and to maintain a separate room for the collection.[11]

Appointed to the committee, Morris quickly became the group's leader. For the next several years, the committee met every Thursday to select specimens and arrange the materials at hand. The committee prepared an operational plan and obtained cabinet cases for the collection.[12] In early 1859, Morris proudly informed the society about the wide range of the committee's collection efforts. Areas covered included paleontology, zoology, mineralogy, geology, general physics, and botany. Such success had its price. He lamented the lack of space available to accommodate needed additional cases.[13] His collection aided scientists in study-ing the state's geologic history and in exploring the interaction between native plants and animals.

Morris's quest to understand the natural world included creating his own sizable collection. He collected shells, fish and bird specimens, and many insects, particularly his beloved butterflies. Throughout his life, as previously noted, he attributed his stamina and good health to "my frequent ramblings in the fields and woods" in search of specimens.[14] In addition to his own efforts, Morris received substantial assistance from another Lutheran clergyman and scientist, John Bachman of Charleston, South Carolina. At the General Synod session of 1850, Bachman gave Morris all his folio volumes of botanical specimens. The delighted Morris told Spencer Baird, "He [Bachman] gave me over 350 species of plants, so that with my own collection I am pretty much *au fait*."[15] By the end of his life, Morris's collection had grown to over 7,000 plant and animal specimens.

Morris's publications were his most valuable scientific contributions. Through his instigation, the Linnaean Association for several years published a monthly journal entitled *The Literary Record and Journal*. In its pages Morris, Baird, and Haldeman, among others, published numerous scientific articles. Morris fo-cused particularly on the need for natural history collections as a fundamental requirement for decent scientific education and on the history of entomological pursuits in the United States.[16]

Morris's greatest scientific achievement came in 1860 when the Smithsonian Institution published his *Catalogue of Described Lepidoptera of North America*. Fas-cinated by the beautiful butterfly, he had a draft of a descriptive catalogue as early as 1842. Driven by his desire to compile a comprehensive listing of all known species, he supplemented information gleaned from studying and classifying his own specimens with research from European and American reference works, as well as data his fellow entomologists had shared with him. From these sources, Morris eventually pulled together all the information then known about species of the North American *Lepidoptera*.

After presenting a portion of his work in a paper at the 1859 meeting of the AAAS, he urged Spencer Baird, by this time the assistant secretary of the Smithsonian, to publish his catalogue.[17] Impressed by the quality of the work, and its enthusiastic reception at the AAAS, Baird accepted the proposal.

In preparing his *Catalogue*, Morris used forty-four published sources. Though using several taxonomic schemes, he principally followed the system devised by German naturalist Gottlieb August Wilhelm Herrich-Schaeffer.[18] When Morris sent his manuscript to his colleague for review, he found himself embroiled in disputes Herrich-Schaeffer was having with other naturalists over the recognition of certain genera and families. An exasperated Morris told Baird he had written Herrich-Schaeffer to inquire, "Am I to ignore their labors, reject their genera and species?"[19]

With relief, Morris later reported that the German had returned his manuscript with only a few proposed revisions, and the suggestion that Morris use the published works of Francis Walker of the British Museum and Achille Guenée, a noted French lepidopterist, as general guides.[20] As Morris divided the order of *Lepidoptera* into its various families, genera, and species, he carefully listed the authority for each item under discussion, and noted any reference work which described the item. The *Catalogue* enumerated 2,000 species, and the realistic Morris predicted that hundreds of new species awaited discovery.[21]

Morris's peers in the scientific community acclaimed his compilation for its scholarly accuracy and practical usefulness. A fellow pioneer entomologist, William Henry Edwards, felt that the *Catalogue*, and a subsequent *Synopsis* published in 1862, "gave a start to American collectors and the work of describing new species went on brisker."[22] Herbert Osborn, professor of natural history and president of the Entomological Society of America in 1911, recognized the *Catalogue* as the only work of its era available to American students. Osborn expressed his debt to Morris when he wrote that "for many years it was the only work by which I could attempt to identify species after the few that were figured or described in popular works were covered."[23] Augustus R. Grote, a noted expert on the *Lepidoptera*, credited Morris's work with first acquainting him with the principles of taxonomy.[24] The indefatigable clergyman had truly broadened the frontiers of American science.

During the 1850s, Morris found another avenue for his scholarly and cultural contributions—history. Interested in literature and the past from youth, Morris felt a natural affinity for interpreting the events of his day through the lens of historical perspective. He focused his historical studies on the social issues which concerned him most. He wanted to preserve the essentially Protestant nature of American society, while maintaining a distinctive confessional identity among American Lutherans. Also, the increasingly hostile reaction in Baltimore and other urban ports to the growing tide of German immigrants alarmed the Lutheran pastor. And the rising level of sectional bitterness, so dangerous for a border state like Maryland, provoked his concern and attention.

His philosophy of history and his approach to the craft emerge in his writings. He believed that divine providence guided human history, which, like the physical world of Morris's scientific writings, was shaped and developed through the actions of eternally valid, natural "principles." The energizing effect on society and human history caused by the emergence of doctrinally pure and "free" religion from the Lutheran Reformation always was for Morris the key to understanding the America of his day. He believed that from Protestantism flowed religious and civic liberties, as well as intellectual, economic, and social progress, a view that he expounded as early as his sermon on the Reformation in 1834.

In this, he reflected the dominant school of history of the antebellum period, romantic nationalism. As with his scientific advancement, Morris's work as an historian benefited from his personal involvement with the leading practitioners. As always, Morris's gregarious personality aided his cause. He recalled with zest, for example, the time he spent with the most eminent of American romantic nationalist historians, George Bancroft.

> This was a most delightful and instructive tour, which continued eight days. We had sleeping and cooking apartments on the cars, and stopped wherever we pleased. I was often alone on our wanderings with Mr. Bancroft, and often tried to draw out his religious and theological views, but could not succeed. It was a subject he avoided, but on historical and literary matters he was open, and let me say inexhaustible. For the remembrance of facts, places, dates, men he was remarkable. It was a week of unmixed enjoyment. Prof. Henry, with his rich stores of learning, and Brantz Mayer, with his sprightliness and literary anecdotes, contributed much to the pleasure of the company.[25]

Morris accepted Bancroft's belief that the basic principles of truth, justice, and morality flow from God, remain immutable, and burst into modern history through the Reformation. The human will in history evolves slowly, yet "moves onward and upward, achieving better states of knowledge and finer patterns of behavior."[26] The revolution in human progress since the sixteenth century had reached its fulfillment in dynamic, Anglo-Saxon, Protestant America.

Like many other Protestants of his day, Morris feared the effect on America of an increasingly aggressive Roman Catholic Church. For Morris, the Roman church represented ignorance, superstition, and a return to the dark medieval past.[27] He expressed his alarm in several historical novels and biographies. In *To Rome and Back*, originally a German novel that he translated and adapted to an American setting, he warned his fellow Protestants about the dangers from a militantly proselytizing Roman Catholicism. Using the romantic technique of stock-characters representing larger historical realities, such as the "spirit of the age," he filled his story with "wily" Jesuits, naive young men, and perceptive females.

In telling the tale of the college-age son of a Lutheran pastor, seduced from his faith by a "subtle" Jesuit priest and saved by his Italian fiancee, he had several points to make. He directly criticized Protestant parents, particularly Lutherans, for not solidly grounding their children in the principles of their religious faith. This left young people, in Morris's opinion, susceptible to falling away from the path of truth, liberty, and progress.[28] While Morris championed Lutheran Protestantism, almost any form of the Protestant communion remained superior to the "errors" of Rome.

The "wily" Jesuit represented the dangers prevalent in a free society. No legal steps, or forceful ones for that matter, could prevent the priest from dissembling and confusing the pastor's son. Yet the yearning for truth, represented by the fiancee's interest in studying the scriptures, ultimately saved the young man. Morris believed that in a free society truth, exemplified by adherence to the Protestant religion, would ultimately prevail.

As expressed in his novel, Morris believed deeply in the triumph of moral purpose. Like a fellow romantic historian he greatly admired, the British writer Thomas Carlyle, Morris felt that the surest path to understanding the moral purpose and lessons taught by history came from the lives of heroic men and women. He always sought "biographical literature of the richest character" to better understand human motivation and the real meaning that lay beneath the surface of events.[29] Apropos of his concerns and abiding interest in people, several biographical works flowed from Morris's pen during the 1850s. In addition to his Gerhard and Arndt works, he wrote *Quaint Sayings and Doings Concerning Luther* and *Catherine De Bora*. In these studies he focused on persons whose life conflicts reflected deeper issues and principles. Individuals such as Luther's wife, Catherine von Bora, and John Arndt represented a piety of "elevated, intellectual character," based on devotion to scripture and a faithfulness to carrying "the doctrine of Christ into practical life."[30] In other words, they were models for Protestant Americans.

Like other Protestants of the day, Morris viewed Luther's work as divinely-inspired, rescuing true, scriptural religion from papal superstition and vice. But as an historian he also sought to understand and explain the human causes and events which influenced the great Reformer. He used the best sources that he could obtain, and sought to separate myth from fact to provide an accurate historical chronology.

In evaluating Luther's marriage and the celibacy question in general, for example, Morris portrayed the personal and political complexities that beset Luther.

He explained the doctrinal and practical implications of Luther's stand that celibacy and the monastic vow of chastity lacked a scriptural foundation and hence were "unnatural." He attempted to weave together the history of clerical celibacy in the Western church and Luther's wish to please his parents by marrying.[31]

Morris also understood the events in the century preceding the outbreak of the Reformation, particularly the ill-will between the Germans and Italians, and the widespread nature of religious and social discontent. Yet, he failed to realize that the Reformation had its roots in medieval thought and history. Though scholarly and well-read, in his writings on Luther and the heroes of the Reformation era he worked from traditional Protestant hagiographic interpretations rather than the views of confessional Lutheran and Reformed historians. Wilhelm Lohe and Philip Schaff, for example, regarded the Reformation as the "legitimate offspring of the Catholic Church" and much of the pre-Reformation church's story as honorable. Morris and most other Protestant historians on the other hand, saw Luther and his Reformation as a complete break from medieval Catholicism and a return to the pristine Apostolic era.

In all this, Morris expressed the duality of romantic history—a sincere respect for accurate facts interpreted through a distinctive, partisan worldview. He could trace the historical evolution of clerical celibacy and yet hail its abrogation in Lutheran lands because it made former priests and monks "patriotic subjects and useful men."[32] Above all else, Morris remained at heart a Lutheran pastor in his analysis and use of history.

In stressing the contributions of the German Luther to European and American progress, Morris had a concern beyond strengthening Lutheran confessional identity and the Protestant nature of contemporary society. He wanted to lessen American antagonism toward German immigrants and, by defusing the hostility, to quicken the "Americanization" of the new immigrants. He wanted to counter, at least from an intellectual point of view, the common opinion of the immigrants as poorly educated, boorish, and somewhat alien. Using the Maryland Historical Society as his venue, with its membership of the city's intellectual and social élite as his audience, Morris sought to convince opinion-makers of German contributions to cultural progress.

On a cold winter's evening in January 1855, Morris presented a paper to the members of the MHS which he hoped would aid in a greater appreciation of Germans and German culture. Morris's topic, "Martin Behaim, the German Astronomer," focused on German contributions in the Age of Discovery. According to Morris, Behaim, a native of Nuremberg, sailed on expeditions to South America and dramatically improved the astrolabe, a piece of equipment used for celestial navigation. Using claims found in secondary sources that Magellan gave credit to Behaim for identifying the strait of water at the tip of South America, Morris buttressed his assertion by noting the lack of any Behaim correspondence between the years 1494 and 1506. To Morris, this proved that Behaim was in the New World at that time and had played a major role in exploring it.[33]

In his zeal to link Germans and America, Morris had relied on faulty sources and a weak assertion. Scholars today credit Behaim for possible contributions to an improved astrolabe, using brass instead of wood, but not at all for voyages of exploration. Though usually more discriminating in ascertaining reliable sources, Morris's use of secondary works and the limits of scholarship in the era before "scientific" history at times adversely affected his work. Whatever his failings in the Behaim case, now, and in the years to come, the point for Morris was to stress continually the preeminent place of Germans in Western culture.

In the last years of the decade of the 1850s, Morris's adopted state found itself beset not only by urban violence against immigrants, but also by escalating rancor over perpetuating the slave system and integrating free blacks into society, and by divergent industrial and agricultural economic interests. To contain these centrifugal forces, civic leaders, such as John Pendleton Kennedy, Brantz Mayer, Severn Teackle Wallace, and John Spear Smith, hoped that the MHS could disseminate culture and knowledge of the state's past and thereby help dampen sectional and partisan conflicts.[34] To the patriotic pastor Morris, no cause seemed more urgent.

In response to the society's stated aim to "collect, preserve and diffuse information relating to the Civil, Natural and Literary History of the State of Maryland," Morris decided to compile a catalogue on books published in Maryland by Maryland authors.[35] This would complement his efforts on the natural history committee, and the fruits of both endeavors would provide a glorious review of the state's "Civil, Natural and Literary History."

In May 1857, Morris proudly told the society that the catalogue's length "will surprise many."[36] Divided into four topical areas—history, literature, drama, and religion—it listed hundreds of books, many buried in obscurity. As with his great *Catalogue of the Described Lepidoptera of North America*, Morris sought to bring together all known information on a given subject. With the catalogue of Maryland books and authors, Morris sought not only to expand knowledge, but also to inculcate a respect for Maryland's past which could help maintain ties and relationships in the increasingly politically fractured state. To Morris, this seemed particularly important for the state's social, intellectual, and economic elite.

He pressed his views through a paper similar to his work on Martin Behaim that he presented at the MHS. He highlighted the successes and setbacks encountered by the state's first major cultural organization, the Maryland Academy of Science and Literature. He vividly described how an act of arson in 1835, in an earlier period of civic unrest, destroyed the academy's library of eight hundred volumes and its cabinet of geological specimens. Morris eloquently expressed his feelings on fate and fortune when he said, "But how soon men are blasted and how suddenly may the fruits of years of arduous labor be destroyed."[37] His real point was the need for leaders not to despair, but to recover and push forward on the path to cultural progress. The academy had rented new rooms, he recalled, and had recommenced purchasing a library. But, because the academy had finally been dissolved in 1844, Morris proclaimed that *now* the Maryland Historical Society had inherited the torch for pushing Maryland's cultural and civic progress forward. In such a task, sectional and sectarian wrangling had no part.

Morris the churchman, scientist, and scholar was now ready for perhaps his greatest challenge as a cultural leader, building cultural institutions for the generations to come.

8

Building Temples
of Culture

By mid-decade of the 1850s, Morris had clearly focused his work as a cultural leader on building institutions of research and learning as the key tools in developing American cultural life. As already seen, Morris the churchman worked assiduously to mold Lutheran institutions as reliable vehicles for the integration of Lutheran confessionalism into American life. As an educator, as well as churchman, he played a key role in advancing the cause of professional higher learning at the college and seminary at Gettysburg. Morris, the scholar, lecturer, and letter-writer, also contributed to the early days of two formidable scientific institutions—the Smithsonian Institution and the American Association for the Advancement of Science. For the next decade or so much of Morris's work as a cultural institution builder revolved around Baltimore and Maryland. Specifically, he took part in the creation and development of the Lutherville Female Seminary and the Peabody Institute and in the nurturing of the young Maryland Historical Society.

Morris's involvement in creating and sustaining a female seminary or academy deeply engaged him on a personal level for the rest of his life. As the enlightened father of several daughters, he cared a great deal about their education and development. This was at a time when many in southern states, including Maryland, began discussing the need for more professional education for women. At the same time, a growing sense of confessional consciousness induced some interest among Lutherans in the church's responsibility to provide educational opportunities for women.

Morris expressed his interest in such matters when he told Charles Philip Krauth about the need for a female academy of a "high order" south of the Mason-Dixon Line.[1] Despite the urging of Morris, Krauth and others, the General Synod never pursued the idea. The Maryland Synod, though, took an interest and, in 1857, created a committee to conduct a subscription campaign to establish a female academy at Hagerstown in the state's western section.[2] The location disappointed Morris, who wanted his venture nearer to Baltimore, so he moved into action.

His educational project went hand in hand with his interest in creating a new community. Baltimore's urban turbulence and the increasing acrimony he experienced in the Lutheran confessional wars deepened the sensitive Morris's need for respite and retreat. So, in 1852, supported financially by his brother Charles and Benjamin Kurtz, Morris took the first steps in bringing his vision to reality.

In February, John G. Morris and Kurtz purchased for $700 a parcel of farmland, called "The Regulation," located ten miles north of downtown Baltimore on York Road. In April 1854, Morris and Kurtz obtained an additional section of land, and by the fall of that year had sold much of the land to the newly-organized trustees for Lutherville Female Seminary for $6,850.[3]

With property in hand and a railroad line nearby, the two clergymen issued a prospectus, stating their purpose and seeking investors to purchase lots:

> First, the erection of a neat and comfortable Hamlet, to be called Lutherville, convenient to Baltimore, easy of access, and comprehending none but reputable families. . . . Second, the establishment in the immediate vicinity of the Female College, a house of Worship, a Primary School for Children, a Park for a promenade ground, and, more remotely, an Orphan Asylum.

To guard against charges of land speculation improper for a minister, the ever-sensitive Morris assured readers that all profits would go to the upkeep of the village's public institutions.[4]

Morris, the project's prime mover, envisioned a secluded, but not too distant, retreat for the city's élite, with the female boarding school as the community's focal point. No doubt, Morris expected that many of the families settling in the village would send their daughters to the "Female College." Naming the village after his hero, Martin Luther, Morris proudly proclaimed his religious stance.

His first efforts involved building a home for his family. In April 1853, the family visited Lutherville, and, to Georgianna Morris's evident relief, they found their new environment "prettier than expected."[5] The Morris summer home, a rambling two-story house with gabled windows and a porch in the front, reflected the romantic, "Gothic Revival" style then prevalent in American architecture.[6]

"Oak Grove," as the family called it, more and more served as the focal point for the Morrises as the years went on. Later, John Morris added a two-story extension and a summer kitchen, as the family spent increasing amounts of time in the small village. The surrounding woodlands and meadows provided the perfect setting for much needed walks and recreational scientific excursions. The restorative effects of Oak Grove and Lutherville would keep Morris in good health for decades to come.

Pastor Morris, with family matters in hand, next turned to getting the school underway. By February 1854, he had won the backing of twenty-seven other investors and obtained the needed act of incorporation from the Maryland General Assembly. Listed as the first of the "Trustees of the Lutherville Female Seminary," Morris with the other trustees had the authority to issue stock in the new corporation, which had as its purpose "the establishment and maintenance of a seminary of learning . . . for the instruction of females in such branches of education . . . deemed suitable and proper." Designed as a joint stock company, the corporation proposed selling 1,000 shares at $50. The trustees also intended to sell scholarships, ranging in cost from $150 to $500. Though the daughters of Lutheran ministers obtained a 25 percent reduction in tuition, the trustees obviously hoped to attract, as well, the daughters of the well-to-do.[7]

Even prior to completing legal incorporation procedures, Morris and the other trustees began building the new seminary. Morris presided at the cornerstone-laying ceremony on June 22, 1853. A pamphlet placed in the cornerstone clearly expressed the founders' aims. It said, "The first and principal object is the establishment of an institution of learning of the first order of excellence, based upon Christian (not sectarian) principles, in which the Holy Scripture will be a subject of daily study and meditation."[8] Though the seminary hoped to obtain students from all denominational affiliations, Morris's strong sense of Lutheran identity prevailed in the charter's requirement that eighteen of the twenty-eight trustees belong to the Lutheran church.

The seminary's first session, with Morris on the faculty, began on October 2, 1854. The seminary building, constructed with limestone in the Tudor style, had a central section augmented with a 96-foot observatory and flanked by two wings.[9] Morris's daughter, Mary Hay (1842-1918), remembered the early years of the school as "very primitive" in terms of furnishings and other provisions.[10] With a continuing influx of students, boarding and day, the school soon seemed on more solid ground.

Tuition, room, and board cost $92.50 per year when the seminary first opened. The curriculum reflected founder Morris's broad intellectual interests and his strong belief in women's education. Courses included philosophy, classical

and modern languages, chemistry, mathematics, and art. In addition, Morris himself gave lectures in geology, botany, and natural history. Also, the seminary offered courses in the "ornamental branches," such as music, painting, and
needlework, for an additional fee. Morris designed the curriculum to "embrace
everything necessary to a solid and finished literary education" that would secure
for a woman "her just and beneficial influence in society."[11]

Slowly, "reputable" families built homes in the village and this provided the
social dimension that an outgoing minister with young daughters needed. With the
new seminary, Morris created the perfect environment for educating his daughters
and testing his own social and intellectual theories of education. He dedicated much
time and energy to developing both the community and the seminary. Lutherville
remained for Morris an almost idyllic setting which nourished and sustained him.
Few ventures would bring him such personal and professional satisfaction.

While still creating his Lutherville experiment, Morris began working on yet
another institution-building project. As a curious intellectual and dedicated
scholar, he had a lifelong love for books, essential tools for advancing knowledge
and improving the tone and caliber of civic life. Antebellum Baltimore had no
major library or reading room open for public use. Prior to the mid-1850s, the only
library services available were offered by the small Library Company of Baltimore.
Typical of the subscription libraries dominant on the American scene from the late
eighteenth century until the Civil War, the Library Company circulated books and
provided reference services only to paying members. In 1854, the Company voted
to close and merge its holdings with the collection the Maryland Historical Society had started to build and maintain in its rooms in the Athenaeum, located at St.
Paul and Saratoga Streets in Baltimore.

The idea of a large library available for members and the public fired Morris's
imagination. In 1855, he sought and won election to the society's library committee. For the next four decades, he provided the energy and direction for the
committee's work in steadily expanding the library. Within a few years, with the
acquisition of the Library Company's collection, the library grew to over 11,300
volumes. Morris and the other members of the committee worked hours each
week cataloguing the books, first by subject and size, then alphabetically by authors' names.[12]

Morris and the committee also devised rules for circulation and use of the
materials by members of the MHS and the public. With over five hundred members by 1858, the society could also afford the services of a paid librarian to
manage the collection. For years, the exacting Morris supervised this employee
and spearheaded campaigns to acquire books on the state's history, economy,

literature, and science. By 1860, Morris and his colleagues had laid the foundations for a major cultural resource.

Morris's leadership position in Baltimore and at the Maryland Historical Society led him at the end of the decade into a venture with fateful and unforeseen consequences. This story began with George Peabody's vision to raise Baltimore's cultural and intellectual level.

Peabody, born into poor circumstances in Massachusetts in 1795, had built a flourishing mercantile business in Baltimore between 1814 and 1838. Then he moved to London and established himself in international banking.[13] Despite his move, Peabody never lost his love for America or his adopted city of Baltimore. From the 1840s until his death in 1869, George Peabody initiated and financially supported numerous philanthropic ventures. Perhaps the most significant venture was in Baltimore.

Shocked that Baltimore, with a population of 200,000, had no educational or cultural institutions worthy of the name, Peabody decided on a bold course of action. In early 1857, he and three prominent Baltimoreans—John Pendleton Kennedy, Charles James Madison Eaton, and William Edward Mayhew—developed a visionary scheme for a library, academy of music, art gallery, public lectures, and prizes for school students. All this would be supported by an initial $300,000 gift from Peabody. By making his new institute available to the public, he hoped to create a vibrant civic cultural life. In a sign of the times, Peabody, in his founding letter of February 12, 1857, "added an injunction against the Institute's ever being used for the nurture of Sectarian theology or political dissension."[14]

Peabody proposed that a board of twenty-five trustees oversee the overall implementation of his plan. He entrusted day-to-day operations of the new institute to the Maryland Historical Society, at that point the city's premier cultural organization.[15] With the majority of new institute trustees also actively involved in the Maryland Historical Society, Peabody's arrangement seemed logical and efficacious.

Peabody's proposal stirred great interest and excitement in the MHS. John Pendleton Kennedy, lawyer, politician, novelist, and one of the society's vice presidents, explained Peabody's offer at the MHS's monthly meeting on March 5, 1857. The fact that Peabody had included space for the society's library, natural history collection, and offices in planning his institute added to the members' enthusiasm. At the April 2 meeting, Kennedy offered a resolution, seconded by Morris, to accept Peabody's proposal.[16] Unable to peer into the future and see the difficulties that ultimately ensued, the members approved the resolution with little hesitation or doubt.

Over the next several years, efforts to bring George Peabody's vision to life went forward. Peabody Institute trustees selected a site, initiated construction of a facility to house the institute, and proposed a plan of organization for the MHS to consider. At the society's general meeting in January 1860, Morris successfully led the effort to secure membership approval for the proposals offered by the Peabody Institute.[17] Serious problems, though, lurked under the surface. Two of the Peabody Institute's trustees, Kennedy and Charles J. M. Eaton, had already locked horns over the location of the new facility and the institute's future direction.

Kennedy argued for a site in the suburbs which provided enough room for an institution of national, as well as local, importance. Eaton's desire for a downtown site ultimately prevailed. The two men also fought over the nature of the institute. In his private journal, Kennedy bitterly criticized Eaton's ideas of having commercial establishments on the first floor of the new building as "quite incompetent" and "not in keeping with Peabody's wish." Eaton, on the other hand, complained to Peabody that Kennedy emphasized the library part of Peabody's plan to the detriment of the other elements.[18] The ill will between these two men eventually had serious consequences for Morris.

Morris's involvement with the fledgling Peabody Institute dramatically expanded in late 1859. In creating the institute and its board of trustees, Peabody drew up a list of 150 prominent Baltimore citizens as replacements when vacancies occurred on the board and placed Morris's name on the list.[19] Morris had grown far from the little-known young minister who had arrived in Baltimore in 1827.

By 1860, Morris had a well-defined public personality. A man with multifaceted interests and talents, he had proved an ambitious, determined, and forceful cultural leader. Though at times petty and querulous, his innate sense of decency and fair play helped him retain a generally optimistic and positive stance toward other people and life in general.

We find a rare glimpse into Morris's private life in the diary his daughter Georgianna kept between 1853 and her marriage in 1863. The portrait that emerges mirrors the man Morris presented to the public. Bluff and hearty, growing stout and weighing about 190 pounds in 1854, Morris the husband, father, brother, and friend proved an emotional man, passionate about people and causes.[20]

For example, Morris clearly stated his feelings about marriage, career, and friendship in a warm, congratulatory letter he sent Spencer F. Baird on the occasion of the latter's marriage and appointment at the Smithsonian Institution:

I have heard of your annexation and congratulate you most cordially. The wives of many great men have aided them . . . in their scientific and literary pursuits, especially during the first year of their marriage—after that, they usually have had other live stock to tend—may your experience be the same.[21]

Clearly Morris hoped that his friend Baird would share the same good fortune he had found with Eliza and his family. Mrs. Morris's involvement with tending "livestock" continued during the 1840s and early 1850s. She gave birth in 1842 to daughter Mary Hay and to a son, John George, in 1845. The death of his second son shortly before the boy's fourth birthday devastated Morris. The anguished father quoted in the family register a poignantly appropriate verse from the twelfth chapter in the second book of Samuel:

> While the child was yet alive I fasted and wept; for I said who can tell whether God will be gracious to me and that the child may live? But now he is dead, wherefore should I fast? I shall go to him, but he shall not return to me.[22]

The birth of Anna Hay (1851-1893) eased the family's grief somewhat. With his daughters, particularly Georgianna, Morris proved, by turns, strict and indulgent. Georgianna, a student and boarder at the Lutherville Female Seminary in the mid-1850s, regularly suffered from fevers, sore throats, and assorted other ailments, which, in her opinion, justified unscheduled returns to her family home. Probably homesickness aggravated the young woman's illnesses. For example, on January 20, 1855, Georgianna felt ill and begged her father to let her return to Baltimore with him. At first, Morris said no, claiming that if he took his daughter home now, any girl who became sick would also demand to go home. Georgianna confided to her diary that she cried all morning and gave herself a "bad headache." After pleading from his other daughter, Mary Hay, the exasperated father finally took Georgianna home.[23] The diary makes clear this pattern was repeated numerous times.

Another example of Morris's basic sympathy and fondness for his daughter occurred during Georgianna's continual conflict with the seminary's headmaster, Mr. Eggers. Georgianna found Eggers "too passionate to get along well here," and they had numerous run-ins. At one point, the headmaster rebuked Georgianna, in the presence of her father, for "improper conduct in singing class." Morris must have realized that all this reflected a conflict between two incompatible personalities. Georgianna wrote that her father took her aside, kissed her, and assured her he would always "take my part when he found that I was imposed on."[24]

Morris's paternal affection extended to his other daughters. When he performed the marriage ceremony for his eldest daughter, Maria Louisa, he seemed "very much agitated when he tied the knot."[25]

Charles and John Morris continued to work closely on church projects. For instance, Charles served with his brother on the board of trustees of Gettysburg College for many decades, leaving $20,000 to the college at his death in 1874.[26] Both brothers worked together on a variety of other church causes, particularly in the mission field.

Though Morris's interests and career had little in common with his second brother's work as a coal merchant and banker in York, he seems to have had an attachment to George Morris as well. The news of George's unexpected death in August 1857 overwhelmed his younger brother. John rushed from the Lutherville train station and burst into Oak Grove exclaiming, "Where is Eliza?" He told his wife, "George is dead," and burst out crying. A few days later, while in York for the funeral, Georgianna noted that "father seems as if he could not possibly sit still for one minute, he and Uncle Charles are dreadfully distressed."[27]

Young Georgianna's diary also gives us another perspective into her father's public affairs. At numerous times the Baltimore pastor lectured the "scholars" at the Female Seminary in Lutherville on the history of women in art, European geography, the geologic information gleaned from his visit to the Alps, and other topics. Morris on at least one occasion prepared exams for the students. He also took upon himself the major responsibility for recruiting students for the fledgling seminary.

Georgianna regularly heard her father preach and she often accompanied him on his expeditions to Washington and the Smithsonian Institution. Georgianna's diary shows that her father's avid interest in Luther and in the need for a strengthened sense of Lutheran identity formed the basis for many of his sermons. Morris preached regularly on Luther's visit to Rome, the nailing of the ninety-five theses, and the conversion of Luther, among other topics. Others noted Morris's skill as a preacher. Margaret Scholl Hood, a friend of Maria Louisa from Frederick, Maryland, often visited Baltimore during the 1850s and commented on Dr. John Morris's "excellent sermons."[28]

Georgianna also noted her father's abilities and appeal as a public lecturer. Early in January 1857, Morris delivered one of his periodic lectures at the Smithsonian. As Georgianna put it, "At night we all went over to the Smithsonian to hear father lecture. He was in a good humor and made the people roar with laughter."[29] Morris's rapport with an audience, public or private, rarely failed him.

These diary entries also allow us a look, albeit at second hand, into Morris's political beliefs. Several times Morris and his wife hosted the veterans of the defense of Baltimore in the War of 1812, known as the "Old Defenders," at picnics held at Oak Grove. Morris clearly expressed his fervent patriotism when he preached "a beautiful sermon" in 1854 to the "Old Defenders," many of whom "had tears in their eyes."[30] Morris put his political allegiance with the Whig Party until the early 1850s. He gave one of the invocations at a session of the party's last convention in June 1852, held in Baltimore.[31]

By the late 1850s, Morris had become an adherent of the newly formed Republican Party. Given that party's abolitionist and anti-Southern stance, supporting it in pre-Civil War Baltimore would prove difficult. Morris, a fervent patriot and personally opposed to slavery, found the Republican Party a logical alternative to the disintegrating Whig party and the fractured Democrats. Georgianna reflected her family's political stance when she lamented the election of the nativist American party (Know Nothing) candidate as Baltimore's mayor in 1856.[32]

Georgianna also spoke for her family when she wrote with indignation about a cruel slave owner the family knew:

> Henrietta went over to Mrs. Talbot's this evening for butter and she came back crying and said there was an awful fuss over at Mrs. Talbot's. She saw a great crowd in the barnyard and Mrs. Talbot standing there. She did not know what it was. So she went near, but soon she ran back for there she saw a poor negro woman stripped bare back, one man beating her with a cowhide, three other men looking on, and that Talbot woman looking to see that it was done right. Henrietta says she never saw such a scene in her life. She said you could hear the strokes of the cowhide and the poor woman's screams were awful. Mrs. Talbot's children were all up at the house crying and one of the other women told Henrietta that Mrs. Talbot was very cruel. I do not know what she was whipped for, but no matter what she did no person has a right to whip his or her fellow creature in that manner, as if they belonged body and soul to them. I am determined never to go to Mrs. Talbot's again and if I can help it never to speak to that fiend in woman's shape again, for if she can stand by and see a fellow creature so beaten, she is no Christian and is not fit company for us. This has put me more against slavery than I ever was. That woman was the mother of 6 children too, and the most valuable slave Mrs. Talbot has."[33]

As 1860 dawned, John G. Morris found himself in an enviable position. He was successful as a churchman, cultural leader, and scholar, and a network of close personal and professional relationships sustained and supported him. Yet the new decade would test Morris's integrity in unexpected ways.

Natural history collection, which JGM helped create and build, in Linnaean Hall, Pennsylvania College. (*Still Picture Branch/79-T-2039A, National Archives.*)

Lutherville Female Seminary. Lithograph by E. Sachse and Company. (*Maryland Historical Society.*)

Dedication of the Peabody Institute, Baltimore, 1866. (*Maryland Historical Society.*)

Oak Grove, JGM's summer residence in Lutherville, Maryland.
(*Maryland Historical Society.*)

Portrait of John Pendleton Kennedy by William Hubbard, Jr. (*Maryland Historical Society.*)

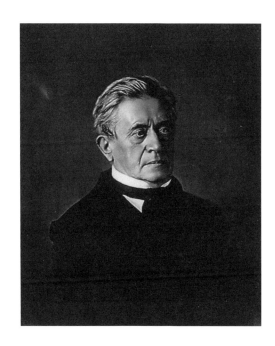

Joseph Henry, first secretary
of the Smithsonian.
(*Still Picture Branch/111-RB-6114,
National Archives.*)

Smithsonian Institution.
(*Still Picture Branch/111-B-4672,
National Archives.*)

Philip Reese Uhler, JGM's colleague and successor as librarian at the Peabody Institute. (*Still Picture Branch/7-H-760, National Archives.*)

Hermann A. Hagen, Harvard professor and reviewer of JGM's most important scientific work. (*Still Picture Branch/7-H-442, National Archives.*)

Herbert Osborn, professor of natural history and president of the Entomological Society of America (1911), recognized the value of JGM's *Catalogue*. (*Still Picture Branch/7-H-315, National Archives.*)

William H. Edwards, scientific colleague of JGM. (*Still Pictures Branch/7-H-530, National Archives.*)

JGM, ca. mid-1880s. (*Still Picture Branch/7-H-516, National Archives.*)

JGM at age ninety. Portrait by Oscar Hallwig. *(Maryland Historical Society.)*

Martin Luther window dedicated to JGM, St. Paul's Lutheran Church, Lutherville, Maryland.
(*Courtesy St. Paul's Lutheran Church.*)

JOHN G. MORRIS, D.D., LL.D.

Part Four

Change and Conflict
1860-1867

At certain revolutions all the damn'd
Are brought: and feel by turns the bitter change
Of fierce extremes, extremes by change more fierce.

JOHN MILTON
Paradise Lost

9

Peabody Interlude

hough well-versed by age fifty-seven in the stresses and strains encountered by a pioneering cultural leader, John G. Morris found the 1860s a decade of unparalleled change and conflict. But emerging from this came one of his greatest accomplishments—creation of a major research library. Morris's election as a trustee of the newly created Peabody Institute in December 1859 inaugurated this period of profound personal and professional change. It began for him the Peabody interlude.

Within seven months of his election, Morris had departed from the pulpit at First Church and begun a new career as the first librarian of the Peabody Institute. The facts involved in the transition seem fairly clear and straightforward. In February 1860, Morris's fellow trustees appointed him to the committees charged with implementing two of the institute's major programs—the library and public lectures. As a member of the Library Committee, Morris worked with chairman John Pendleton Kennedy in preparing a report for the Board of Trustees on organizing the library. The committee proposed using $25,000 of George Peabody's gift to purchase 50,000 volumes for a collection that emphasized history, literature and science. Further, the committee suggested hiring a librarian with an annual salary of $1,500. The board accepted the committee's report, and on April 13, 1860, directed the Library Committee to begin a public search for a full-time librarian. They also stipulated that the librarian could hold no other employment.[1]

Within a few weeks, Morris wrote Kennedy expressing his strong interest in obtaining the new post. Tackling the main obstacle to his desires, Morris told Kennedy he knew that the latter favored poet and editor John R. Thompson for the job. However, Morris went on, he believed Thompson had accepted an editorship in Georgia and thus probably would not accept the librarian post. Morris continued his campaign by resigning from the Board of Trustees or June 2, and again telling Kennedy of his own keen interest and that Thompson had a post elsewhere.[2] The board met on June 7 and considered eight candidates. Morris later recollected, "I was certain I would be chosen." Though we do not know the reasons for his certainty, Morris did indeed receive the highest number of votes and became the institute's first librarian.[3] No doubt Morris's scholarly acumen and long years of cultural leadership in Baltimore made his selection an eminently suitable one. His membership in the élite Conversational Club and in the Maryland Historical Society, for example, clearly indicated his good standing in the eyes of the city's social and intellectual leaders. The most intriguing questions, though, concern what precipitated this new direction for Morris after thirty-three years as a parish pastor.

Many years after the fact, he recounted his thoughts as he wrestled with his momentous decision:

> If I do not leave now and accept this respectable place, so well suited to my tastes, I may never have a better opportunity of bettering my condition. If I stay here much longer I will be considered too old to be called to any other church, and my own people will get tired of me and give me unmistakable evidences that I had better leave. Worn out among them, and no longer a young man whom any other church would want (for few men over fifty receive calls), had I not better quietly withdraw and give the church an opportunity of securing another man?[4]

Morris's decision-making with his career change bears some resemblance to his original "call to the ministry." He rationally analyzed his talents, interests, and selected the option most suitable for him. But there was much more to it than this. Almost fifty-seven years old, Morris faced a late mid-life crisis. He was restless after all his years at First English. Ever sensitive and blunt, he felt that "The Church had never supported me, and the deficiency was made up from my own private income to an amount upwards of $15,000, at a low calculation." The scholarly and now theologically correct pastor resented the congregation's continued "methodistic" tendencies. Emotionally and physically, Morris was exhausted from over three decades of toil spent in nurturing his church. He remembered that he "had served that church 33 years, having built it up from the beginning, enlarged the house of worship several times, sent off two colonies, built the parsonage, paid off a large portion of the debt, and left everything in a prosperous condition."[5] He was tired and he wanted a change. Most of all, he feared hanging on too long, losing control of the situation, and being forced out.

Furthermore, Morris's growing national reputation as a scientist and scholar made the unique offer presented by the Peabody Institute an irresistible opportunity "of bettering my own condition." Intellectually and theologically, he had outgrown First Church and needed to move on. As always, he needed the support of those closest to him.

Eliza Morris played an influential role in her husband's career change. As Morris put it, his move had the "sanction of one whose opinion on such a subject I valued more highly than that of any other person living. My brother also sanctioned it."[6] As with his decision to enter the ministry, significant family members influenced and supported him. Eliza Morris's motivations are uncertain. Leaving the active parish ministry and focusing his career at the Peabody Institute meant Morris would have more time and energy for his family, and for the other interests and activities that he continued to pursue. Perhaps she also hoped for an easing of the many church conflicts which had embroiled her husband for so long.

Not all members of Morris's family understood the change that was about to occur. Twenty-one year old Georgianna noted in her diary on June 8 her father's election the day before as librarian of the Peabody Institute. While the young woman had not "paid much attention," she found the idea of her father anything but a pastor "absurd."[7] Morris took care to assure family, friends, and fellow Lutherans that he did not intend abandoning the pulpit "altogether." He would continue as a preacher when needed, though he "might for a season cease to be pastor." Morris promised them that undertaking a "secular office" did not mean a lessening of his basic commitment to preaching and the church. As he left the parsonage, Morris found that his "mind was at ease."[8] He did not realize that he was moving into the most difficult period of his life.

In keeping with George Peabody's vision that the library for his institute should "be furnished in every department of knowledge with the most approved literature . . . maintained for the free use of all persons who desire to consult it," Morris and the library committee first turned their attention to developing a long-range plan to collect the world's finest books.[9] By early August, Morris had begun scouring catalogues from the best European and American libraries to identify books the library wished to acquire. By April 1861, Morris had compiled a catalogue, or "desiderata" as he called it, listing 20,000 titles representing over 50,000 volumes that the Peabody Institute planned to obtain. With $500 provided by the trustees, Morris published the catalogue and distributed it to booksellers, publishers, and libraries in Europe and America.[10]

Morris's "desiderata" would last as the basis for the library's collection policy until a major reorganization took place in 1916. The comprehensive catalogue focused on both ancient and modern history, philosophy, the fine arts, natural science, and modern languages. With the catalogue completed, Morris next turned his efforts to creating the collection. In addition to mailing out the catalogue, Morris traveled to New York and Boston several times visiting bookstores, publishers, and libraries. Slowly the collection grew. By the end of Morris's tenure in September 1867, he had acquired over 20,000 volumes for the library.[11]

Morris's zeal for history led him to one of his most innovative accomplishments at the Peabody Library. The outbreak of the Civil War stimulated a flood of pamphlets arguing the merits of each side. Morris informed the library committee that he intended to obtain as many of these pamphlets as possible. He explained, "The present troubles of the country have been the occasion of a vast number of pamphlets, which we should possess as a source of current historical facts, to any future writer or reader."[12] Though a strong Union man, Morris saw the need for the historical record to reflect all points of view. By the end of the war, he had obtained hundreds of war pamphlets.

Much of his time went to less congenial tasks than developing the library's collection. He had to study what he termed "library economy" and develop policies and procedures for diverse activities including designing the new library, purchasing books at the lowest possible price, cataloguing new acquisitions, and binding books for preservation purposes. All of these were common problems nineteenth-century library managers faced. For, in fact, Morris and others like him were laying the foundations for a network of research and public libraries accessible to the public.

Morris worked closely with Charles J. M. Eaton, who had replaced John Pendleton Kennedy as chairman of the Library Committee, and in dealing with the architects in the design of the library and its reading room. Though not opened to the general public until the formal dedication of the institute's building in November 1866, the reading room gradually attracted serious readers and students. Located on the second floor at the top of the wrought-iron staircase, the library was Morris's proudest creation. The 100-foot-long and 33-foot-wide reading room had a gallery running along two sides where the books were stored. Morris glowingly noted that the reading room "has six large tables and more than half of the extent of the walls for about seven feet high are shelved with walnut and made to appear like furniture rather than like shelves." Lush walnut book ends, bookcases, and catalogue cases complemented the walnut and cane-back library armchairs and the carpeted floors.

The gas lights, among the earliest used in an American library, set off the elegant room. Morris's private office, walnut-paneled with a beautiful view from atop Mt. Vernon Square looking down toward the Baltimore harbor, made his satisfaction complete. To top off the scene, in the reading room he placed on the shelves "all the encyclopedias, dictionaries, some reviews, bound in elegant Morocco binding."[13]

Perhaps Morris's penchant for Morocco binding explains in part the bitter relationship that developed between him and Eaton. At the Library Committee chairman's insistence, the board of trustees adopted "Rules and Regulations" for the library which clearly placed Morris in a subordinate position. The committee controlled the hiring and firing of employees, and charged the librarian with maintaining all books and accounts; noting all acquisitions in a register; cataloguing, arranging, and labeling all books; keeping a daily record of all visitors; and personally closing the library each night.[14]

At Eaton's insistence, Morris submitted a detailed plan explaining his strategy for purchasing books, and noted in his annual reports that his purchases averaged $1.52 per book. In his plan, he promised to show all lists of books for purchase to the chairman for his approval. Further, he assured Eaton he would only purchase books in "library condition." Morris explained to Philip Uhler, a young entomologist who served for a time as Morris's assistant at the Peabody, that Eaton "was angry about broken old dilapidated books needing restoration." To counter accusations that he lacked business ability, Morris stressed that purchases of foreign books would depend on favorable exchange rates.[15]

Despite Eaton's concern about the cost of binding, Morris insisted that each book have its own cover. He conceded that binding should bear some relation to the book's cost and usefulness, and that binding together small books or pamphlets on similar subjects could meet his "absolute" rule that each book have a cover.[16] For the seven years of his tenure, Morris and Eaton argued endlessly over the library's operations and Morris's acquisition practices. Gradually, all this wore Morris down and engendered a deep bitterness which lasted for the rest of his life.

Morris referred privately to Eaton in 1864 as "his lordship." By 1866 the two men waged open war. He shared with Uhler that now he had "begun to insist also and usually get what I want, even though violently resisted" by Eaton. "You know how it *was* formerly, when I yielded for the most part but it is no longer," he told his friend.[17] In October, George Peabody visited Baltimore for the institute's official opening, and Morris experienced a brief burst of hope that his situation might improve. Exultantly, he told Uhler, "The library committee is to meet every week and I am no longer to be responsible *to Eaton only*, but to the Committee. I am to lay before *them* every week, my correspondence, my wants and wishes and recommendations and they are to act on them and not as heretofore C. J. F. M. E. *alone*. I am sure he does not like it, for a fellow who has wielded the power so long, doesn't like to give it up."[18]

Within a month, though, Morris experienced deep disappointment when he realized that Eaton had retained his dominance of the Library Committee, and planned to hire a business manager for library operations. On Christmas Eve of 1866, Morris at last openly faced Eaton for a final, climactic showdown. Distraught, he complained to Eaton that hiring a new man "is really a discharge." Eaton, appearing "mild and gentle," denied that he blamed Morris (as Uhler had reported) for slow progress. Rather, he praised Morris for his "ability, energy, and industry." But, Eaton acidly noted, Morris had no "mercantile education" and thus was "not the best man to buy books." Morris threatened to "leave immediately" if Eaton carried through with his plan. He concluded by telling Eaton that "my dismission will reflect more discreditably on the Peabody than on me, for the people know me and this concern is very unpopular."[19] Given no reassurance, Morris rushed from Eaton's room and fled to his office. His humiliation was complete.

Morris's allusion to the institute's unpopularity referred to yet another situation that sorely aggravated and helped end his tenure at the Peabody. He was a prominent member of the Maryland Historical Society's Library Committee, which had the responsibility of fulfilling George Peabody's injunction that the MHS move its library, natural history collection, and reading room to the institute, and then manage the institute's operations under the general supervision of the Peabody's board of trustees. Placing the society's 30,000 volume library in proximity to Morris's collection at the Peabody would immediately create a cultural resource of national importance. Despite the fact that the Peabody trustees had completed construction of a new building by February 1862, and had proposed a plan of organization acceptable to the MHS as early as 1860, no further steps in implementing George Peabody's plan occurred.

In part, this reflected the bitter split among the Peabody's trustees caused by the outbreak of the Civil War. With the trustees almost evenly divided between Union and Confederate supporters, the board never met during the war years.[20] Charles J. M. Eaton and the board's president, John Pendleton Kennedy, filled the vacuum. Almost from the beginning, Eaton doubted the efficacy of Peabody's arrangement. He feared that the Maryland Historical Society, with over 500 members and "easy access to membership and committees," would eventually dominate the Peabody Institute and undermine the aims of the founder. Gradually

Kennedy began to share Eaton's doubts. When the Peabody trustees refused in March 1866 to finalize arrangements with the society, the anger of the society's members boiled over.[21] No wonder the dejected Morris wrote that "I would not be surprised if *the whole* concern were shut up before a month elapses!!"[22]

The Maryand Historical Society argued that the institute's legal incorporation required that the society receive space in a new building and assume day-to-day responsibility for the institute's operations. Furthermore, the society noted that it had "the same literary, artistic, and scientific purposes" as the Peabody, angrily rejecting accusations of lax membership policies by stressing that any three members of the society could blackball a prospective member. The leaders of the society expressed their basic incredulity over Eaton's and Kennedy's wariness by reminding the institute that its trustees (most of them MHS members) had final control over nominations for all administrative positions. The society also plaintively noted that the institute's librarian "is one of our most respected and heeded associates."[23] Hardly a plea to warm Eaton's heart.

In the spring of 1866, George Peabody returned to the United States for a brief visit. He had to resolve the bitter impasse so the institute could officially open. With patience and tact, Peabody sought an acceptable resolution. He acknowledged the Maryland Historical Society's legal rights, but stressed the impossibility of union after so much controversy. In response to the society's acceptance of this bitter fact, a grateful George Peabody donated $20,000 as a permanent investment and income for the society.[24] With his dream of a great, unified cultural collection shattered and faced with the continued dominance of his nemesis at the Peabody, Morris decided to resign.

Even with the perspective of many years, Morris remembered Charles J. M. Eaton with anger and resentment. In caustic terms not found elsewhere in *Life Reminiscences*, Morris described Eaton as a man "unsympathetic in his nature, haughty in his manners, and most absurd in his pretensions. He knew no poetry nor literature nor science, and yet this man was my master in the selection of books and my superior in authority in all things. Never before had I been placed in such a humiliating position. I was mortified beyond expression at my enforced subserviency." Taking full revenge on the deceased Eaton, Morris steamed that, "He treated me and my assistant as if we were apprentices in a dry goods store; he had no respect for our labors, and never gave us credit for anything we did; he was constantly finding fault."[25]

Did Eaton deserve such venom? Undoubtedly the two men were temperamentally quite different and surely ill-suited for a mutually acceptable working relationship. Though Eaton's perspective on how the institute should develop differed from that of Morris and John Pendleton Kennedy, he was as devoted as they to realizing George Peabody's vision. He spent years of his life laboring for the growth of the institute. Morris, basically used to running his own show, little realized what it meant to become an employee and operate under a daily regimen of rules and procedures. It grated on him and he came to hate it. Rather than acknowledge this incompatibility, Morris lashed out at the symbol of his problem, Charles J. M. Eaton. Certainly Eaton lacked tact and empathy in dealing with the proud and sensitive Morris, but he did not deserve the posthumous vilification he received.

Though Morris's tenure at the Peabody, begun with such great expectations, ended in frustration and disappointment, he accomplished much of enduring value. His sensible collection policy and aggressive acquisition efforts created the nucleus of a major research library. Morris's skillful "library economy" resulted in the design and construction of handsome and useful library space, as well as the establishment of orderly procedures for cataloguing and preserving thousands of books. Created from nothing by the first librarian's indefatigable industry and scholarly ability, the library program continued along the basic lines set down by Morris for almost fifty years. Perhaps as important, Peabody's vision and Morris's success inspired another prominent civic leader, Enoch Pratt, to found the Baltimore public library, one of the pioneer events in the emerging taxpayer-supported public library system developing in America.

Though working at the Peabody Institute proved difficult indeed, Morris found the other parts of his life equally troublesome and challenging.[25]

10

Standing by Conviction

The outbreak of the Civil War tested John G. Morris's integrity and character. Though personally opposed to slavery, he had refrained before the war from any involvement with militant abolitionism. As an early supporter of the American Colonization Society, he favored a policy of gradual emancipation and relocation of the ex-slaves (and free blacks as well) to Africa. Yet, Morris had no personal animus toward blacks. In February 1850, for example, he signed a memorial to the mayor and city council of Baltimore protesting that the free blacks had to pay taxes for public schools, yet could not attend them. Morris's stance paralleled that of the Maryland Synod which twice (1824, 1834) commended the merits of the colonization society to the support of the "patriot, of the philanthropist, and the Christian." The synod avoided any discussion of slavery during the war, though by 1864 it did adopt "a ringing resolution of loyalty"[1] to the Union.

The synod's diffidence reflected conditions in a border state which had over 87,000 slaves and 84,000 free blacks within its boundaries. Marylanders for the most part wanted both to preserve the union and maintain southern property and political rights. Though Baltimore conducted 60 percent of its trade with the North, old southern families had a dominant influence. The hotly contested election of 1860 exposed the deep fissures in society. In the four-way party split, most city and state voters supported the candidate of the southern Democrats, John C. Breckinridge. John Bell, candidate of the hastily created Constitutional Union Party, ran close behind. Stephen A. Douglas (northern Democrat) and Abraham Lincoln (Republican) received only scattered support. In fact, only 1,087 Baltimore voters cast their ballots for Lincoln.[2]

Georgianna Morris's diary entry on the day after Lincoln's election reveals the concerns prevalent in the Morris family and their basic stance on the issue of union. She wrote, "Old Abe Lincoln has been elected President of these United States—God grant they may always be United—though there is great fussing in the South and talk of secession."[3] Though less vocal on slavery, John G. Morris never wavered in his public support for the Union. During the tumultuous day in April 1861 when pro-southern mobs in Baltimore threatened Morris and other pro-government supporters, the clergyman remembered, "It cost something to be an uncompromising Union man in those early days. . . . For one or two days, we were threatened with an order of expulsion from the city, and we were forbidden for a short time to display the Union flag, but a change of sentiment soon occurred."[4] Morris's invitation to John Pendleton Kennedy to join senior Union officers at the Morris home on Greene Street for a social evening indicates that the atmosphere in the city had indeed turned for the better.[5]

Though most of Morris's former congregation remained on the Union side, "some men and women whose pastor I had been for many years, whose children I had baptized, and some of whom I had buried, whose friend and comforter I had been in trouble, and their welcome guest always, . . . broke up all intercourse with me and my family." Morris believed that those "who sighed to be respectable" joined the "aristocracy" and "fashionable people" who adhered to the South in hopes of personal and social advancement. Always sensitive to losing church members over a "respectability" issue, the acute Morris noted with no little satisfaction that the "aristocracy" dropped these people "when no longer needed."[6] When Union troops passed through Lutherville on southbound trains, Morris and other "loyal citizens would rush down the road and welcome them as they passed by waving the Union flag and giving them enthusiastic hurrahs. Their response came with a will."[7] Morris felt the touch of war at Oak Grove, as well as in Baltimore. Shortly before the battle of Monocacy in July 1864, he and other Lutherville residents experienced a sharp scare when Confederate raiders appeared in the neighborhood. As news spread of the rebels' approach, Morris hurried from church to Oak Grove, concealed his valuables under a woodpile, and put his horses in nearby woods. Fortunately, the enemy turned in a different direction and the villagers remained unharmed. Morris was calm throughout the incident, secure in the belief that he could prevent the rebel commander, a local man named Gilmore, from plundering the village because Gilmore and his father had taken tea with Morris a few months earlier.[8] Morris's unshakable faith in social bonds among gentlemen clearly comes out in this vignette. Though a bit naive in this instance,

Morris's attitude undergirded his approach in all his social and professional trans-
actions with the men of his class. He never forgave breaches of this trust.

As the end of war approached, Morris helped organize a meeting of "loyal
ministers" in Baltimore. To his utter disgust, he had to withdraw his resolutions
defining "loyal minister" because others found them "too strong for some
weak-kneed gentlemen present." Morris's strong sense of probity and honor
stands out clearly in his resolutions. No minister who remained silent, changed his
tune depending on the group, refused to pray for the president, or only now loudly
professed loyalty deserved the appellation "loyal." The continuing split in the Baltimore clergy angered Morris. He wrote, "Nothing came out of the meeting. Most
of those present were opposed to the government; others better disposed were
afraid of offending their rebel parishioners. The few faithful could do nothing."[9]
The honest and forthright Morris remained steadfast in support of the Union
through the long and bitter conflict. No pressure to remain silent or neutral could
deter him. Wartime Baltimore revealed the granite in John G. Morris's character.

Despite his wartime preoccupation and deep involvement in the affairs of
the Peabody Institute, Morris remained surprisingly active in the affairs of the
Maryland Synod and the General Synod. He had reported at the conclusion of
his pastorate at First Church that over his long years of service he had baptized
1,204 infants and adults, confirmed 458 individuals, buried 217 infants and 270
adults, married 508 couples, presided over the Lord's Supper 128 times, and
preached 4,000 sermons. All this was in addition to improving First Church
physically and establishing two flourishing congregations as offshoots of his own
church.[10] Morris held pride of place as the synod's senior member and because of
his great accomplishments.

Though the secessionist crisis loomed large in the fall of 1860, Morris and
other Maryland Synod leaders pushed forward with a proposal to merge with the
Virginia Synod. Ostensibly this effort was based on a desire to merge with smaller
synods and thus achieve greater effectiveness, but internal Maryland politics
played an important part.. At the 1860 synod meeting, Morris and two other ministers formed a committee to review the president's annual report and prepare a
response. In its report, the committee used the concept of synodical mergers to
urge postponing any effort to set boundaries and recognize the Melanchthon
Synod, formed in the late 1850s by disgruntled "American Lutherans" from western Maryland.[11] The Maryland Synod, which had previously rejected the
Melanchthon Synod's organizing principle of "elective affinity," concurred with

the committee's position. The proposal to merge "small synods" reflected not only the historical ties between the Maryland and Virginia synods dating back to 1820, but also the Maryland Synod's desire to repair the schism caused by the Melanchthon Synod. Further, Morris and his companions hoped that such a merger could help Lutherans of the General Synod stay united, despite the political difficulties enveloping the country.

Morris, appointed chairman of a five-man delegation to the Virginia Synod, vainly sought to achieve a merger. He attended a meeting of the Virginia Synod and presented the Maryland proposal in the best possible light. Virginians resisted the proposal for two reasons: the increasing drift to war made separation more likely than union, and most Virginia pastors felt, as they had at the time of the 1829 split, that they had little in common with their distant Maryland colleagues. Though the Virginians appointed a committee to correspond with Morris about the Maryland proposal, nothing further came of the effort. As Morris reported in 1861, secession had put "kebosh" to it all.[12] Similarly, efforts to bring back the Melanchthon Synod pastors proved unavailing. Reunion came only in 1868, three years after the death of Benjamin Kurtz, the guiding spirit of the Melanchthon Synod.

Though the Maryland Synod, reflecting divisions and conditions within the state, remained silent on the war until its 1864 session, the General Synod took a different approach. On the eve of the Civil War, the General Synod had achieved its greatest extent and influence. It claimed 864 out of 1313 Lutheran ministers in America as members and 164,000 out of 235,000 Lutherans as communicants.[13] The war, and continuing political and confessional differences within the General Synod, marked the 1860s as a traumatic period for the national body.

The biennial session was originally scheduled for May 1861, but the General Synod postponed it, hoping that somehow or other the southern synods would remain in fellowship with the parent organization. The formation of a permanent Confederate government in February 1862 and the onslaught of ever more bloody battles dashed these hopes.[14] Finally, the General Synod convened in Lancaster, Pennsylvania, in May 1862. The refusal of the southern synods to respond to the convention's call proclaimed the split in the church.

At the Lancaster session, Morris served as the Maryland Synod representative on a committee charged with preparing a document on "the present crisis and the duty of Christians." Without the constraints of southern synods, the national church openly proclaimed its allegiance to the federal government. The resolution, unanimously adopted by the General Synod, stated that the Word of God "requires loyal subjection to the `powers that be,'" and declared at the same time that they "who resist the power shall receive to themselves condemnation." The

General Synod acknowledged that "in the suppression of this rebellion and in the maintenance of the Constitution and the Union by the sword, we recognize an unavoidable necessity and sacred duty."[15]

Like many other Christians, the members of the General Synod believed that the war resulted from God's judgment of individual and national sins, though they also recognized a more immediate cause. Morris and his colleagues on the committee saw the "continuance and spread of domestic slavery" as the precipitating factor in the outbreak of war. For the first time in its history, the General Synod supported any state moves initiating "constitutional emancipation."[16] Though finally condemning slavery, the socially conservative General Synod expressed its concern for proper constitutional order and respect for property rights. The General Synod's unabashed support for the Union and its social conservatism mirrored the views of delegate Morris.

Political and confessional strife continued to plague the General Synod. The situation exploded at the York, Pennsylvania, session in 1864. The bitterness engendered over the "Definite Platform" battle in the 1850s had never really ended. Conservative district synods, particularly the Pennsylvania Ministerium, warily eyed the "American Lutherans" and vowed to withdraw from the General Synod if the latter changed its confessional stance, or sought to extend its control over the district synod. The General Synod's admission of the Melanchthon Synod in 1859 only increased the Pennsylvania Ministerium's unease. The Franckean Synod's request for admission as a member of the General Synod in 1864 precipitated the final explosion.[17]

Long an advocate of "American Lutheran" principles, the ardently abolitionist Franckean Synod in upper New York state stood poles apart from the Pennsylvania Ministerium, with its concern for adherence to traditional Lutheran doctrine and liturgical practices. At the York meeting, a long and contentious debate ensued. At first delegates refused the request for admission on the grounds that the Franckean Synod's declaration of faith "was devoid of Lutheranism's distinctive doctrines."[18] After the Franckean Synod representatives reassured the delegates that membership in the General Synod implied acceptance of its confessional stance, particularly the traditional acceptance of the Augsburg Confession as a "substantially correct" exhibition of scriptural doctrine, the delegates approved admission by a vote of ninety-seven to forty-three. The General Synod's injunction that the Franckean Synod at its next meeting publicly accept the national body's confessional stance did nothing to mollify the opposition. At this critical turning point, Morris, long a foe of "American Lutheranism" and proponent of increased confessional subscription, joined the dissenters.[19]

The delegates from the Pennsylvania Ministerium, in accordance with the implied threat in its conditional return to the General Synod in 1853, withdrew in protest from the convention. In the midst of the uproar, Morris and other leaders steered through the General Synod a resolution strengthening its acceptance of the Augsburg Confession. Now, the General Synod viewed "the Augsburg Confession as a correct exhibition of the fundamental doctrines of the Divine Word, and of the faith of our Church founded upon that Word."[20] Further, delegates adopted a resolution passed by the Pittsburgh Synod in 1856 rejecting the "American Lutheran" claim that the Augsburg Confession contained doctrinal errors. These efforts at amelioration proved futile.

At the meeting of the General Synod in 1866, President Samuel W. Sprecher refused to accept the credentials of the ministerium's delegates, claiming that their 1864 withdrawal constituted secession and now the ministerium would have to apply for readmission. The majority of the delegates sustained Sprecher's decision. Further efforts at compromise collapsed. Within a year, eleven synods formed a new national body, the General Council, holding a middle position between the General Synod's moderate confessional stance and the Missouri Synod's acceptance of all the Lutheran confessional statements from the sixteenth century.[21] Devastated by southern and conservative defections, the General Synod, by 1868 had only 590 ministers and 86,198 communicants.[22] In the ensuing decades, John G. Morris would lead the efforts at reunion.

The situation at Gettysburg Seminary reflected both the personal and doctrinal battles and the exacerbated tensions of the era. Morris's feelings about Samuel Simon Schmucker continued unabated. In a letter to the Reverend Henry Louis Baugher, president of Pennsylvania College, Morris lamented what he considered Schmucker's continuing deleterious influence, particularly in regard to the sacrament of the Lord's Supper. "Such *unlutheran* views," Morris wrote, "of a doctrine characteristically Lutheran, I cannot sanction in a man sworn to maintain a different ground. Surely, Sir, it is the lowest sort of Zwinglianism that will end in Rationalism."[23]

As a longtime member of the seminary's board of directors, Morris sought to steer the institution through stormy times. When Schmucker announced his resignation in early 1864, the struggle to replace him began. Leaders of the Pennsylvania Ministerium proposed Charles Philip Krauth's son, Charles Porterfield Krauth, as the most suitable candidate. The younger Krauth, a staunch confessionalist, represented a clean break from Schmucker's pan-Protestant evangelical sympathies. His ardent conservative partisanship, and the fact that the Pennsylvania Ministerium announced the creation of its own seminary after withdrawing from the General Synod, doomed Krauth's chances. Instead the Gettysburg directors selected James A. Brown, also a Schmucker critic and an East Pennsylvania Synod leader.[24] Though very fond of Charles Porterfield Krauth, Morris felt that Brown represented an adequately orthodox theological stance, while avoiding the pitfalls of the General Synod-Pennsylvania Ministerium struggle. The withdrawal of the ministerium's representatives from the seminary's board and the resignation of Charles F. Schaeffer from the college and seminary faculties, sealed the split.

Brown's opposition to the "Definite Platform" and his moderate views on confessional subscription earned Morris's support. A bit earlier than this, Morris had expressed support for Brown as a potential candidate for the Franklin Professorship at Gettysburg College. He viewed Brown as a "ripe scholar" with valuable experience as a teacher.[25] With the installation of James Brown, the seminary's board and faculty entered a period of harmony not known since the days of Schmucker's undisputed leadership.

In the midst of all the turmoil and conflict, John G. Morris's scholarly endeavors continued at full force. In fact, intellectual activities afforded the beleaguered Morris some relief. His major scientific work of the period appeared in 1862. At Joseph Henry's request, he compiled a companion piece to his *Catalogue of Described Lepidoptera*. Morris's new work, entitled *Synopsis of the Described Lepidoptera of North America*, focused on two Lepidoptera genera, active in the daylight and twilight hours, which shared common structural characteristics. Drawing on the published works of Breckinridge Clemens and several other entomologists, he showed how knowledge of anatomical structure led to identifying genus and species without the need for dissection. Referring readers to his *Catalogue* for complete reference citation, Morris stressed in this new work distinctive physical features involving insect heads, wings, undersides, and bodies. The *Synopsis*, as well as the continuing good reception of the *Catalogue*, added immeasurably to spreading understanding about the basic principles involved in scientific classification.[26]

During the early 1860s, Morris also continued working with the Maryland Historical Society's Natural History Committee. In addition to collecting and labeling specimens, he published research papers. He read one of these, on the Ailanthus silk worm of China, to the society in December 1861. He demonstrated for his audience silk spun from American species of the worm he had cultivated.[27] The newly created United States Department of Agriculture published his paper in 1862.

Morris complemented his scientific research with work on a variety of historical subjects. Not surprisingly, his role in the Maryland Historical Society led him to focus on Maryland history. In November 1864, Morris reported to the MHS that he had collected 713 names of Maryland authors who had produced 1,877 volumes or pamphlets. In addition, Morris had a list of 158 periodicals published in Maryland, with fifty-three of these printed and issued in Baltimore.[28] In addition to his own research efforts, Morris sought help from others, such as Joseph Henry, in gathering data for this project.

Morris's bibliographical interests were expressed also in research he undertook in compiling a catalogue of the writings of the Lords Baltimore. The MHS, charged by the state with preserving the records of Maryland's colonial past, had a great deal of interest in Morris's project. He presented a paper on December 1, 1864, entitled "The Lords Baltimore as Authors," which briefly described the major writings of Maryland's six proprietors.[29] These literary and historical projects again demonstrate Morris's zeal to further knowledge by creating reference works and his commitment to one of the main aims of an historical society of the era—preserving the deeds and accomplishments of great men.

Morris's interest went beyond the merely literary or the state's long-distant colonial past. Just as he had done at the Peabody Institute, he successfully proposed that the historical society's Library Committee gather newspapers, periodicals, and pamphlets documenting "current events." Clearly Morris felt the responsibility as an historian and librarian to preserve the historical record for future generations.[30] Further, he hoped that knowledge of and respect for the state's past could help ameliorate the war's divisiveness.

Morris's involvement in the course of Lutheran church history took a new direction in this period. He began to increase his work in the Lutheran Historical Society, founded at First Church in 1843 at the conclusion of the General Synod's session. Though Schmucker continued as president of the society, Morris served as one of the vice presidents and began to focus his scholarly intellect on the society's work.

At the bitterly contentious York meeting of the General Synod, Morris presented a paper to the Lutheran Historical Society, entitled "The Literature of the Lutheran Church in the United States." He argued that the production of "good books" by Lutheran ministers and laymen inspired the respect of fellow Lutherans and the good opinion of other churches. He stated that "great literary works survive for ages and they influence multitudes in all future time," and that "authors, at all respectable, are the chief glory of the people."[31] Morris felt the society had to collect the almost six hundred books, pamphlets, and tracts written by

Lutheran pastors from all parts of the church. He hoped that appreciation for Lutheran contributions to American church life could provide a rallying point for all Lutherans. And he saw the Lutheran Historical Society playing a similar role as the Maryland Historical Society, i.e., providing an arena where contending parties could find some common ground. The cause of Lutheran unity and the work of the Lutheran Historical Society would consume much of Morris's energy in the years to come.

When Morris's duties at the Peabody at last drew to a close, the sixty-four-year-old clergyman cast about for new directions. He plaintively informed Joseph Henry of his availability after July 1 of 1867 for any "translation work" from German and French.[32] Fortunately for Morris, the pastorate at Third English Lutheran Church became available. Morris had strong ties to the congregation because of his missionary efforts which had led to the church's organization in the 1840s. Also, he had served as part-time, interim pastor on two occasions over the previous seven years. With the position officially vacant, the congregation unanimously elected Morris pastor in August 1867.[33] The president of the Maryland Synod expressed the feelings of many when he wrote, "The Synod will hail with pleasure the return to the pastoral work of the senior of the Ministerium, Rev. F. G. [sic] Morris, D.D., who has accepted a call to the Third Church in Baltimore."[34] The return to active ministry marked a period of renewed vigor in Morris's work as a cultural pioneer and leader.

Part Five

Renewed Vigor
1867-1895

Curiosity is one of the permanent and certain characteristics of a vigorous mind.

SAMUEL JOHNSON
The Rambler, 1751

11

Crusader for Unity

After leaving the Peabody Institute, Morris once again focused his energy and talents on issues he held most dear. Now sixty-nine-years-old, he initiated a sustained campaign to heal the breaches in Lutheran unity caused by doctrinal, sectional, and ethnic conflict. As a passionate advocate of history, he also had a creative burst of energy that bore fruit. And, lastly, the mature Morris's scholarship reflected his perspective on man, society, history, and religion. Yet, when he officially departed the Peabody Institute on September 1, 1867, he could not have foreseen the work and achievement that lay ahead.

The condition of the General Synod in the late 1860s caused Morris a great deal of anxiety. From a peak in 1860 when its district synods encompassed two-thirds of the Lutheran church in America, by 1868 the General Synod had lost almost half of its membership.[1] And by the early 1870s, yet a fourth national church body had appeared, the Synodical Conference (led by the Missouri Synod). To make matters even more complicated, numerous independent synods, organized along ethnic lines, had appeared.

Feelings between the General Synod and the General Council remained especially antagonistic. The minutes of the 1868 General Synod reported the bitter observation: "That but three entire Synods and parts of three others have thus seceded from us, and had been led into the narrow and intolerant particularity of Lutheranism now attempted to be combined in this country."[2] In fact, within a short time, the General Council would outdistance the older organization in membership.

Morris wanted to see the General Synod, General Council, and General Synod, South (after 1886, the United Synod, South) reunite and form once again a bulwark of English-speaking Lutheranism. This bulwark would eventually encompass, he hoped, all but the most doctrinaire and separatist Lutherans. Feeling that the various groups held more beliefs in common than not, Morris embarked on a three-part campaign: dialogue, doctrinal clarification, and raising Lutheran historical consciousness.

He began his crusade at the 1873 General Synod convention in Canton, Ohio. He supported the members of the Committee on Correspondence with Other Church Bodies when they held out an olive branch to the General Council, and proposed an "interchange of correspondence and fraternal greetings by exchange of delegates."[3] He saw this as the first step toward reconciliation, and led efforts on the convention floor to get the measure adopted. With some enthusiasm, the General Synod approved the proposal, and sent it on to the General Council.

Members of the General Council did not share Morris's opinion on how much the opposing sides held in common. Bitter memories of battles at York and Fort Wayne remained fresh. Instead of agreeing to exchange delegates, the General Council proposed a colloquium for all Lutheran church bodies accepting the unaltered Augsburg Confession.[4] There participants could discuss and debate varying views on the Confession and other doctrinal issues which, the council maintained, did divide Lutherans. The General Council extended the same offer to the Synodical Conference and the General Synod, South, which both promptly accepted.

With anger, the General Synod rejected the idea of a colloquium as a far cry from the mutual recognition and church fellowship implied in the exchange of delegates and official correspondence. Morris's colleagues could not abide what they saw as continued doubts about the orthodoxy and legitimacy of General Synod Lutheranism.[5]

With his effort at a conciliating gesture in tatters, Morris pondered his next step. He understood that the colloquium concept loomed as the only practical vehicle for achieving his goal of beginning a dialogue. With the General Synod officially refusing to endorse the idea, he decided to take the lead in organizing an unofficial "Free Diet."

Morris turned for help to an old friend and former colleague, Joseph A. Seiss, a prominent pastor in the General Council. Seiss agreed, and the two men worked through 1876 and 1877 to get the meeting off the ground. Both men realized that, with the volatile state of feelings, they had to retain control over both the substance and the format of the diet. They sought speakers of acknowledged intellectual stature not tainted by excessive partisanship, and topics that explored differences and similarities in doctrine and practices.[6]

After much discussion, Morris and Seiss agreed on speakers and topics. From the General Synod came Morris himself, on the thirty-nine articles of the Anglican Church and its Lutheran roots; James A. Brown, Schmucker's successor at Gettysburg, on the four Lutheran general bodies and their areas of agreement and potential cooperation; Gettysburg College president Milton A. Valentine on Lutheran education; and F. W. Conrad, editor of the *Lutheran Observer*, on the salient characteristics of the Augsburg Confession.[7]

General Council speakers included Charles Porterfield Krauth, son of Morris's old friend, on the relationship of the Lutheran church to other denominations; church historian Henry Eyster Jacobs on the history of the Lutheran Church in America; and Seiss, who analyzed common misunderstandings and misinterpretations which divided Lutherans.[8]

In setting Philadelphia as the site for the diet, Morris and Seiss in practical terms limited participation from beyond the mid-Atlantic region. Given the lack of official sponsorship and support, the two pastors had no other realistic alternative. They did hope that meeting dates of December 27 and 28 [1877] came at a quiet time for otherwise busy pastors and educators.

Morris looked toward the diet with some trepidation. Some churchmen still worried about the "American Lutheran" elements in the General Synod which they viewed as "indistinguishable . . . from Methodism."[9] Seiss did not help Morris's peace of mind when he wrote, "Your men are too intolerably flabby and nothingarian to make any headway at this rate."[10] F. W. Conrad, editor of the *Observer*, worried that Seiss's attitudes had "affected his catholic spirit."[11] Clearly the fact that the General Synod tolerated "symbolists" and "anti-symbolists," as long as all accepted the Augsburg Confession, did not sit well with the men of the General Council.

Despite his fears, the diet lived up to Morris's hopes and expectations. Over a hundred clergymen paid their way to Philadelphia and participated in the two-day event. The papers presented stimulated spirited, but civil, exchanges. Morris, as chairman, used all his wit, humor, and verbal skills to maintain a positive tone. Participants responded with enthusiasm to the frank and informative environment, and formed a committee to organize another diet. With support from the *Lutheran Observer* and *Our Church Paper*, Morris and Seiss led a follow-up session in November 1878, once again in Philadelphia.[12]

Though the diets did not lead to the quick merger that Morris sought, they did contribute to an increased civility in the intra-church debates. Diet participants and assiduous readers of church papers now had a much improved, and less polemical, understanding of differing positions on confessional subscription, the sacraments, church polity, and relationships with other Christians. Morris's diets began the dialogue which eventually culminated in 1917 in the great merger of the General Synod, the General Council, and the United Synod, South, into the United Lutheran Church in America.

After the diets, Morris continued his crusade. At one of his final major appearances on the stage of the General Synod, he preached the opening sermon at the 1885 convention. Concluding a two-year term as synod president, he preached on Nehemiah 4:17: "Everyone with one of his hands wrought in the work and with the other hand held a weapon." Just as Nehemiah worked to refurbish the Temple, Lutherans in America had to retain the allegiance of German and Scandinavian immigrants to the "good old ways of the fathers." Morris argued that home mission work based on God's Word, Luther's catechisms, and the Augsburg Confession had to combat the "frivolous, shallow, and vacillating religious experience and practice of many of the sects around us."

The retiring president professed to see few doctrinal, linguistic, or ethnic differences genuinely separating Lutherans. "Our work," he said, "is to promote harmony and unity of action among ourselves." For Morris, two major issues separating the General Council and the General Synod—altar fellowship and Lutheran pulpits for Lutheran pastors—posed no particular problems. He saw both sides holding essentially similar views. Using humor to make his point about the issues around which Lutherans had to rally, he attributed the encroachment on the "Lutheran sheep-fold" by other denominations to the "quality of the mutton!"[13] Morris's zeal in fostering dialogue and common action reflected his unwavering dedication to a broadly inclusive English-speaking Lutheranism—a Lutheranism adaptive to the American environment, yet faithful to the essence of its doctrinal heritage.

Morris's efforts as a leader in the struggle for church unity were based on the belief that most Lutherans shared a common theological perspective. As a theologian, he focused principally on the nature of the church, as defined in the Augsburg Confession, and on the sacraments. He always stressed the primacy of the Augsburg Confession, the only Lutheran creed sanctioned by the General Synod, as the indissoluble link uniting all Lutherans.

In 1872, Gettysburg Seminary selected its longtime director to give the annual Holman Lecture on some aspect of the Augsburg Confession. Morris selected articles VII and VIII of the Confession, which dealt with the nature of the church.

In his lengthy lecture, he drew a picture of the church which he believed all Lutherans, except the "American Lutherans," could accept.

Like the confessors, as he called them, Morris saw the church as a spiritual union of believers united by faith through the ages with the church's head, Christ. He acknowledged, as did Luther and his followers, that the church contained both the pious and the unbelieving, the good and the wicked. Here Morris clearly denied the Calvinist (and, in his opinion, the "American Lutheran") concept of the true church as the assembly of the elect and those destined for salvation.

Morris quoted approvingly from the Confession that "the preaching of the Gospel in its purity and the administration of the sacraments according to the Gospel" comprised the distinguishing characteristics of the "true church." To Morris, "scriptural purity" for the "true church" rested both on the doctrine of justification by faith, a hallmark of the Lutheran Reformation, and on retaining the sacramental elements of water in baptism and bread and wine in the Lord's Supper. The elderly church leader's views on the sacraments stood in sharp contrast to those he expressed in his 1831 editorial debut in the *Lutheran Observer*. The Morris of the 1870s "unhesitatingly" found in the Lutheran Church those distinguishing characteristics, "which exhibit the marks of the true church most prominently."[14]

By identifying the Lutheran Church with articles VII and VIII of the Confession, Morris sought to raise Lutheran consciousness about the primacy of their church in the Protestant tradition and to stress those beliefs which united most Lutherans. With the exception of the "American Lutherans," according to Morris, almost all Lutherans in America adhered, at a minimum, to the unaltered Augsburg Confession and traditional interpretations of the sacraments and the nature of the church.

In his paper at the 1877 Philadelphia "Free Diet," churchman Morris had again brought the Augsburg Confession to the fore. For the benefit of the General Council members in the audience, he explored "The Augsburg Confession and the Thirty-Nine Articles of the Anglican Church." Using a variety of secondary sources, particularly the works of his diet colleague Seiss and church historian Philip Schaff's *Creeds of Christendom*, he portrayed the Augsburg Confession as "the standard of pure Protestantism," and the basis for all similar declarations of faith. In part, he intended his presentation as an indirect response to renewed calls at that time from the Anglican and Episcopal Churches for Christian union. Morris and other Lutheran leaders wanted credal primacy of place given to the venerable Augsburg Confession, and offered it as the most suitable basis for union efforts.

Morris's primary motivation, though, lay in explaining how much of the doctrinal bases for both the Anglican and Reformed traditions rested on the work of

German Lutherans. Morris argued that "all Protestant organizations have based their Formulas of Faith upon the greater 'Bill of Rights' extorted from Charles V in Augsburg, 1530." Morris portrayed this as analogous to extracting the Magna Charta from King John in 1215. The drawing of such an analogy reflected Morris's traditional, Protestant-oriented "Whig" interpretation of history, along with his pro-Lutheran bias.

Morris, quoting from Schaff, Seiss, and Anglican Archbishop Lawrence, stressed that the various articles of faith promulgated under Henry VIII, Edward VI, and Elizabeth I reflected Lutheran thought and sometimes even the exact wording of the Augsburg Confession. He felt that this was particularly true in regard to theological and doctrinal issues such as original sin, justification by faith, the efficacy of works, and freedom of the will. He also sketched the influence of German Lutheran worship services in the development of the English reformed liturgy, and the continued interest of English reformers in obtaining advice from Luther's closest colleague, Philip Melanchthon.[15] Though he overlooked non-Lutheran influences in the Thirty-Nine Articles, as well as its theological ambiguity in places, Morris impressed upon his listeners the spiritual primacy of the mother church of the Reformation. In particular, he stressed the place occupied by the Augsburg Confession as the credal statement to which all true Lutherans and Protestants subscribed.

Besides tackling the nature of the church and the Lutheran confessions, Morris the theologian addressed another doctrinal issue, "which is perhaps the least understood by many of our good people." In a lengthy article in 1883, he evaluated for his readers "the Lutheran Doctrine of the Real Presence of the Body and Blood of Christ in the Lord's Supper." The issue of the Real Presence had played a major part in the bitter debate and conflict between the "American Lutherans" and the confessionalists. By clarifying traditional teaching, Morris again stressed what he considered the uniquely correct Lutheran understanding of doctrinal matters, in this case the sacrament of the Lord's Supper.

He refuted three interpretations of the Lord's Supper which he believed conflicted with Lutheran tradition. First, he denied the Roman Catholic doctrine of transubstantiation, which claimed that the priest at Mass sacramentally transformed the elements of bread and wine into the physical (albeit invisible) body and blood of Christ. Morris, consistent with traditional Protestant thought, denied that the bread and wine underwent an essential change, and attacked transubstantiation as lacking a scriptural base.

Morris defended Lutherans against the accusation that their church taught consubstantiation, or the commingling of the bread, wine, body and blood of Christ into one mass. Again, he argued that the words of scripture did not support such a view. "The words of institution," Morris wrote, "do not say take, eat, in this bread is included or enclosed my body; in this cup is included (or enclosed) my blood."

Morris also used scripture to refute those "American Lutherans" and other Protestants who accepted the sacramental teaching of Ulrich Zwingli, the sixteenth-century Swiss reformer. Zwingli viewed the Lord's Supper as a memorial, and Christ's words of institution as figurative, not literal. Morris completely rejected this point of view, reversing the position he took in his 1832 *Catechism* and 1840 *Popular Exposition of the Gospels*. He charged that by reducing the words of institution to purely symbolic meaning, Christ's atonement in which his body and blood "was given for us" became symbolic, not real.

Morris explained to his readers that correct Lutheran teaching, in accordance with Article X of the Augsburg Confession, taught that though the elements of bread and wine remained unchanged, "the true body and blood of Christ are really present under the form of bread." He stated that "we believe in a true, substantial presence of the body and blood of Christ, although we do not comprehend the mode, for that is divine and beyond human conception."

He argued that the accuracy of traditional Lutheran sacramental teaching rested on interpreting "passages of Scripture according to their plain, natural meaning. . . . It is a fundamental rule of Scriptural interpretation not to depart from the real, natural sense of the language, without absolute necessity and when the Scriptures themselves direct us to do so." Using the standards of lower biblical criticism, he argued that the words of Jesus at the Last Supper meant that "the body and blood of Christ are truly present in the Holy Supper."[16]

In this, one of his most extensive theological treatises, the aged church leader defended and, he hoped, justified the Lutheran doctrinal position most open to criticism from within and without the church. Morris buttressed his case two years later when he translated Luther's ninety-five theses and three other primary works of the Reformer. He quoted from Luther, the Wittenberg Concord (1536), and the Formula of Concord (1581) to prove the scriptural soundness of the Lutheran position.[17] Once more, Morris sought to prove to his fellow Lutherans the correctness of their church's traditional teachings, and the primacy of place in the Protestant Christian tradition that rightfully belonged to the Lutheran church.

Raising Lutheran historical consciousness became a third front in Morris's campaign for Lutheran unity. From 1875 onward, Morris focused much of his energy in this area on the Lutheran Historical Society. As president of the society for the last two decades of his life, Morris, assisted by his nephew, Charles A. Hay, brought new direction and purpose to the organization. Morris and Hay were determined to use the mission of the society—collecting written materials documenting the life of the church in America—to build bridges among Lutheran factions. In this they hoped to emulate organizations such as the Luther Society of New York, the Lutheran Social Union of Philadelphia, the Luther League, and various Lutheran educators' conferences.

Morris and Hay, Gettysburg Seminary professor and curator of the society's collection, worked throughout the 1870s and 1880s to create interest in the society. Both men wrote numerous articles for the *Observer* and the *Lutheran Quarterly* stressing the pan-Lutheran nature of the society's goals and objectives. Hay wrote that, though the society had started in the General Synod, it had "a catholic spirit which has attracted confidence and support from all portions of the church." In words which Morris heartily supported, Hay claimed that Lutherans now realized their heritage as "children of one household."[18]

Morris urged that all efforts in the church to collect Lutheran-related books, articles, or manuscripts focus around the Lutheran Historical Society. He argued that, unlike the divided Presbyterians, the Lutherans should have only one society. In Morris's opinion, a comprehensive collection formed the basis for writing a history of the church, which would clearly portray for contemporary Lutherans and future generations the church's Reformation heritage as expressed in its doctrine, liturgy, and polity.[19] He saw the society as the ultimate repository of Lutheran historical documentation, from which would flow books and articles attesting to the common heritage that, at heart, united Lutherans in America.

Once gain, his zeal for collecting came to the fore. In 1876 he compiled the *Bibliotheca Lutherana: A Complete List of the Publications of All Lutheran Ministers in the United States*, the latest in the long line of his scholarly and scientific compilations. He hoped this work would increase Lutheran pride in "the achievements of our ministers," as well as help to unite Lutherans around the literary heritage of their pastors. He wanted to document and proclaim Lutheran contributions to the religious and cultural life of the nation. He included books, pamphlets, and book reviews from the periodical press of the church, which he viewed as "an index of its literary character."[20]

The indefatigable Morris traveled regularly to Gettysburg to assist Hay in cataloguing the society's collection and soliciting new materials. In April 1886, for example, the eighty-two-year-old Morris spent eight or nine days in Gettysburg cataloging over 500 bound volumes.[21] In the early 1860s, the collection had consisted of approximately 211 bound volumes of sermons, addresses, and synod minutes, as well as eighteen manuscripts, 145 unbound pamphlets, and forty-five miscellaneous articles. By the end of Morris's life in 1895, the society had 1,998 bound volumes and 1,000 unbound pamphlets, manuscripts, and letters.[22] Even more significant to the enhancement of the society's pan-Lutheran aspirations, Morris had convinced the publishing houses of the Missouri Synod and the General Council to provide the society with copies of all their synodical publications.

In the mid-1880s, President Morris had even persuaded the General Synod's board of publication to begin providing grants on a regular basis for the society's purchasing efforts. With a $500 grant in hand, he obtained a valuable collection of American Lutheran books and pamphlets owned by the Reverend Matthias Sheeleigh.[23] Morris's zeal as a churchman and bibliophile had created yet another invaluable cultural resource around which all Lutherans could rally.

Morris worked for unity on a local as well as national level. After all, the Maryland Synod had experienced a bitter schism beginning with the creation of the Melanchthon Synod on its territory in 1857. The death of Benjamin Kurtz in December 1865 made a reconciliation possible. Morris, as Maryland Synod president in 1867, worked assiduously to persuade the pastors of the breakaway synod that the reasons for disunion had passed. Though the General Synod had strengthened its position on the Augsburg Confession, it still permitted a wide latitude of opinion among its members. Home mission labors and geographical proximity argued for a union of combined efforts.

With the Melanchthon Synod pastors agreeable to reunion, Morris and his colleagues accepted their demand to support Kurtz's Missionary Institute at Selinsgrove, Pennsylvania. The Maryland Synod men agreed to support the Missionary Institute in its original purpose (i.e., training men for home mission work), if all members of a reconstituted Synod acknowledged the seminary and college at Gettysburg as the church's primary educational institutions. With the Melanchthon Synod's assent to this formula, the two synods reunited in 1869.[24]

Morris had less success in his efforts to reunite the Missionary Institute and Gettysburg Seminary. Always opposed to a second, competing institution, he accepted the charge of the seminary's board to engineer a merger. This effort stirred the antagonism of certain "American Lutherans." One critic, Peter Anstadt, doubted the sincerity of Morris and his colleagues' interest in the institute. Further, another critic viewed the seminary as "mainly a feeder for the symbolical school at Philadelphia, to the inexpressible grief of American Lutherans all over the land." With pride, the institute's advocate noted that its forty-one graduates favored "revivals and active measures for the conversion of sinners."[25] Despite Morris's wishes to the contrary, the wounds from the "American Lutheran" battle still split the General Synod, and nothing came of his efforts to effect a merger.

On a personal level, perhaps the most significant work for Morris involved his return to active parish ministry. As a pastor, he once again returned to the bedrock of his personal and professional identity. Called to the pulpit of Third English Lutheran Church in September 1867, he came to a church and people that he understood. Founded in 1841 with his active support and as an offshoot of First Church, the church on Monument Street in downtown Baltimore had already used Morris's services during previous periods of pastoral vacancy. In 1867, the congregation, with limited resources at its disposal, offered a permanent pastoral call to Morris. Already financially stable and anxious to restart his pastoral career, Morris accepted the offer without hesitation.[26] Using pent-up energy from his ordeal at the Peabody, he once again visited parishioners, led Bible studies, and delivered weekly sermons and lectures.

The seasoned pastor's organizational skill, manifested time and again at First Church, reasserted itself. With Morris's leadership, the congregation enlarged and remodeled the church, the first such effort since the original construction in 1852.[27]

From Morris's point of view, the people of Third English "were, in general, a plain sincere people, who never gave me more trouble than usually falls to the lot of most ministers."[28] Though the situation at Third English appeared less complicated than his first pastoral charge, the two congregations shared one characteristic. In his memoirs, Morris reported that both congregations "had very vague theological, and some of them fanatical, notions and very loose ideas of true Lutheranism."[29] This continuing concern of Morris reflected not only his finely developed sense of confessional and denominational identity, but also the varied religious backgrounds and experiences of the parishioners. Despite this concern, his years at Third English helped reestablish his equilibrium and sense of confidence, badly shaken after the tumultuous relationship with Charles J. M. Eaton.

As Morris approached age seventy, he decided in 1873 to retire from full-time pastoral work. He wanted to conserve his energy for the great crusade for Lutheran unity which dominated the last decades of his life. But the time at Third English had rejuvenated him. Morris looked on his six years there with more satisfaction than he ever viewed his work at the Peabody Institute. He always remembered that the congregation "treated me kindly and my services are gratefully remembered to this day. . . . My reminiscences of that church are on the whole pleasant."[30]

Despite the intensity of his work as a national church leader, Third English, in fact, did not mark the end of Morris's pastoral career. In January 1879, the small Lutheran congregation in Lutherville, St. Paul's, needed a replacement for the Reverend J. R. Dimm, who had resigned as principal of the seminary and pastor of the village church. Organized in 1856 as a nondenominational church, the congregation became Lutheran and a member of the Maryland Synod in 1869, primarily through the efforts of Morris.[31] Because of its size—the church had fewer than fifty members—the congregation could offer a prospective pastor very modest compensation at best. Morris explained that "as there was no one else who could take charge of it on account of the small salary, I assumed the care of it."[32] As the founder and chief resident of the village, Morris agreed to preach each Sunday, and attend to the limited pastoral responsibilities. Emblematic of his commitment to Lutherville, he preached at the small church for ten years, retiring at last from all pastoral work in 1889.

During these years of renewed vigor, Morris also found the intellectual energy to bring the other passionate interests of his life to maturity and fulfillment. All this brought balm and healing to a life vigorously pursued.

12

Mature Scholar

As a respected churchman, John G. Morris's books, articles, and speeches reached a wide audience. Though he remained an adherent of natural theology, combining a Christian world-view with elements of romanticism, Morris matured as a scholar in his post-Peabody era. He articulated his philosophical positions in greater depth, exploring the nature of man, society, religion, and history. Motivated by his twin passions, the quest for Lutheran unity and preserving the Protestant essence of America, he wrote prodigiously during the 1870s and 1880s.

The period around the four-hundredth anniversary of Martin Luther's birth in 1883 proved a particularly fertile time. One article in particular, "The Translated Portions of Luther's Writings" (1882), revealed Morris's understanding of human nature. Basing his stance on Luther and the Apostle Paul, he saw a "duplex nature" in man: an inner, renewed spiritual nature and an old, external carnal one or, in Lutheran terms, "a free master over all things . . . and a bound servant to all things." As did Luther, Morris viewed this "duplex nature" as part of a whole, with man as both saint and sinner at the same time.[1]

Redeemed by God's free gift of salvation, a Christian man, according to Pastor Morris, found himself linked to God and neighbor (society) through faith and love. To Morris, the Protestant religion played the key role in the linkage between God, man, and society. For the Baltimore churchman, and others who thought as he did, true religion and Protestantism were one and the same thing.

Even more clearly than in the 1830s, the Morris of this period interpreted Martin Luther as the human agent of the divine will through whose work "truth triumphed and the gospel became free." Before ten thousand spectators at the May 1886 unveiling of a statue of Luther in front of the Luther Place Memorial Church in Washington, D.C., he proclaimed that the work of Luther and his Reformation had led to the regeneration of church and society. Only Protestantism, according to Morris, fostered human liberty and preserved the rights of individual conscience and private judgment.

The strength and continued religious purity of Protestantism, Morris told the enthusiastic crowd, rested on adherence to the Bible, the "religion of Protestants." In a classic Protestant cry, he stated, "It was this bible which gave liberty to Luther, and it was Luther who gave liberty to the world." In a period of rising immigration from Catholic countries, Morris saw the Church of Rome as a renewed potential threat to Bible-based Protestantism. In distinguishing for his audience the difference between Protestants and "Romanists," he portrayed Protestants as people who based their beliefs on scripture, questioned their leaders, and exercised at all times the prerogative of private judgment in religious matters. "Romanists," on the other hand, accepted church teachings without question and deferred totally to tradition and the rulings of the church's hierarchy. To Morris, this perverted true religion, stifled society, and destroyed the freedom of the Christian.[2]

Remaining true to his earlier belief that human history represented the unfolding of the divine will, he viewed the Reformation as the start of a new era, the "mightiest revolution of modern times." In this act of providence, as Morris portrayed it, "conceived in the divine mind and controlled by the divine hand," the monk Luther played the role of God's chief actor. For Morris, Luther remained the man of "unshaken fortitude; dauntless courage; indefatigable industry; burning zeal; devoted piety; great learning."[3]

This deterministic, near hagiographic, view of Luther carried within it a seed of contradiction. Morris believed that even without Luther the Reformation would have eventually occurred, but "it would not have been so good."[4] This implicit contradiction in Morris's logic reflects a subtle conflict between his religiously grounded, deterministic view of history, and his romantic notion of history as the "biography of great men." For some romantic historians, the "great man" theory did not require divine providence as an interpretive framework. Morris, as a religious believer and devout Protestant, assumed a necessary linkage.

As a devotee of the "great man" school, Morris lavished attention on Luther as the greatest religious figure since St. Paul. He used Luther's letters and other works, earlier church historians, and the writings of contemporary historians, such as Jacob Burckhardt and Jules Michelet, to dispel what he termed myths about Luther. He discredited, for example, the old story about Luther hurling an inkstand at the devil while in hiding at the Wartburg. The historian Morris acidly noted the regular refurbishment of the ink mark on the castle wall. Reflecting his careful respect for historical evidence, Morris noted that the incident never appeared in Luther's letters, "a rich source of information concerning all events happening to him at this period."[5]

Despite his best efforts, Morris's understanding of Luther reflected the limitations of scholarship prior to the early twentieth-century renaissance in Luther studies. He accepted, for example, the old belief that Luther grew up in a poor family and had to sing for his food while a student. A more thorough understanding of the social and economic background of Luther's family came much later.

Morris's belief in the notion of progress in history flowed from his understanding of divine providence, the impact of true religion, and the roles of "predestinated" great men. Like most of his contemporaries, he saw nineteenth- century Anglo-American Protestant society as the highwater mark of moral, intellectual, and material progress. For Morris, Luther and the Reformation not only purged the church "of papal sin and gloom," but also broke the intellectual shackles inhibiting individual and national liberty, scientific inquiry, educational reform, and the pursuit of commerce.[6] In his opinion, the evolution of vigorous, healthy, and free Protestant nations, particularly the United States, flowed directly from the divinely-inspired Reformation. Like the Reformation itself, he saw this triumph of progress as inevitable.

Morris's occasional criticisms of his hero Luther reflected his notions of historical progress. For instance, he deplored Luther's "asperity" of language. He acknowledged that the strident polemical language of the era, and the personal assaults which Luther endured, played a role in the intemperate outburst of the Wittenburg professor. But Morris saw a deeper meaning. He viewed Luther's time as "not so far advanced in what we call civilization." He speculated "whether most of the learned men did not enjoy the benefits of refined home education, or whether the monastic training of not a few of them did not contribute to the coarseness of their manner and the vulgarity of their language."[7] In seeing the falling away of violent language in public life as a sign of progress, Morris believed, as did his fellow Victorians, that the use of such "bitter invective . . . would at the present time blast the character of any reputable author, and exclude him from the circle of refined society."[8] Luther's "asperity" of language also reflected the fact that the Reformer's "lively imagination easily embodied the emotions of his heart, and the superstitions of the Middle Ages." The scientific and rational Morris felt that "history must still record this failing in the Reformer."[9]

In this, Morris clearly shows himself a staunch supporter of that decorum and propriety so valued by the middle and upper classes in late nineteenth-century society. From the 1830s onward, whether talking about the scientific pursuits of Lutheran ministers or some other issue, he always referred to the need for "respectability" in personal and professional conduct. For Morris, the quest for "respectability" remained a sincere, single-minded pursuit. His belief that "respectability" had reached a high level in contemporary America illustrates his subscription to the notion of civilization's progress—at least Anglo-American Protestant civilization's progress.

But history did more than chronicle the unfolding of divine providence and human progress. History indeed could teach important lessons. In his most creative historical work, "The Young and German Luther," Morris found a psychological lesson. He posited the theory that "most great events in Church, State, literature, art, science, etc., have been conceived and advanced by young men." Before Freud and the onset of modern psychology, historian Morris found in the young Luther a model to explain, from the biographical perspective, human progress.

Morris argued that an older man in Luther's place, with more at stake personally and professionally, would have hesitated to risk everything in public battle with Rome. He saw older men as "sensitive to reproach and persecution," and often hesitant in action and fearful of peril.[10] The boldness of youth, exemplified by Luther, dared to risk all in pursuit of a great goal or belief. These kinds of risks advanced religion, knowledge, and society.

Though thirty-four years old at the posting of the ninety-five theses, with much at stake in his monastic career, Luther did stand ready to risk and lose everything. Morris attributed this to the monk's lack of worldly experience, which prevented him from understanding the difficulties ahead. For Morris, such audacity and rigorous energy remained the domain of a young man.

Though simplistic about the Luther of 1517, Morris had an insight into individual endurance and achievement. Some individuals do have a spark of genius or courage, which often surfaces early in their life. Though not all great events in history are attributable to young men, he did correctly sense that a man well along in life or career probably made poor material for leading revolutionary change. "The Young and German Luther" contains hints of psychological understanding and perspective later explored by authors such as Erik Erikson in *Young Man Luther*.

Morris also gleaned more traditional, moral lessons from history. In *The Lords Baltimore*, published in 1874 after he read it to an enthusiastic Maryland Historical

Society audience, the aging author stated a basic premise: "The memory of founders of States and of great institutions, benevolent, literary or civil, should be cherished with patriotic fervor."[11] History, through the biography of great men, had patriotic and moral lessons to teach.

Though dedicated to creating a "chronological order and historical sequence" that would bring the Calvert family to life, Morris's philosophical stance affected his interpretation of history's lessons. Using as he always did the best available published sources (including Brantz Mayer's *Calvert and Penn*, John Pentleton Kennedy's *Life and Character of Calvert*, and John Nichol's *Progress of James I*), he drew a portrait of each Lord Baltimore.

Treading gingerly over the first Lord Baltimore's conversion to Roman Catholicism, Morris asserted that no direct evidence proved that George Calvert desired a site in the New World for his co-religionists.[12] His staunch Protestantism affected his historical judgment about Maryland's origins. Nothing for Morris could detract from viewing America as a Protestant nation; patriotism and Protestantism went hand in hand.

In considering Maryland's proprietors, Morris evaluated each man's probity, conduct as a gentleman, and stance toward the family's reconversion to Protestantism in 1713, in assessing their utility as moral role models. This comes across most clearly in Morris's treatment of the fifth and sixth Lords Baltimore. He used the views of Frederick the Great and other contemporaries in judging Charles Calvert, the fifth lord. An honest, good-natured but weak man, Charles Calvert elicited no approval from the Maryland pastor.

Frederick, the last Lord Baltimore, drew Morris's active disapproval. Scorning what he called Frederick's sybaritic lifestyle and dilettantish ways, Morris deemed it most appropriate that Frederick left no legitimate heir. The death of the last Calvert family descendant in an English debtor's prison in 1860 elicited a classic moral judgment—"sic transit gloria mundi."[13]

Morris based his biographically-derived moral lessons on Victorian standards. From Luther's "asperity" of language to the foibles of eighteenth-century aristocrats, Morris reflected the *mores* of his era. He judged the past from what he considered the advanced standards of his day. His biographical approach, slighting social, economic, and political factors, along with his moralistic point of view, limited the long-term value of *The Lords Baltimore* and other historical writings.

Morris's scientific interests, of course, continued. Though his advancing years restricted some of his outdoor collecting work, he remained closely involved with events in the entomological community. He maintained correspondence with other scientists, exchanged specimens, and contributed information for a biographical dictionary of American scientists. He continued as the years went on with his natural history lectures at Pennsylvania College and the seminary.

His major scientific contributions in this period involved his work as chairman of the American Association for the Advancement of Science's Entomology Subsection. He compiled lists of recent entomological publications and urged on his colleagues the "German model" in describing each order in the animal kingdom. In his ceaseless efforts to expand the frontiers of American scientific knowledge, he also advocated a survey of the large public and private scientific collections.[14] This, he hoped, would make more information generally available.

The elderly Morris's commitment to building cultural institutions and collections of enduring value remained constant. After the difficult years at the Peabody Institute, Morris stayed deeply involved with Baltimore's other premier cultural institution—the Maryland Historical Society. Yearly, from 1867 onward, Morris won election as a vice president of the Society, and he served on the Library Committee throughout the period. By 1885, Morris and the Library Committee could proudly report that after decades of labor, the Society had 20,000 volumes and pamphlets in its holdings, as well as 3,300 manuscripts.[15]

Besides efforts directed toward increasing the library, Morris also sought to disseminate what he considered interesting or important information about Maryland history. Appointed to a three-man Committee on Publication in April 1870, Vice President Morris and his colleagues suggested that the society publish the diary of the first Jesuit priest in the colony of Maryland. Despite his opposition to Roman Catholicism, historian Morris recognized the significance of "Father White's Relation of Maryland." He argued on behalf of the committee that the society should appropriate $300 to publish the journal in Latin and English. The document's age and witness to historic events made it a suitable first volume in a new series of MHS publications.[16]

Morris's interest in early Maryland history clearly stands out in the papers he presented at MHS meetings. Topics included the "Tuesday Club" of eighteenth-century Annapolis, the origins of a portrait of Lord Baltimore in the society's possession, and, on February 10, 1873, the paper which resulted in *The Lords Baltimore*.[17]

Morris's most notable venture during these years reflected another of his lifelong concerns. From his beginnings in a German-American family through his long involvement with the German issue in the Lutheran Church, he always cared about German acceptance into American society. He continuously tried to foster this by showing German contributions to history in general and American society in particular.

On the evening of January 5, 1886, Morris helped create a vehicle to further this cause. At a meeting in the rooms of the Maryland Historical Society, he discussed with other prominent Baltimore German-Americans, such as Louis P. Hennighausen, Edward F. Leyh, and Charles F. Raddak, the feasibility of establishing a new historical society. After some debate, the men decided to draft a constitution for an organization dedicated "to collect and preserve material for the history . . . of the Germans in the growth and development of the American Nation, especially in Maryland."[18]

A month later on February 16, twenty-three men gathered, approved the draft constitution, and elected Morris as the first president of the Society for the History of the Germans in Maryland. Despite his devotion to his German heritage, Morris's primary identification as an American came through when he successfully argued for recording the minutes of society meetings in English.[19] Within a year, membership grew to seventy-two. Until his death, the old scholar presided at the new society's nine meetings each year and "discharged his duties faithfully."[20]

President Morris stimulated interest in the German society through a stream of papers he read at the monthly meetings. In one noteworthy paper, on the Egyptologist Gustavus Seyffarth, he explained to members that the society also had a duty to "exhibit the career of German individuals who have distinguished themselves in any department of human effort." With obvious pride, Morris observed that he had entertained the eminent scientist in his home.[21]

As he did in all his scholarly ventures, Morris prepared a compilation—this one a list of all printed descriptions of America published by German settlers and visitors prepared from 1673 onward. He also donated books on German-American topics to build up the society's fledgling collection. In the years remaining to him, Morris did all he could to ensure that the German society kept on a firm footing.

In 1886 Morris made another, less successful, foray into stimulating interest in history. With a group of neighbors, he founded the first Baltimore County Historical Society. Though the organizers met a few times, their efforts drew little public interest, and the county society folded.

While John G. Morris maintained an extremely active professional life, the decades following the Civil War brought significant changes in his personal affairs. As time went on, the healthy and robust Morris outlived more and more of his colleagues and family. In 1873, Samuel Simon Schmucker died in Gettysburg, and Morris lost one of his oldest links to York and the early days of his church career.

Profoundly ambivalent about his mentor, he must have had intense feelings as he delivered one of Schmucker's funeral orations. Before his own life ended, Morris would find himself in a public controversy over his attitudes toward Schmucker. Despite their conflicted relationship, he and Schmucker had spent many years in common endeavors and shared experiences.

A more personal loss occurred with the death of Charles A. Morris on April 10, 1874. With the passing of his oldest brother and guardian, John Morris lost his functional father. He felt lifelong gratitude for the care and attention Charles had lavished on him as a youth. This care and attention provided the structure and direction the young John Gottlieb had needed. It had set him on a path to professional success and fulfillment. Without Charles Morris's strong hand, his youngest brother would have had a far more difficult time. Though their careers took them in different directions, the two brothers shared a strong interest in advancing the cause of the Lutheran Church. With pride, brother John noted that Charles had given over $80,000 to charity in the course of his long life.[22]

An even more bitter blow fell in July of the next year. In the family register a sorrowful Morris wrote:

> July 16, 1875 was the saddest day in our family history. The kind mother, the wise counselor, the spotless exemplar, the holy woman, the perfect Christian, left me and went before. "A woman that feareth the Lord shall be praised." Proverbs 31:30.[23]

According to nephew Charles, Eliza, though in feeble health, went to Baltimore on July 9 for a reception in honor of an old Morris family friend, the Reverend Charles A. Stork. She became ill and remained at her daughter Maria's house, dying a week later.[24] Though his wife's death was not totally unexpected, the elderly Morris felt a deep and abiding sense of loss. Granddaughter Louise Morris Leisenring Reese remembered years later the toll Eliza's death took. "After the death of his dearly beloved wife in 1875," Louise wrote, "busy and active as he was, there was an unfilled space in his heart and he was very lonely."[25]

The deaths of Charles and Eliza severed all the old man's links to his early years. He found respite in his work and joy and rejuvenation in the idyllic setting of Oak Grove in Lutherville. By the 1880s, Morris spent all but the coldest months of the year at his summer residence. He regaled readers of the *Lutheran Observer* with how he spent his time "at my Tusculum at Lutherville." The following letter bears extensive quotation:

> MY DEAR DR. S—: . . . But you ask me what are my special employments and my regular everyday pursuits? Well, as far as amusement is concerned, I receive my daily mail at nine o'clock, and then an hour is spent in reading the morning papers and

my letters. Those of the latter requiring answers are immediately attended to. I go fishing three or four times every week, on which account my neighbors call me Old Izaak Walton! give several lessons a week in botany to a lad of my family; I capture moths at night in my study--well, if they *will* come in and fly about my lamp, I think it well to *press* them to stay, and they do! I play croquet with my girls and my neighbors' girls and boys! . . . These are my chief amusements, but I do a great deal of work beside. I carefully prepare one sermon a week; I go to town several times a week; I read the principal reviews and monthlies and a few of the weeklies, beside skimming over more than a dozen of our own Church papers, especially the German; I conduct a considerable correspondence with friends and the press; I am writing several fresh lectures for next winter's campaign. I try to keep up with the current literature of the day, which I find it very hard to do; I am constantly making efforts to increase my collection of books concerning Luther, and of the productions of Lutheran divines in America.[26]

As his letter gives witness, Morris in old age retained his ready wit, humor, and *joie de vivre*. These traits shone forth in his social "amusements and pastimes," as well as in the church work and scholarship that had informed his life since young adulthood. His resiliency and optimism smoothed the sharp edges of his sometimes "blunt and brusque" manner. This allowed a heart "as big as his brain" to prevail in the personality of the strong-willed pastor.

Despite Morris's love for Lutherville, he decided by the mid-1880s that his advancing age required that he sell the female seminary. Proprietor of the school since the 1860s, the elderly pastor had the full responsibility for procuring the capital needed for improvements, securing competent instructors, and, most difficult of all, finding a capable principal and wife to run the boarding school. With the school rarely turning a profit, and the need to secure the school's future paramount, the time for change had arrived.

In early 1884, Morris put out a circular announcing his desire to sell, and making the proposition that the Lutheran Church, either through its national or local bodies, buy it. He maintained that while twelve or thirteen Lutheran colleges for men operated under church auspices, Lutheran academies for women operated only under private ownership. Morris argued that a school more closely tied to the church would always teach "our distinctive church doctrines, a proper regard for our time-honored usages and church festivals and holidays, the outline, at least, of our grand old church history." To spur interest, Morris offered to sell the school and eleven acres of property for $10,000, half of what he considered its true value. To ensure the seminary's continued Lutheran identity, he urged that an incorporated board of directors, all Lutheran in composition, manage the school, with a legal proviso that it must always remain a Lutheran educational institution.

He also felt that a formal affiliation with the church would strengthen the school's character and enhance its longevity.[27]

A great deal of letter writing ensued in the *Lutheran Observer*. Those supporting Morris, such as the seminary's principal, the Reverend J. H. Turner, and fellow clergyman S. E. Furst, argued that the Lutheran Church neglected the education of women, and misunderstood the key role of women in church and society.[28] Some even feared that the school could eventually fall into Roman Catholic hands. Other writers, while supporting Morris's motives, disputed his analysis of the danger facing Lutheran female education. These writers pointed out that all the schools in question either had self-perpetuating boards of trustees with a majority of Lutherans on them or had sole Lutheran ownership. So, these writers argued, the schools were in effect church institutions.[29] This argument, in part, begged the question. Private owners could close their schools or sell them to *any* individual or group, as Morris had pointed out. Some others, generally in support, nonetheless voiced some doubt about the true value of closer church affiliation.

One pastor, Joel D. Schwartz, doubted the practicality of Morris's goal to inculcate "a genuine and true Lutheranism" in a reconstituted Lutherville Female Seminary. To Schwartz, the divisions among Lutherans in America meant that church bodies would never have the sense of cooperation needed to make Morris's proposal a success.[30]

Just as he found in the 1850s, the church did not share his intense interest in female education, and no offers, official or otherwise, materialized. After much discussion, J. H. Turner bought the school from Morris in April 1886. Turner signed a promissory note for $15,000, payable to Morris over a ten-year period at 5 percent interest. Morris held the mortgage for the period of the promissory note.[31] Though he had wanted to leave his school with a closer permanent tie to the church, at least he had freed himself from a major burden and responsibility.

Morris's intense commitment to the seminary and the cause of female education enabled the school to survive over three tumultuous decades. During the time Morris supervised the education of his wards, he insisted upon liberal arts and religion classes, as well as "finishing school" refinements. He aimed to produce educated and refined women capable of successfully influencing home, church, and society. Though traditional in outlook from one perspective, those like Morris who insisted on giving young women a good education contributed to the eventual opening up of new opportunities for women.

Another of Morris's joys and pleasures involved his work at the House of Refuge for Juvenile Delinquents. Founded in December 1855 and jointly operated by the state and city, the House of Refuge sought to teach homeless boys or those in trouble with the law some useful trade, as well as basic educational and religious instruction.[32]

Elected in 1881 by the mayor and city council of Baltimore as one of the institution's managers, the seventy-eight-year-old Morris served for the rest of his life as chairman of the School and Chapel Committee. Sensitive to the problems caused by the lack of a father, and sorrowful over the loss of his own sons, he poured his heart and energy into the task at hand. He oversaw the work of three teachers who taught the boys arithmetic, geography, spelling, reading, writing, history, and his favorite subject, entomology. By the end of his first year, he had rejuvenated the religious part of the boys' training. He brought in ministers on a volunteer basis to lead chapel services, and laymen to teach Sunday school and Bible classes.

Morris spent many long hours talking with the boys, monitoring their education, and keeping up with many who graduated from the reformatory. He did all he could to ensure that the House of Refuge did not become a mere prison or warehouse. This sort of social concern had surfaced as early as the 1820s, when he had spent many long hours working with the American Bible and Tract Societies. These concerns only grew stronger in the post-Civil War era, with the high human cost of rapid industrialization. Urban centers, such as Baltimore, experienced the full impact of social and economic change. The pastor in John G. Morris always remained front and center.

13

Finale

In the closing years of his life, Morris remained focused on his dearest concerns—his church and the advance of American culture, particularly through the pursuit of history. Blessed with continuing remarkable vigor in his tenth decade, Morris the pastor and scholar retained the respect of his colleagues for undimmed clarity of purpose and goals.

As he faced the inevitable end of his work, the elderly Morris shared his experience and insight for the benefit of fellow Lutherans. Ever the teacher and always concerned for young people, Morris particularly sought to aid young clergymen. As one example of this continuing pastoral concern, he wrote an article less than three months before his death for the *Lutheran Observer*, primarily aimed at the young pastors in his audience. Entitled "How Should A Pastor Know When His Usefulness Has Ended?," it identified four factors Morris considered essential measurements of a pastor's usefulness.

First, a pastor should experience success in "turning men to righteousness" and firmly rooting believers in their faith through effective and powerful preaching. Second, he should retain members and add "solid material." As a third, and related, factor, the pastor should keep the allegiance of the young and old members of the congregation. The fourth factor, according to Morris, lay in the pastor's ability "in furthering the spiritual, social, and financial interest of the congregation as a church of Jesus Christ." The practical Morris realized that a successful pastor must have good organizational and business skills.[1]

In short, he urged his clerical readers to focus on their preaching, pay attention to membership retention, particularly in the key constituencies of youth and the elderly, and to approach their work in a businesslike, professional manner. How could a pastor tell that his usefulness had ended? It's very simple, Morris declared. If Sunday attendance declined, then the minister would know the time to depart had arrived.[2] Though personally successful in a variety of pastoral assignments, Morris knew from long observation that when a congregation did not attend Sunday services and support the church, they had, in effect, discharged the pastor. The pastor should acknowledge the situation and move on. Based on his experience at First English Lutheran Church, Morris felt the perceptive pastor should anticipate the end of his "usefulness," an inevitable event in every pastoral career, and move on before congregational decline or disaffection set in.

Morris's pastoral concerns for clergy and laity alike appeared in an 1891 dispute over publishing a new English translation of Luther's commentary on St. Paul's epistle to the Galatians. Morris argued the need for a new translation because of inadequate earlier versions and, more important, because nowhere else had Luther "so thoroughly elaborated the doctrine of justification," and delineated the difference between law and gospel.[3] To Morris the doctrine of justification represented the foundation for "true" religion, and thus required public understanding and acceptance. Though he doubted the financial feasibility of selling the entire commentary, he did advocate publishing key passages from Luther's work. Morris the pastor supported any effort that disseminated what he considered Luther's most significant scriptural writings, and the insights that made Lutheranism central to the story of Protestantism.

In these last years of his life, Morris's pastoral concerns continued to include the cause of Lutheran unity. The Lutheran Historical Society remained one of his favorite forums for advancing Lutheran historical knowledge and solidarity. Morris and his diligent co-worker Charles Hay continually solicited new acquisitions for the society's library. To Morris's great delight, the seminary constructed a fireproof room for the society's bound volumes, pamphlets, articles, and manuscripts.[4] With safe quarters available, he gave to the society one of his most cherished possessions—a large volume of newspaper clippings and pictures he had compiled in 1883 documenting the four-hundredth anniversary celebration of Luther's birth.

Advanced age did not dim Morris's sharp wit. At the last meeting of the Lutheran Historical Society he attended, at the close of the 1895 session of the General Synod, he gave a lengthy report on the society's activities and accomplishments. In passing, he mentioned that the Missouri Synod's seminary had sent pictures of its professors to the society for inclusion in the library. One of the attendees, the Reverend Adam Stump, called out, "Are they better looking than the professors in our Seminary?" Without pausing, Morris fired back, "Yes, they are a good deal better looking than you are." Loud laughter and applause greeted the old man's riposte.[5]

Though an ardent advocate of the historical society, Morris feared that Lutherans outside the General Synod viewed the organization as purely an auxiliary to the larger body. This frustrated his goal of having the entire Lutheran Church accept and support the society. Given the realities of the day, he understood the need for a different vehicle to bring others more actively into the cause of Lutheran history.

In 1894, he worked with his old General Council ally Joseph A. Seiss to organize the Philadelphia-based Academy of Church History. Obviously meant to stimulate interest among the adherents of the General Council, the Academy had an initial burst of success. Within a year, with Morris as its president, the academy had sixty-nine members, and in April 1895 met at Seiss's Philadelphia church with ten papers on the agenda. Morris opened the meeting with a devotional service, followed by his own talk on "The History of Local Churches, Chiefly in Maryland." He never stopped working to spread through all means available a better understanding of what he considered an accurate perspective on Lutheran history and doctrine.[6] Only from this perspective, he believed, could church unity eventually emerge.

His venture with the Academy of Church History had a more subtle and personal aspect to it. The aged Morris felt at home with the confessionally stricter philosophy of the General Council. His partnership with Seiss in the "free diets" experiment certainly indicated as much. Though he always remained loyal to the General Synod and its institutions at Gettysburg, Morris had developed over time an affinity for the General Council's more defined ethnic German cultural identity. He realized that the process of ethnic and confessional assimilation would take time before his goal of a united progressive English-language Lutheran church in America would come to pass; hence, the founding of the academy in the heart of General Council territory. Last, but not least, Morris had close personal relationships with prominent General Council leaders. These included, among many others, Seiss and Morris's former protégé, Charles Porterfield Krauth, now the General Council's leading theologian.

The bitterness that Morris's quest for a confessionally-based and united church still evoked spilled into public during Morris's last year. Peter Anstadt, a Schmucker partisan and biographer, took Morris to task for describing Samuel Simon Schmucker as the "severest moralist" he had ever met. This comment, part of a generally critical evaluation, appeared in Morris's *Fifty Years in the Lutheran Ministry*, published in 1878, several years after Schmucker's death. Why Anstadt waited until 1895 to rebuke Morris publically remains unclear. Anstadt vigorously defended Schmucker's rejection of cards, theater, circus, tobacco, and alcohol. According to Anstadt, ministers should follow Schmucker's example and forsake "innocent amusements" if any might give public offense. Further, he vigorously disputed Morris's interpretation of the fateful 1846 trip to Europe with Schmucker. The lack of invitations to preach in German churches merely reflected the law and custom of the country. No doubt Morris's role in defeating "American Lutheranism" provoked Anstadt's ire, and fueled the latter's ridicule of Morris's interest in Luther "relics."[7] Bitter wounds had yet to heal. Morris refrained as usual from any public comment.

Along with his pastoral and church interests, Morris remained deeply committed to secular historical pursuits. Besides church history societies, Morris put his energy principally into the Society for the History of the Germans in Maryland and the Maryland Historical Society. He was convinced as always that only organized effort could bear fruit, He felt such societies existed "to verify doubtful facts, develop and record unwritten events, correct popular errors, authenticate disputed facts, to delineate the character and deeds of illustrious men."[8] The search for truth combined with the didactic purpose of great lives.

Always conscious of his heritage as a second-generation American, Morris continued to use the Society for the History of the Germans in Maryland to build bridges with other Americans. Giving a stream of papers at monthly society meetings, he returned over and over to the theme of German cultural and patriotic contributions to the nation. He made his points in biographical essays on the Muhlenbergs, Conrad Weiser, and Baltimore pastor John Uhlhorn, among others. He explored for his listeners the treatment of black slaves by Germans and the German experience in Baltimore, along with translations of numerous articles and essays.[9]

Morris remained a leading figure at the Maryland Historical Society. For most of the 1890s, he continued as one of the Society's vice presidents, and in 1892, he began a term as librarian. Morris's work ethic, and gruffness, comes through in a June 1893 letter to his assistant librarian, John Gatchell. Though ill and confined temporarily to Oak Grove, Morris urged Gatchell to make sure the rearranging of the book collection continued, and to keep the library staff "busy at it."[10] The MHS recognized Morris's unique and long-term contributions to the organization, and the advancement of culture, by electing him its fifth president on February 11, 1895. This was the last of the many honors which had filled his life. With John G.

Morris's death, on October 10, 1895, the labors of a true cultural pioneer at last came to an end. A number of important legacies remained.

Morris provided his three surviving daughters with a sizable estate valued at almost $50,000. He divided his Baltimore and Lutherville properties, as well as the proceeds from selling his stocks and bonds, among his children. He also took great care in managing his intellectual bequests. He left to his grandson, Pastor Charles R. Trowbridge, his extensive collection of Luther books, the writings of American Lutheran ministers, and his scientific lectures and letters "from distinguished men." Within a few years, Trowbridge entrusted these important materials into the care of the Lutheran Historical Society. Morris willed his collection of shells and herbarium to Pennsylvania College, the scene of his earliest scientific endeavors. In typical fashion, he wrote, "I hope they may when received by said college be arranged in systematic and scientific order so they may be useful for study."[11] To the end, he combined scholarly scientific methodology and practical application.

Many eulogies marked the passing of John G. Morris, and they attempted to assess his legacy to church and country. Several characteristics of the man emerge from the many resolutions of respect which hit the heart of Morris's contributions as an American cultural leader. He was remembered by the president of the Maryland Synod as the "nineteenth century reincarnation of Luther" and as a man of "fine literary taste." The Maryland Historical Society saluted its late leader for his "intense patriotism and love of historical detail."[12] Above all, love of country and church had motivated Morris. In serving both, the ambitious clergyman capitalized on his vast reservoir of natural energy and optimism and the keen intellect and wit that observers always noted. From his ardent patriotism flowed his contributions to American cultural life.

Most important to Morris was his lifelong effort to assimilate the Lutheran church into American Protestantism. As a young leader in the 1820s and 1830s, he worked indefatigably to win the battle to use English in the church. This was the key struggle if Lutherans were to enter the mainstream of American religious life. In this pioneering effort, Morris created three flourishing English-language churches in Baltimore which helped transform the relationship between Lutherans and other Protestants in the city. Lutherans were no longer aloof and isolated, but instead became full partners in Baltimore's religious life. During the mid-century wave of German immigration, Morris mobilized the Maryland Synod to try and assimilate the newcomers into the American Lutheran church. A daunting task and never totally successful, but one at which he labored throughout his entire career.

At the regional and national levels, Morris's greatest contribution to American Lutheranism took place at Gettysburg. Involved from the earliest years of Pennsylvania College and Gettysburg Seminary, Morris's leadership helped sustain these bastions of progressive, English-speaking Lutheranism. As trustee, director, and instructor, Morris worked for over half a century to ensure that both institutions survived a myriad of crises, particularly the confessional battle which ripped at the heart of the seminary. Amid doctrinal conflict and disputes over the role of German at the college and seminary, he sought the principled compromises necessary to prevent collapse.

Morris's literary talents and love of history immeasurably aided his understanding of what Lutheran identity and unity meant in the American context. His wide reading in German theology and church history, buttressed by the stunning impact of German immigrants on the church in America, guided the Baltimore pastor in his evolution from revivalism to a moderately conservative confessionalism. Taking a long perspective, he realized that a successful English-language Lutheranism had to rest on those doctrinal and historical traditions that, to him, made the Lutheran church the "mother church" of Protestantism.

In pursuit of this goal, and to document the contributions of Lutherans to America, Morris created an invaluable research collection under the auspices of the Lutheran Historical Society. Morris and his colleague Charles Hay gathered thousands of pamphlets, manuscripts, and printed materials from all corners of the church. Whether through the Lutheran Historical Society, the Academy of Church History, the "free diets" or his own writings, Morris's work in spreading knowledge about Lutheran history and traditions helped lay the foundation for improved understanding and mutual respect among the church's warring factions. The 1917 merger of the General Synod, the General Council, and the United Synod, South, owed a great deal to the pioneering efforts of Morris, among others, in building lines of theological and historical communication.

Morris's pastoral, theological, and historical publications reflect his literary ability and, with his work as church leader, stand as monuments to his determined efforts to strengthen Lutheran identity and unity. Though not particularly original in his theological or historical thinking, he always wrote with style and a fine attention to detail and accuracy. His writings on Luther, other figures from church history, and doctrinal issues, such as the sacraments, marked not only Morris's evolution but also the journey of much of American Lutheranism. As a cultural leader, Morris never ceased striving for a Lutheranism that flourished in the new American soil of religious freedom.

His "intense patriotism" was expressed in other cultural arenas. His pioneering scientific publications, the *Catalogue* and *Synopsis of the Described Lepidoptera*, laid the foundations for further progress in entomology. Though he rejected Darwinism and remained a scientific and religious adherent of natural theology, his assiduous work in creating natural history collections, exchanging information, and organizing scientific societies aided the development of the American scientific community. A cosmopolitan in acquiring knowledge, Morris remained at heart a nationalist. He sought American preeminence in American science.

In pursuit of this quest, Morris focused much of his energy on education in both public and academic forums. Many of his lectures, whether under the auspices of the Baltimore Lyceum or other similar sponsors; sought to inform the public about the practical value of scientific knowledge. Hundreds of lectures and articles stressed the economic and national benefits arising from a strong scientific community. Often using humor, Morris taught hearers and readers about the basic facts of scientific classification and analysis, and how this would strengthen American agriculture and commerce.

In a similar fashion, Morris lead the founding of one of the first college-level student natural history societies. Organized at Pennsylvania College, the new society, at Morris's direction, helped construct the first student-built science building on a college campus. Further, he edited one of the earliest scientific journals, a skillful and polished product for the era.

Morris's lifelong fascination with science reflected not only his personal predilection, but also his belief that scientific pursuits added to a minister's utility and "respectability." This was the essential Morris: the man who believed the clergy must be well-educated, involved in more than church affairs, and part of the effort to raise the tone and quality of public life. Self-assured as a speaker and writer, Morris exemplified that nineteenth-century phenomenon, the clergyman as the man of letters prolific in public service.

Similar sentiments animated Morris's work as an historian and cultural institution builder. His wide range of activities encompassing the Lutheran Historical Society, the Maryland Historical Society, the Peabody Institute, and the Society for the History of Germans in Maryland had a common thread. Whether in secular or religious arenas, Morris fought to raise the level of public appreciation for history and, a particular concern, the contributions of American Germans to Maryland and the nation. An appreciation for the past and the contributions of "great men" would solidify the twin pillars of American freedom and prosperity—a republican form of government rooted in the Protestant ethos.

As with his scientific principles, Morris remained true to the tenets of an earlier historical tradition. In tone and substance, his work exhibited all the characteristics associated with the "Whig" school of history. To him, Protestantism guaranteed political, intellectual, and religious freedom and made inevitable the progress of Western (i.e., Protestant) civilization. Morris's biographical interest in Luther and other major religious and secular leaders reflected the Romantic era's fascination with the heroic figure. His subscription to the "spirit of the age" and belief in overarching natural principles also marked Morris as a follower of the Romantic tradition.

Yet Morris's philosophical orientation did not interfere with objectivity and truth, at least as he understood it. He always sought to present an accurate historical chronology and the causes and relationships affecting historical events. Though not of the rank of a Joseph Henry or a George Bancroft, Morris shone in the next tier of talented and ambitious men who created the research collections and built the scientific and historical societies.

As a cultural leader, Morris remained rooted in the antebellum world which formed him. Gentlemen of education and means had a responsibility to combat social disorder and elevate the character of public discourse. Heading the Baltimore Lyceum and the Maryland Academy of Science and Literature, Morris, like others of his class, sought to counteract the economic, social, and political pressures tearing city, state, and nation apart. Creating great libraries at the Maryland Historical Society and Peabody Institute were efforts not only to sustain the cultural life of the well-to-do, but the beginning of making knowledge and culture more accessible to society at large. Morris's endeavors complemented those of Enoch Pratt and the founding of Baltimore's first free public library in the 1870s.

What Morris built as a cultural leader endures. An English-speaking Lutheranism rooted in America is a reality. This and the continued success of the Lutheran institutions at Gettysburg reflect the success of Morris's long, sustained labors. The collections of the Maryland Historical Society and the Peabody Institute, which Morris established, continue as essential core elements in the life of both organizations. The Society for the History of the Germans in Maryland has operated for well over a hundred years along the lines Morris laid down.

In all aspects of his professional life, Morris demonstrated a sustained commitment to knowledge and a passionate zeal for excellence. Morris's work contributed significantly to the cultural journey of nineteenth-century America and helped influence the era that followed.

Morris the man remains in many ways a more elusive figure than Morris the cultural leader. This reflects the relative paucity of private records in comparison to his public activities. Yet a reasonably complete and complex figure does emerge. A passionate, highly principled man, Morris was in certain ways the "nineteenth century reincarnation of Luther." Though certainly not a religious revolutionary, Morris, like Luther, struggled with inner tensions. For Morris, these tensions revolved around the need for independence and recognition, an early paternal loss and the success that a strong ego demanded. As with Luther, his inner tensions resulted not in paralysis but a lifetime of prodigious labors and accomplishments.

These inner tensions at times led to fractious and explosive relationships. Sensitive to slights, real or perceived, the high-strung Morris often complained to his confidants about offending individuals. In *Fifty Years* and *Life Reminiscences*, he expressed his personal disagreements with Samuel Simon Schmucker and his utter detestation of Charles J. M. Eaton. He held grudges for decades and, at least with Schmucker and Eaton, took posthumous revenge. Filled with a strong sense of his own worth, Morris resented anyone who did not sufficiently recognize it. This perhaps explains his marked coolness when leaving First English Lutheran Church.

Yet Morris's personality also had great depths of loyalty and friendship. To his family, brother Charles in particular, Morris exhibited great devotion. Never one to wear his heart on his sleeve, Morris poured out on the pages of his diary the concern and love he felt for his family. Family losses profoundly moved him. To his old friend Charles Philip Krauth, he remained steadfast. Morris cared a great deal for all those closest to him.

Though known for his gruff manner, Morris showed an abiding and sincere interest in young people, as witness his years of work aiding young pastors, such as William Passavant and Charles Porterfield Krauth, and the girls at Lutherville Female Seminary and the boys lodged at the House of Refuge. Basically gregarious, Morris enjoyed the companionship of others and continued his many personal and professional relationships to within a few weeks of his death.

A complex man indeed. Yet, he more than honorably acquitted himself as a man of his time. John Gottlieb Morris's strong personality and native intelligence, disciplined by a lifetime of study and work, enabled him to earn an honored place in the history of American culture and religion.

Notes

Chapter 1: Journey's End

1. Charles S. Albert, "The Rev. Dr. John G. Morris: A Tribute to His Character," *Lutheran Observer*, 25 October 1895.

2. John G. Morris, *Life Reminiscences of an Old Lutheran Minister* (Philadelphia: Lutheran Publication Society, 1896), 362.

3. Ibid., 364.

4. Louise Morris Leisenring Reese, "Memories of Oak Grove," Archives of the Baltimore County Historical Society, Cockeysville, Maryland.

5. Morris, *Life Reminiscences*, 369-371.

6. Ibid.

7. Ibid., 378-381.

Chapter 2: Early Years

1. There are several sources for information on the life and career of Dr. John Morris. There are excerpts from a diary Dr. Morris kept that is now lost. These excerpts are part of a collection of personal and family papers maintained by Helen Berry, a descendant of John G. Morris in Lutherville, Maryland. See also John G. Morris, "Biographical Sketch of Dr. John Morris, Surgeon of Armand's First Partisan Legion," The *Pennsylvania Magazine of History and Biography*, XVII (1883): 200-203.

2. Morris, *Life Reminiscences*, 8-9. Much of our information about John G. Morris's family and his early years are found only in his *Reminiscences*. Though Morris jotted down diary entries through much of his life, these memoirs reflect compilation in the last years of his life. Much of what he writes, therefore, is recollected from the perspective of old age. Judging by incidents where facts can be checked with other sources, Morris, for the most part, remembered dates and events accurately. His interpretations of personalities and events are of course subject to other interpretations and points of view.

3. Stephen J. Vicchio, "Baltimore's Burial Practices, Mortuary Art and Notions of Grief and Bereavement, 1780-1900," *Maryland Historical Magazine*, 81 (Summer 1986): 137-138.

4. Morris, *Life Reminiscences*, 10.

5. *Men of Mark in Maryland*, Vol. IV (Baltimore, Washington, and Richmond: B. F. Johnson, Inc., 1912), 420. This biographical essay on John G. Morris includes a brief section on his father in an attempt to discern the "paternal inheritance."

6. Charles H. Glatfelter, "John Gottlieb Morris (1803-1895): A Sketch," 1973, Papers of John G. Morris, Lutheran Theological Seminary, Gettysburg, Pennsylvania, 5. See also Account of August 10, 1815, Register of Wills Office, York County, York, Pennsylvania.

7. Morris, *Life Reminiscences*, 10-11, 15-16.

8. Ibid., 45.

9. Ibid., 16, 28.

10. Ibid., 14.

11. Information on the Morris family is available in files 1334 and 14153, Historical Society of York County, York, Pennsylvania. See also papers of Helen Berry.

12. George R. Prowell, ed. A History *of York County Pennsylvania*, 2 vols. (Chicago: J. H. Beers and Co , 1907), 737, 766, 806. See also John Gibson, ed. A History *of York County Pennsylvania* (Chicago: F. A. Battey Publishing Co., 1886), 257, 307.

13. James Lawton Haney, "John George Schmucker and the Roots of His Spirituality," Es*says and Reports of the Lutheran Historical Conference*, XIV (1990): 67-95; Morris, *Life Reminiscences*, 13.

14. Peter Anstadt, *Life and Times of Rev. S. S. Schmucker, D.D.* (York, PA: P. A. Anstadt and Sons, 1896), 366-368.

15. Morris, Life *Reminiscences*, 13.

16. Ibid., 20.

17. Ibid., 19-20.

18. Ibid., 11, 19.

19. Ibid., 12-13, 17-19.

20. Ibid., 19.

21. Ibid., 26.

22. Ibid.

23. Ibid., 27.

24. Ibid., 35.

25. Ibid., 19, 38.

26. Herbert HovenKamp, *Science and Religion in America, 1830-1860* (Harrisburg: University of Pennsylvania Press, 1978), 7-9.

27. Ibid., 10-11.

28. Morris, Life *Reminiscences*, 27, 34-35.

29. Ibid., 40.

30. Ibid., 43, 45; "Deaths Doings," *Gettysburg Star and Sentinel*, 15 October 1895.

31. Ibid., 44.

32. Ibid., 44-45.

33. Ibid., 43-44.

34. Ibid., 45.

35. Ibid., 46.

Chapter 3: Call to Ministry

1. Morris, *Life Reminiscences*, 46.

2. Ibid., 47.

3. Ibid., 46-47.

4. Ibid.

5. John G. Morris, *Fifty Years in the Lutheran Ministry* (Baltimore: James Young, 1878), 119-121.

6. Because of Samuel Simon Schmucker's prominent role in Morris's life as teacher and colleague, his theological beliefs and the various intellectual sources for those beliefs are significant. See Anstadt, *Life and Times of Rev. S. S. Schmucker* and Abdel Ross Wentz, *Pioneer in Christian Unity: Samuel Simon Schmucker* (Philadelphia: Fortress Press, 1967); see also Morris's sketches of Schmucker in *Fifty Years*, 121-131, and *Life Reminiscences*, 50, 94, 95, 312.

7. Frank H. Seilhamer, "The New Measures Movement in the Lutheran Church in America, 1820-1860" (Bachelor of Divinity thesis, Lutheran Theological Seminary at Gettysburg, 1959), 2, 10-15. See also *Lutheran Quarterly* (May 1960): 121.

8. The American religious ethos of the first half of the nineteenth century is well documented. Some general accounts which provide the historical context for the era include: Sydney E. Ahlstrom, *A Religious History of the American People*, Vol. 1 (Garden City, New York: Image Books, 1975); Edwin Scott Gaustad, *A Religious History of America* (New York: Harper and Row, 1966); Winthrop S. Hudson, *Religion in America*, 2nd ed. (New York: Charles Scribner's Sons, 1973); Martin E. Marty, *Righteous Empire: The Protestant Experience in America* (New York: The Dial Press, 1970); Sidney E. Mead, *The Lively Experiment: The Shaping of Christianity in America* (New York: Harper and Row, 1963); William Warren Sweet, *Revivalism in America: Its Origin, Growth and Decline* (New York: Charles Scribner's Sons, 1944).

9. H. George Anderson, "The Early National Period, 1790-1840," in *The Lutherans in North America*, rev. ed., E. Clifford Nelson, ed. (Philadelphia: Fortress Press, 1980), 95-100, 134-135.

10. Lutheran pastors and local congregations by the middle of the eighteenth century began to organize themselves into ministeriums or synods to foster cooperation in reacting to issues or needs that exceeded the resources of local congregations. The first such organization was the Pennsylvania Ministerium, founded in 1748 at the behest of Lutheran patriarch Henry Melchior Muhlenberg. Synods at first conformed, more or less, to state boundaries. From the mid-nineteenth century on, many synods were also formed on ethnic or theological grounds.

11. Nelson, *Lutherans in North America*, 134-135.

12. Sydney E. Ahlstrom, *A Religious History of the American People*, 622-624.

13. Nelson, *Lutherans in North America*, 108. See also Todd W. Nichol, "Lutheran Revivalism: A Request for a Reappraisal," *Essays and Reports of the Lutheran Historical Conference*, Vol. XII (1986); Raymond M. Bost, "Catechism or Revival," *Lutheran Quarterly* (Winter 1989); Paul P. Kuenning, *The Rise and Fall of American Lutheran Pietism: The Rejection of an Activist Heritage* (Macon, GA: Mercer University Press, 1988).

14. For information on the organization and early days of the General Synod, see Morris, *Fifty Years*, 257-260, 349; Vergilius A. Ferm, *The Crisis in American Lutheran Theology* (New York: The Century Co., 1927), 5, 14, 19-23, 51, 82; Nelson, *Lutherans in North America*, 14, 115-125.

15. Wentz, *Pioneer in Christian Unity*, 49.

16. Ferm, *The Crisis in American Lutheran Theology*, 82. Licensure was one of several ministerial offices that informally developed in the early nineteenth century. This was the step prior to ordination and usually limited performance of ministerial functions to a specific area for a limited period of time. Synods and ministeriums examined candidates and granted licenses.

17. Morris, *Life Reminiscences*, 51.

18. Ibid., 55.

19. Luke Schmucker, *The Schmucker Family and the Lutheran Church in America* (privately published, 1937), 35.

20. Morris, *Life Reminiscences*, 57, 59-60.

21. The relationship of German Lutheran pietism, English Puritanism and, ultimately, evangelical American Protestantism is complex. Several sources assist in understanding the pietist-Puritan connection in American Lutheranism. These include: Ferm, *The Crisis in American Lutheran Theology*, 5, 14,19-23, 51, 91-92; Ahlstrom, *A Religious History of the American People*, Vol. 1, 297-300; Wentz, *Pioneer in Christian Unity*, iv, 34-38, 50, 53; Nelson, *Lutherans in North America*, 62-67, 71-72, 149-150; Kuenning, *The Rise and Fall of American Lutheran Pietism*, 78-79; Robert F. Scholz, "The Confessional Stance of Henry Melchior Muhlenberg and the Early Pennsylvania Ministerium," *Lutheran Quarterly* (Winter 1987).

22. Morris, *Fifty Years*, 128; Anstadt, *Life and Times of Rev. S. S. Schmucker*, 114-115; Morris, *Life Reminiscences*, 57.

23. Morris, *Life Reminiscences*, 49; *Fifty Years*, 11.

24. Morris, *Fifty Years*, 11.

25. Haney, "John George Schmucker and the Roots of His Spirituality"; Wentz, *Pioneer in Christian Unity*, 50, 53.

26. Morris, *Life Reminiscences*, 52.

27. Ibid., 58

28. Ibid., 65-70.

29. Wentz, *Pioneer in Christian Unity*, 17-19, 22-23, 26-27, 31; Morris, *Life Reminiscences*, 73-83.

30. Morris, *Life Reminiscences*, 73-83.

31. Ibid., 73, 80.

32. Ibid., 76.

33. The Maryland-Virginia Synod, formerly a conference in the Pennsylvania Ministerium, organized as a separate entity in 1820 and became a district synod in the General Synod. In 1829, the Maryland-Virginia Synod reorganized along state boundaries and broke into two district synods.

34. Morris, *Life Reminiscences*, 85.

35. Ibid., 86.

36. Ibid., 87.

37. Ibid., 92-93.

38. Ibid., 97.

39. Ibid.

Chapter 4: Emerging Church Leader

1. Raphael Semmes, Baltimore *as Seen by Visitors, 1783-1860* (Baltimore: Maryland Historical Society, 1953), 104.

2. Background material for the Baltimore and Maryland context of the 1820s and 1830s is found in: Robert J. Brugger, *Maryland: A Middle Temperament, 1634-1980* (Baltimore: The Johns Hopkins University Press, 1988), 187-189, 191, 196, 199, 203, 206,

221-222, 230, 240, 250; Suzanne Ellery Greene, *An Illustrated History: Baltimore* (Woodland Hills, California: Windsor Publications, Inc., 1980), 76, 82, 100; Sherry H. Olson, *Baltimore: The Building of an American City* (Baltimore: The Johns Hopkins University Press, 1980), 71, 80, 83, 91-92, 98, 102, 108; Richard Walsh and William Lloyd Fox, eds., *Maryland: A History* (Annapolis, MD: Hall of Record Commission, Department of General Services, 1983), 161, 170, 183, 188, 199-200, 203-204; *Maryland: A Guide to the Old Line State*, (New York: Oxford University Press, 1940), 133-135.

3. Anna Margaret (Suppes) Hay, *Genealogical Sketches of the Hay, Suppes and Allied Families* (Johnstown PA: Wm. H. Raab and Son, 1923), 15, 37-38.

4. Morris, *Life Reminiscences*, 79-80.

5. Ibid., 143, 177.

6. Sylvia D. Hoffert, "A Very Peculiar Sorrow: Attitudes Toward Infant Death in the Urban Northeast, 1800-1860," *American Quarterly*, Vol. 39 (Winter 1987): 601, 605.

7. Papers of Helen Berry; The Diary of John G. Morris, 1827-1836, 1885-1890; 24 June 1828, 2 May 1829. Special Collections, Manuscripts, Gettysburg College, Gettysburg, Pennsylvania.

8. Diary of John G. Morris, 25 May 1830.

9. Hay, Genealogical *Sketches of the Hay, Suppes and Allied Families*, 16; John G. Morris to Charles P. Krauth, April 1838, Papers of John G. Morris.

10. Morris, *Life Reminiscences*, 99, 114, 121.

11. Ibid., 114; John G. Morris to Charles P. Krauth, 22 January [1834?], Papers of John G. Morris.

12. Diary of John G. Morris, 29 March 1827, 27 April 1827, 20 May 1827.

13. Morris, *Life Reminiscences*, 111-112.

14. Ibid., 113; "First Annual Report of the Sunday School of the English Lutheran Church," *Lutheran Observer*, 16 April 1832; John G. Morris to Charles P. Krauth, 19 July 1832, Papers of John G. Morris; Diary of John G. Morris, 29 March 1827.

15. Morris, *Life Reminiscences*, 112-113; Evangelical Lutheran Synod of Maryland, *Proceedings of the Twentieth Annual Session* (Baltimore: John Murphy, 1839), 6.

16. Morris, *Life Reminiscences*, 126-127, 129; John G. Morris to Charles P. Krauth, n.d. [1833?], Papers of John G. Morris.

17. Morris, *Life Reminiscences*, 115-116; Mary Ellen Gleason to Michael J. Kurtz, 5 April 1988, identifying Morris's life membership (6 December 1830) from the records of the American Bible Society, New York, New York.

18. John G. Morris, Compiler, *Register of the First English Lutheran Church From February 1857 to March 1859* (Baltimore: Frederick A. Hanzsche, 1859), 6-7.

19. Morris, *Life Reminiscences*, 105.

20. Evangelical Lutheran Synod of Maryland and Virginia, *Proceedings of the Annual Session*, 1827, in *The Evangelical Lutheran Intelligencer*, 2 (1827-1828), 215; *Proceedings of the Annual Session*, 1828, 3 (1828-1829), 212; *Proceedings of the Annual Session*, 1833 (Baltimore: Cloud and Pauter, 1833), 9; *Proceedings of the Annual Session*, 1834 (Baltimore: J. H. Dieger and Son, 1834), 5; *Proceedings of the Annual Session*, 1835 (Baltimore: Jas. Lucas and E. K. Deaver, 1835), 5; *Proceedings of the Annual Session*, 1836 (Baltimore: John W. Woods, 1836), 5; *Proceedings of the Annual Session*, 1837 (Baltimore: J. W. Woods, 1837), 4; Morris, *Fifty Years*, 9; General Synod of the Evangelical Lutheran Church in the United States,

Proceedings of the Fifth Convention (Gettysburg PA: H. C. Neinstedt, 1829), 5; *Proceedings of the Seventh Convention* (Albany: Hoffman and White, 1833), 8-9; *Proceedings of the Tenth Convention* (Gettysburg PA: H. C. Neinstedt, 1839), 5.

21. "To Our Readers," *Lutheran Observer*, 31 August 1831.

22. Ibid.

23. "Regeneration," *Lutheran Observer*, 2 April 1832; John G. Morris, *The Catechumen's and Communicant's Companion; Designed for the Use of Young Persons of the Lutheran Church, Receiving Instructions Preparatory to Confirmation and the Lord's Supper* (Baltimore: Lucas and Deaver, 1832), v, 63-65.

24. Ibid.

25. Morris, *The Catechumen's and Communicant's Companion*, 67.

26. John G. Morris to Charles P. Krauth, April 1838, Papers of John G. Morris. Schmucker's concept of a union was a confederation of evangelical denominations united by adherence to the early Christian creeds, with each denomination retaining its own polity, usages and "peculiarities" in matters doctrinally "non-essential." This great union would facilitate evangelization in America and the world, and thus defeat the forces of irreligion, impiety, and Romanism. From the mid-1830s onward, Protestants expressed growing fears over what they considered an aggressively expanding and proselytizing American Catholic church.

27. General Synod of the Evangelical Lutheran Church in the United States, *Proceedings of the Seventh Convention*, 20; *Proceedings of the Eighth Convention* (Troy NY: N. Tuttle, 1835), 16.

28. *Lutheran Observer*, editorial, 16 April 1832; editorial, 15 May 1832. When Morris relinquished the editorship of the *Observer* in 1833, he had built the subscribership up to 700 and estimated a yearly profit of $1,300. Morris unsuccessfully urged his friend Krauth to take the editorship, which Benjamin Kurtz subsequently took. See John G. Morris to Charles P. Krauth, [1833?], Papers of John G. Morris; Abdel Ross Wentz, *History of the Evangelical Lutheran Synod of Maryland of the United Lutheran Church in America, 1820-1920* (Harrisburg PA : Evangelical Press, 1920), 65.

29. Evangelical Lutheran Synod of Maryland, *Proceedings of the Annual Session*, 1832, in *Lutheran Observer*, 2 (1832-1833), 74; Wentz, *History of the Maryland Synod*, 155; Morris, *Fifty Years*, 262; *Lutheran Observer*, 30 March 1838.

30. John G. Morris to Charles P. Krauth, 23 November [no year], 18 March [no year], Papers of John G. Morris.

31. Ibid., 5 February and 13 March 1839; Morris, *Life Reminiscences*, 116.

32. Abdel Ross Wentz, *History of the Gettysburg Theological Seminary of the General Synod of the Evangelical Lutheran Church in the United States and of the United Lutheran Church in America, Gettysburg, Pennsylvania, 1826-1926* (Philadelphia: The United Lutheran Publication House, 1926), 245, 341-342; Charles H. Glatfelter, A *Salutary Influence: Gettysburg College, 1832-1985* (Gettysburg PA: Gettysburg College, 1987), 27, 75-77.

33. Wentz, *History of Gettysburg Seminary*, 137; John G. Morris to Charles P. Krauth, 12 April 1830, Papers of John G. Morris; Diary of John G. Morris, 24 June 1830.

34. William B. Sprague, ed., *Annals of the American Pulpit*, Vol. IX (New York: Robert Carter and Brothers, 1869), 139-140.

35. John G. Morris to Charles P. Krauth, n.d., Papers of John G. Morris.

36. Ibid.

37. Meeting of the Board of Trustees of Pennsylvania College, 18 April 1838, September 1838, Records of Gettysburg College, Gettysburg, Pennsylvania; John G. Morris to Samuel Simon Schmucker, David Gilbert, John B. McPherson, 30 May 1838, Correspondence of the Board of Trustees of Pennsylvania College to 1839, Records of Gettysburg College.

38. Minutes of the Board of Trustees of Pennsylvania College, Meeting of 18 September 1839.

39. Ibid., Meetings of 18 September 1839, 22 April 1840, 16 September 1840; John G. Morris to David Gilbert, 21 September 1839, Correspondence of the Board of Trustees of Pennsylvania College to 1839.

40. Morris, *Life Reminiscences*, 290-291.

41. Douglas C. Stange, "Benjamin Kurtz of the *Lutheran Observer* and the Slavery Crisis," *Maryland Historical Magazine,* 62 (September 1967): 287.

42. General Synod of the Evangelical Lutheran Church in the United States, *Proceedings of the Eighth Convention,* 27; Wentz, *History of the Maryland Synod*, 107.

43. John G. Morris, "Sketch of a History of the Maryland Synod, October 1870," Papers of John G. Morris; Wentz, *History of the Maryland Synod,* 125.

44. Stange, "Benjamin Kurtz of the *Lutheran Observer* and the Slavery Crisis," 291.

45. *Lutheran Herald and Journal of the Franckean Synod,* I (16 November 1835): 169.

Chapter 5: A Passion for Scholarship

1. HovenKamp, *Science and Religion in America*, ix.

2. David Levin, *History as Romantic Art: Bancroft, Prescott, Motley, and Parkman* (Stanford CA: Stanford University Press, 1959), 27.

3. HovenKamp, *Science and Religion in America*, xi -xi i .

4. Morris, *Life Reminiscences*, 110-111.

5. Ibid.

6. Donald M. Scott, "The Popular Lecture and the Creation of a Public in Mid-Nineteenth Century America," *The Journal of American History*, 66 (March 1980): 791-795; Kevin B. Sheets, "Saving History: The Maryland Historical Society and Its Founders," *Maryland Historical Magazine*, 89 (Summer 1994): 135-142.

7. Morris, *Life Reminiscences*, 197-198.

8. Ibid., 191-193; Diary of John G. Morris, 3 July 1830.

9. James R. Moore, "Geologists and Interpreters of Genesis in the Nineteenth Century," *God and Nature: Historical Essays on the Encounter Between Christianity and Science,* David C. Lindberg and Ronald L. Numbers, eds. (Berkeley CA: University of California Press, 1986), 327-328.

10. Ibid.

11. John G. Morris, "Geology and Revelation," American *Museum of Literature and the Arts*, 1 (November 1838): 281.

12. Ibid., 278-279.

13. Ibid., 280-281.

14. Ibid., 283.

15. Jonathan Horwitz, A *Defense of the Cosmogony of Moses* (Baltimore: Richard J. Matchett, 1838), 3-5.

16. Ibid.

17. Moore, "Geologists and Interpreters of Genesis in the Nineteenth Century," 335.

18. Arnold Mallis, *American Entomologists* (New Brunswick NJ: Rutgers University Press, 1971), 284-285.

19. The manuscript diary of Charles A. Hay, 1859-1889, 9 November 1862, Adams County Historical Society, Gettysburg, Pennsylvania.

20. Morris, *Life Reminiscences,* pp. 166-167.

21. John G. Morris to Charles P. Krauth, April 1838, Papers of John G. Morris; Morris, *Life Reminiscences,* 168.

22. John G. Morris to Thaddeus W. Harris, 23 July 1839, bmu 1966.10.2, Museum of Comparative Zoology, Harvard University, Cambridge, Massachusetts,

23. Thaddeus W. Harris to John G. Morris, 17 September 1839, bmu 1308.10.25, ibid.

24. John G. Morris, "Necessities and Blessings of the Reformation," *The Year-Book of the Reformation,* Benjamin Kurtz and John G. Morris, eds. (Baltimore: Publication Rooms, 1844), 11-31; Lewis W. Spitz, "The Lutheran Reformation in American Historiography," in *The Maturing of American Lutheranism,* Herbert T. Neve and Benjamin A. Johnson, eds. (Minneapolis: Augsburg Press, 1968), 102.

25. Levin, *History as Romantic Art,* ix, 24-27.

26. Morris, "Necessities and Blessings of the Reformation," 24; Levin, *History as Romantic Art,* 14-15, 74-78.

27. Morris, "Necessities and Blessings of the Reformation," 14-15.

28. Levin, *History as Romantic Art,* 24-27.

29. John G. Morris, "German Literature," *The Baltimore Book,* W. H. Carpenter and T. S. Arthur, eds. (Baltimore: Bayly and Burns, 1838), 224-235.

Chapter 6: Denominational Warrior

1. Dieter Cunz, *The Maryland Germans* (Port Washington NY: Kennikat Press, 1948), 202.

2. Olson, *Baltimore: The Building of an American City,* 123.

3. Evangelical Lutheran Synod of Maryland, *Proceedings of the Twentieth Annual Session* (Baltimore: John Murphy, 1839), 14-15, 17.

4. Ferm, The *Crisis in American Lutheran Theology,* 123-124, 127.

5. Evangelical Lutheran Synod of Maryland, *Proceedings of the Twenty-Third Annual Session* (Baltimore: Publication Rooms, 1841), 32. During the 1840s and 1850s Morris aided a group of younger ministers—Charles Porterfield Krauth, William A. Passavant, Joseph A. Seiss, and Samuel Simon Schmucker's son, Beale—in developing an enhanced appreciation for the Lutheran Confessions. Eventually all of them would reject "American Lutheranism" and join the conservative tide sweeping the church. Morris was more than just a theological mentor. He took young Krauth into his family when the latter arrived in Baltimore, and he conducted Passavant's marriage, setting the example for all by being the first to kiss the bride! He was instrumental in having both men called to their churches in Baltimore. He encouraged Krauth to view Second English "as a receiving ship where raw

recruits are exercised in naval tactics and prepared for more important points." Morris's kindness and shrewdness in nurturing young talent go far to explain his wide influence in the church. See Adolph Spaeth, *Charles Porterfield Krauth*, Vol. 1, 1823-1859 (New York: The Christian Literature Co., 1898) and G. H. Gerberding, *The Life and Letters of William A. Passavant* (Greenville PA: The Young Lutheran Co., 1906).

6. General Synod of the Evangelical Lutheran Church in the United States, *Proceedings of the Twelfth Convention* (Baltimore: Publication Rooms, 1843), 8, 11-12

7. Evangelical Lutheran Synod of Maryland, *Proceedings of the Twenty-Fourth Annual Session* (Baltimore: Publication Rooms, 1842), 17.

8. General Synod of the Evangelical Lutheran Church in the United States, *Proceedings of the Thirteenth Convention* (Baltimore: Publication Rooms, 1845), 80-82.

9. Wentz, *History of the Maryland Synod*, 108-109.

10. Ibid.

11. Ibid., "Missionary Convention in Baltimore," *The Missionary*, 5 (April 1852): 28.

12. General Synod of the Evangelical Lutheran Church in the United States, *Proceedings of the Eleventh Convention* (Baltimore: Publication Rooms, 1841), 11-12.

13. Ibid., *Proceedings of the Twelfth Convention*, 19.

14. Ibid., *Proceedings of the Thirteenth Convention*, 43-44.

15. Ibid., *Proceedings of the Fifteenth Convention* (Gettysburg: H. C. Neinstedt, 1850), 14.

16. Ahlstrom, A *Religious History of the American People*, 626.

17. Evangelical Lutheran Synod of Maryland, *Proceedings of the Twenty-Fifth Annual Session* (Baltimore: Publication Rooms, 1843), 14-15, 17-18; *Proceedings of the Twenty-Seventh Annual Session* (Baltimore: Publication Rooms, 1845), 13-14.

18. General Synod of the Evangelical Lutheran Church in the United States, *Proceedings of the Thirteenth Convention*, 29-30, 32, 38-39.

19. Samuel Simon Schmucker, *The Patriarchs of American Lutheranism* (Baltimore: Publication Rooms, 1845), 3-5, 7, 54-55. The Lutheran Historical Society, one of several such denominational societies founded in the 1840s and 1850s, reflected the increasingly sectarian and denominational tone in American Protestantism. The threads of unity woven by the interdenominational benevolent societies of the 1820s and 1830s began to unravel. For further information on the Lutheran Historical Society, see Michael J. Kurtz, "The First Lutheran Historical Society," Lutheran *Quarterly* (Spring 1991): 77-92.

20. August R. Suelflow and E. Clifford Nelson, "Following the Frontier," *The Lutherans in North America*, 220.

21. Anstadt, *Life and Times of Rev. S. S. Schmucker*, 242-243.

22. Morris, *Fifty Years*, 122-123.

23. Anstadt, *Life and Times of Rev. S. S. Schmucker*, 253-255. Interestingly enough, Charles Porterfield Krauth reported to his father that John G. Morris, on the eve of his trip to Europe, was "in fine humor, very sanguine." In fact, according to the younger Krauth, Morris would probably write sketches of his adventures in Europe while still on the voyage over to relieve the tedium of the trip. The man Krauth referred to as "our theological Dumas" seemed not at all anxious about his reception in Germany. See Spaeth, *Charles Porterfield Krauth*, 108-109.

24. Alumni Association of the Lutheran Theological Seminary at Gettysburg, Minutes of Association Meetings, 1841-1881, Meeting of 19 September 1848.

25. John G. Morris, "Luther's Larger and Smaller Catechisms," *The Evangelical Review*, 1 (July 1849): 62-81.

26. John G. Morris, "Paul Gerhard," *The Evangelical Review*, 6 (October 1850): 282-296.

27. John G. Morris to Charles Philip Krauth, 20 November [1849], Papers of John G. Morris.

28. Wentz, *History of Gettysburg Seminary*, 162, 172; Samuel Simon Schmucker to Beale M. Schmucker, 29 July 1850, Schmucker Manuscript Collection, Special Collections-Manuscripts, Gettysburg College.

29. Morris, *Fifty Years*, 103.

30. Wentz, *History of Gettysburg Seminary*, 171, 173.

31. John G. Morris to Samuel Simon Schmucker, 13 July 1853, Papers of John G. Morris.

32. Wentz, *History of Gettysburg Seminary*, 173.

33. Ibid., 176-177.

34. Minutes of the Board of Trustees of Pennsylvania College, Meetings of 16 September 1857, 16 September 1858.

35. Ibid., Meeting of 27 April 1859.

36. Morris, *Fifty Years*, 337.

37. Ibid.

38. Evangelical Lutheran Synod of Maryland, *Proceedings of the Thirty-Seventh Annual Session* (Gettysburg PA: H. C. Neinstedt, 1855), 18; Wentz, *History of the Maryland Synod*, 152-153; Ferm, *The Crisis in American Lutheran Theology*, 254.

39. "Inconsistency—Then and Now," *Lutheran Observer*, 4 January 1856.

40. John G. Morris, *The Life of John Arndt, Author of "True Christianity"* (Baltimore: T. Newton Kurtz,]853), 48-49, 201.

Chapter 7: National Recognition

1. John G. Morris to Spencer F. Baird, 18 July 1844, Spencer F. Baird Collection, Spencer F. Baird Incoming Correspondence, 1845-1887, Archives of the Smithsonian Institution, Washington, DC.

2. John G. Morris, "Collections of Natural History in Colleges," *The Literary Record and Journal of the Linnaean Association of Pennsylvania College*, 1 (November 1844): 3-52.

3. Morris, *Life Reminiscences*, 208-209.

4. John G. Morris to Spencer F. Baird, 30 June 1845, Spencer F. Baird Incoming Correspondence.

5. Morris, *Life Reminiscences*, 209.

6. John G. Morris, "Natural History as Applied to Farming and Gardening," *Tenth Annual Report of the Board of Regents of the Smithsonian Institution* (Washington, DC: A. O. P. Nicholson, 1846), 131-140.

7. Ibid.

8. Glatfelter, *A Salutary Influence*, 103-111.

9. John G. Morris, "Cabinet of the Linnaean Association," *The Literary Record and Journal of the Linnaean Association*, 1 (March 1845): 102-103.

10. John G. Morris, *An Address Delivered Before the Linnaean Association of Pennsylvania College, September 14, 1847* (Gettysburg PA: H. C. Neinstedt, 1847), 3.

11. Maryland Historical Society, Minutes of Society Meetings, 1851-1895 (MS 2008), Meeting of 7 May 1857, Records of the Maryland Historical Society, Baltimore, Maryland.

12. Ibid., Meetings of 4 June 1857 and 1 October 1857.

13. Ibid., Meeting of 6 January 1859.

14. Morris, *Life Reminiscences*, 166-167.

15. John G. Morris to Spencer F. Baird, 19 July 1850, Spencer F. Baird Incoming Correspondence.

16. John G. Morris, "American Zoology No 1: Entomology," *The Literary Record and Journal of the Linnaean Association of Pennsylvania College*, 1 (August 1845): 201-203.

17. American Association for the Advancement of Science, *Proceedings of the American Association for the Advancement of Science, August 1859* (Cambridge, MA: Joseph Lovering, 1860), 355; John G. Morris to Spencer F. Baird, 20 October and 27 October 1859, Records of the Assistant Secretary (RU52), Incoming Correspondence, 1850-1877, Vol. 17, 486-487, Archives of the Smithsonian Institution, Washington, DC

18. John G. Morris, "Catalogue of the Described Lepidoptera of North America," Smithsonian Miscellaneous Collections, Vol. 3, 2 (Washington, DC: Smithsonian Institution, 1860), iii.

19. John G. Morris to Spencer F. Baird, 2 March 1859, Records of the Assistant Secretary (RU52), Incoming Correspondence, Vol. 17, 483.

20. John G. Morris to Spencer F. Baird, 16 June 1859, Ibid., 484.

21. Morris, *Catalogue of the Described Lepidoptera*, iii-iv.

22. "Entomological Reminiscences of William H. Edwards," *Journal of the New York Entomological Society* LIX (June 1951): 135-136.

23. Herbert Osborn, *Fragments of Entomological History, Including Some Personal Recollections of Men and Events* (Columbus OH: privately published, 1937), 167-168.

24. Mallis, *American Entomologists*, 304-308.

25. Morris, *Life Reminiscences*, 321-322.

26. Ray Allen Billington, comp., *Alan Nevins on History* (New York: Charles Scribner's Sons, 1975), 308-309.

27. From his first years in Baltimore, Morris publicly sided with those Protestants who were fearful of Roman Catholicism. In *Life Reminiscences* (129), Morris stated, "I have so acquired the habit that I seldom let pass an opportunity of giving Romanism a hit, but it is done mildly and kindly." He rejected all violent protests against the Roman Church typical of the period. Many years after his trip to Europe in 1846, Morris recounted a night he spent at a Roman Catholic monastery in the Swiss Alps. He talked far into the night with an old monk about the history and theology of the Roman Church. Morris expressed his basic attitude toward Roman Catholics when he wrote "yet this old man was a simple, inoffensive and religious man as far as his corrupt theology would allow him to be." In fact, the next day, Morris accepted the old man's blessing and attended mass! ("A Night with the Monks on the Alps," *Lutheran Observer*, 10 July 1885). Though he rejected Roman Catholicism as such, Morris was not a mindless bigot.

28. John G. Morris, *To Rome and Back Again; or the Two Proselytes* (Baltimore: T. Newton Kurtz, 1856), 12, 18, 24, 32.

29. Morris, *The Life of John Arndt*, vii.

30. John G. Morris, *Catherine De Bora; or Social and Domestic Scenes in the Home of Luther* (Philadelphia: Lindsay and Blackiston, 1858), 122; Morris, *Life of John Arndt*, 109.

31. Morris, *Catherine De Bora*, 9-10, 13, 15, 27, 31-32, 34.

32. Ibid., 11.

33. John G. Morris, *Martin Behaim, the German Astronomer*, Pre-Fund Publications of the Maryland Historical Society, Vol. 2 (Baltimore: The Maryland Historical Society, 1855), 39-40.

34. Brugger, *Maryland: A Middle Temperament*, 233-234.

35. Leslie W. Dunlap, *American Historical Societies, 1790-1860* (Madison, WI: Cantwell Publishing Co., 1944), 163-164.

36. Maryland Historical Society, Minutes of Society Meetings, Meeting of 7 May 1857.

37. John G. Morris, "The Maryland Academy of Science and Literature," *Maryland Historical Magazine* 2 (1907): 263.

Chapter 8: Building Temples of Culture

1. John G. Morris to Charles Philip Krauth, 20 November [1849], Papers of John G. Morris.

2. "Church Intelligence," *The Missionary* 4 (April 1851): 28.

3. Baltimore County Circuit Court, Land Records, 11 February 1852, Vol. 1, 183; 3 April 1854, 15 September 1854, Vol. 9, 264-268.

4. John G. Morris and Benjamin Kurtz, *Lutherville and Lutherville Female College* (Baltimore: John W. Woods, 1852), 3.

5. 28 April 1853, Diary of Georgianna Morris, Papers of Helen Berry.

6. Pamphlet--*Lutherville Historical Tour No. 447, 5 October 1973, The Orchard* 4 (November 1959), Archives of the Baltimore County Historical Society, Cockeysville, Maryland.

7. Morris and Kurtz, *Lutherville and Lutherville Female College*, 4-8.

8. "Lutherville School 75 Years Old," *Baltimore Sun*, 10 June 1928.

9. "The Early History of Maryland College," *The Maryland Collegian*, 34 (February 1917): 1.

10. Mary Hay Morris, "Reminiscences by an Old Pupil," *The Maryland Collegian*, ibid.: 4-5.

11. Neal A. Brooks and Eric G. Rockel, *A History of Baltimore County* (Towson, Maryland: Friends of the Towson Library, Inc., 1979), 286-287.

12. Thomas L. Hollowak, *A History of the Maryland Historical Society Library, 1844-1975* (Baltimore: Maryland Historical Society, 1982), 4-6.

13. The *Biographical Cyclopedia of Representative Men of Maryland and the District of Columbia* (Baltimore: National Biographical Publishing Co., 1879), 685-686.

14. Franklin Parker, *George Peabody: A Biography* (Nashville: Vanderbilt University Press, 1971), 88-90; Elisabeth Schaaf, comp., *Guide to the Archives: The Peabody Institute of the City of Baltimore, 1857-1977* (Baltimore: The Peabody Institute, 1987), 59.

15. Parker, *George Peabody*, 89-90.

16. Maryland Historical Society, Minutes of Society Meetings, Meetings of 5 March 1857 and 2 April 1857.

17. Ibid., Meeting of 26 January 1860.

18. Franklin Parker, "An Abstract of George Peabody, Founder of Modern Philanthropy" (Ph.D. dissertation, The George Peabody College for Teachers, 1956), 441-451.

19. John G. Morris to William E. Mayhew, 2 December 1859, Record Group II, Board of Trustees of the Peabody Institute, Letters Received, The Archives of the Peabody Institute of The Johns Hopkins University, Baltimore, Maryland.

20. Diary of Georgianna Morris, 26 April 1854, Papers of Helen Berry.

21. John G. Morris to Spencer F. Baird, 9 November 1846, Spencer F. Baird Incoming Correspondence.

22. John G. Morris, *Family Register,* Papers of Helen Berry.

23. Diary of Georgianna Morris, 20 January 1855, Papers of Helen Berry.

24. 12 February 1855, Ibid.

25. 27 November 1856, Ibid.

26. Glatfelter, *A Salutary Influence*, 212.

27. Diary of Georgianna Morris, 12, 13 August 1856, Papers of Helen Berry.

28. Rose Barquist, Mary Frear Keeler, and Ann Lebheiz, eds., The *Diaries of Margaret Scholl Hood, 1851-1861* (Camden ME: Picton Press, 1992), 7, 9, 131.

29. 2 January 1857, Diary of Georgianna Morris, Papers of Helen Berry.

30. 23 August 1853, Ibid.

31. Charles R. Schultz, "The Last Great Conclave of the Whigs," *Maryland Historical Magazine*, 63 (December 1968): 393.

32. 9 October 1856, Diary of Georgianna Morris, Papers of Helen Berry.

33. Robert I. Cottom, Jr., and May Ellen Hayward, *Maryland in the Civil War: A House Divided* (Baltimore: The Maryland Historical Society, 1994), 12.

Chapter 9: Peabody Interlude

1. Minutes of the Board of Trustees, 1857-1976, 13 February 1860, 5 April 1860, 13 April 1860, Record Group II, Board of Trustees of the Peabody Institute.

2. Ibid., Meetings of 30 April 1860 and 2 June 1860.

3. Ibid., Meeting of 7 June 1860; Morris, *Life Reminiscences*, 181.

4. Morris, *Life Reminiscences*, 176-177.

5. Ibid.

6. Ibid.

7. 8 June 1860, Diary of Georgianna Morris, Papers of Helen Berry.

8. Morris, *Life Reminiscences*, 177.

9. Schaaf, comp., *Guide to the Archives: The Peabody Institute of the City of Baltimore, 1857-1977,* 15, 59.

10. Peabody Institute, Annual Report of the Librarian, 1 August 1861, Record Group VI, Peabody Library; Morris, *Life Reminiscences*, 182.

11. Peabody Institute, "Report on Trip to Boston and New York," 30 April 1862, Library Committee, Record Group II, Board of Trustees of the Peabody Institute; Annual Report of the Librarian, 17 February 1868, Record Group VI, Peabody Library.

12. Peabody Institute, "Report on Trip to Boston and New York," 30 April 1862, Library Committee, Record Group II, Board of Trustees of the Peabody Institute.

13. John G. Morris to Philip Reese Uhler, n.d., Morris/ Uhler Correspondence, 1862-1865, Record Group III, Office of the Provost, Archives of the Peabody Institute.

14. Peabody Institute, "Rules and Regulations for the Government of the Library," 12 February 1862, Record Group VI, Peabody Library.

15. John G. Morris to Charles J. M. Eaton, 6 May 1863, Library Committee, Record Group II, Board of Trustees of the Peabody Institute; Morris to Uhler, September 1864, Morris/ Uhler Correspondence, Record Group III, Office of the Provost, Archives of the Peabody Institute.

16. Peabody Institute, "Report on Binding," 8 April 1863, Record Group VI, Peabody Library.

17. Morris to Uhler, September 1864, 4-6 June [1866?], Morris/Uhler Correspondence, Record Group III, Office of the Provost, Archives of the Peabody Institute.

18. Morris to Uhler, 25 November [1866?], Morris/Uhler Correspondence, Record Group III, Office of the Provost, Archives of the Peabody Institute.

19. Morris to Uhler, 24 December [1866?], Morris/Uhler Correspondence, Record Group III, Office of the Provost, Archives of the Peabody Institute.

20. Parker, *George Peabody: A Biography*, 157

21. Maryland Historical Society, Minutes of Society Meetings, Meeting of 1 March 1866.

22. Morris to Uhler, n.d., Morris/Uhler Correspondence, Record Group III, Office of the Provost, Archives of the Peabody Institute.

23. *The Maryland Historical Society and the Peabody Institute Trustees: A Report from a Special Committee of the Maryland Historical Society, 5 March 1866* (Baltimore: John Murphy and Co., 1866), 4-15.

24. Parker, "An Abstract of George Peabody, Founder of Modern Philanthropy," 654-655.

25. Morris, *Life Reminiscences*, 184-186.

Chapter 10: Standing by Conviction

1. Wentz, *History of the Maryland Synod*, 124-125; Memorial to Mayor and City Council of Baltimore, 7 February 1850, City Council Records, Record Group 16, Series 1, Item 457, Baltimore City Archives, Baltimore, MD.

2. Brugger, *Maryland: A Middle Temperament*, 268-270; Greene, *An Illustrated History: Baltimore*, 116.

3. 7 November 1860, Diary of Georgianna Morris, Papers of Helen Berry.

4. Morris, *Life Reminiscences*, 326.

5. John G. Morris to John Pendleton Kennedy, November 1861, Vol. 10, 9, Letters Received, Papers of John Pendleton Kennedy, Archives of the Peabody Institute.

6. Morris, *Life Reminiscences*, 325-326.

7. Ibid., 327-328.

Notes

8. Ibid., 329-330.

9. Ibid., 330-332.

10. Morris, Register *of the First English Lutheran Church,* 8-9.

11. Evangelical Lutheran Synod of Maryland, *Proceedings of the Forty-Second Annual Session* (Gettysburg PA: H. C. Neinstedt, 1860), 11.

12. Ibid., *Proceedings of the Forty-Third Annual Session* (Gettysburg PA: H. C. Neinstedt, 1861), 10.

13. Abdel Ross Wentz, A *Basic History of Lutheranism in America,* rev. ed. (Philadelphia: Fortress Press, 1955), 146.

14. Suelflow and Nelson, "Following the Frontier, 1840-1875," in *The Lutherans in North America,* 242-243.

15. General Synod of the Evangelical Lutheran Church in the United States, *Proceedings of the Twentieth Convention* (Gettysburg PA: H. C. Neinstedt, 1862), 30.

16. Ibid.

17. Suelflow and Nelson, "Following the Frontier, 1840-1875," in *The Lutherans in North America,* 231.

18. Ibid.

19. General Synod of the Evangelical Lutheran Church in the United States, *Proceedings of the Twenty-First Convention* (Gettysburg PA: H. C. Neinstedt, 1864), 19.

20. Suelflow and Nelson, "Following the Frontier, 1840-1875," in *The Lutherans in North America,* 232.

21. Ibid.,232-235.

22. General Synod of the Evangelical Lutheran Church in the United States, *Proceedings of the Twenty-Third Convention* (Philadelphia: Jas. B. Rodgers, Printer, 1868), 46.

23. John G. Morris to Henry Louis Baugher, ca. 1860-1862, Papers of John G. Morris.

24. Wentz, H*istory of the Gettysburg Theological Seminary,* 185-186.

25. Benjamin Keller to John G. Morris, 23 September 1863, Special Collections—Manuscripts, Gettysburg College.

26. John G. Morris, "Synopsis of the Described Lepidoptera of North America, Part 1: Diurnal and Crepuscular Lepidoptera," *Smithsonian Miscellaneous Collections,* Vol. IV (Washington, DC: The Smithsonian Institution, 1862), iii-iv.

27. Maryland Historical Society, Minutes of Society Meetings, Meeting of 5 December 1861.

28. Ibid., Meeting of 3 November 1864.

29. Ibid., Meeting of 1 December 1864.

30. Ibid., Meeting of 3 November 1864.

31. John G. Morris, "The Literature of the Lutheran Church in the United States," *The Quarterly Evangelical Review,* LIX (July 1864): 416-417.

32. John G. Morris to Joseph Henry, 27 March 1867, Records of the Secretary (RU 26), Incoming Correspondence, 1863-1869, MCA-OW, Archives of the Smithsonian Institution, Washington, DC

33. "Monument Street Church, Baltimore," *Lutheran Observer,* 9 August 1867.

34. Evangelical Lutheran Synod of Maryland, *Proceedings of the Forty-Ninth Annual Session* (Baltimore: Sherwood and Co., 1867), 25.

Notes

Chapter 11: Crusader for Unity

1. Wentz, A Basic History of Lutheranism in America, 155.
2. General Synod of the Evangelical Lutheran Church in the United States, *Proceedings of the Twenty Third Convention*, 46.
3. Ibid., *Proceedings of the Twenty Sixth Convention* (Philadelphia: Lutheran Publication House, 1873), 36.
4. Ibid., *Proceedings of the Twenty Seventh Convention* (Philadelphia: Lutheran Publication House, 1875), 29-32.
5. Ibid.
6. Joseph A. Seiss to John G. Morris, 15 June 1877, 13 August 1877, 8 September 1877, 19 September 1877, 26 October 1877, Papers of John G. Morris.
7. John G. Morris, "Diet Scrapbook," Papers of John G. Morris.
8. Ibid.
9. Augustus Charles Wedekind to John G. Morris, 4 September 1877, Papers of John G. Morris.
10. Joseph A. Seiss to John G. Morris, 15 June 1877, Ibid.
11. F. W. Conrad to John G. Morris, 4 September 1877, Ibid.
12. "The Diet," *Our Church Paper*, 10 January 1878; "The Diet," *Our Church Paper*, 15 August 1878.
13. "The General Synod," *Lutheran Observer*, 5 June 1885.
14. John G. Morris, "The Church," *The Quarterly Review of the Evangelical Lutheran Church*, 3 (October 1872): 481-494.
15. John G. Morris, "The Augsburg Confession and the Thirty-Nine Articles of the Anglican Church," *The Quarterly Review of the Evangelical Lutheran Church*, 8 (January 1878): 79-92.
16. John G. Morris, "The Lutheran Doctrine of the Real Presence of the Body and Blood of Christ in the Lord's Supper," *The Quarterly Review of the Evangelical Lutheran Church*, 13 (April 1883): 249-271.
17. Henry Ware and C. A. Buckheim, ed., *First Principles of the Reformation or the Ninety-Five Theses and the Three Primary Works of Dr. Martin Luther*, John G. Morris, trans. (Philadelphia: Lutheran Publication Society, 1885), 1-4.
18. Charles A. Hay, "The Lutheran Historical Society," *The Lutheran Quarterly*, 18 (April 1888): 183-184.
19. John G. Morris, "Address Before the Historical Society of the Lutheran Church at the Springfield Meeting, May 1883," Records and Correspondence of the Lutheran Historical Society, Lutheran Theological Seminary, Gettysburg, Pennsylvania.
20. John G. Morris, *Bibliotheca Lutherana: A Complete List of the Publications of All Lutheran Ministers in the United States* (Philadelphia: Lutheran Board of Publications, 1876), 5-6.
21. John G. Morris, "Letter from Gettysburg," *Lutheran Observer*, 9 April 1886.
22. General Synod of the Evangelical Lutheran Church in the United States, *Proceedings of the Thirty Seventh Convention* (Philadelphia: Lutheran Publication Society, 1895), 203.
23. Ibid., *Proceedings of the Thirty Second Convention* (Philadelphia: Lutheran Publication Society, 1885), 168.

24. Wentz, *History of the Maryland Synod*, 165-168.

25. "Selinsgrove and Gettysburg," *Lutheran Observer*, 25 October 1867.

26. Morris, *Life Reminiscences*, 178.

27. Ibid.

28. Ibid.

29. Ibid .

30. Ibid .

31. St. Paul's Evangelical Lutheran Church: 1853-1953 (Lutherville, MD: Published by the Church, September 1953), 1.

32. Morris, *Life Reminiscences*, 180.

Chapter 12: Mature Scholar

1. John G. Morris, "The Translated Portions of Luther's Writings," The *Quarterly Review of the Evangelical Lutheran Church*, 12 (April 1882): 195-196.

2. J. G. Butler, ed., *The Luther Statue at the National Capital: History—Unveiling—Addresses* (Washington, DC: R. Beresford, 1886), 30-42.

3. Ibid.

4. Ibid.

5. John G. Morris, *Luther at the Wartburg: A Reformation Story of 1521* (Philadelphia: Lutheran Publication Society, 1882), 13-14.

6. Butler, *The Luther Statue*, 32.

7. John G. Morris, "The Asperity of Luther's Language," *The Lutheran Quarterly*, 11 (January 1881): 1-13.

8. Ibid.

9. Morris, *Luther at the Wartburg*, 57.

10. John G. Morris, "The Young and German Luther," *The Lutheran Quarterly*, 12 (January 1882): 7-12.

11. John G. Morris, *The Lords Baltimore*, Fund Publication no. 8 (Baltimore: John Murphy and Company, 1874), 5-6.

12. Ibid., 19.

13. Ibid., 46, 50, 54, 61.

14. Morris, *Life Reminiscences*, 169-172.

15. *Annual Report of the Officers and Committees of the Maryland Historical Society for 1884-1885* (Baltimore: John Murphy and Company, 1885), 8-10.

16. Maryland Historical Society, Minutes of Society Meetings, Meeting of 2 June 1870.

17. Ibid., Meetings of 10 February 1873, 12 May 1873.

18. *First Annual Report of the Secretary of the Society for the History of the Germans in Maryland* (Baltimore: Isaac Friedenwald, Printer, 1887), 15.

19. Ibid., 16-17.

20. *The Second Annual Report of the Secretary of the Society for the History of the Germans in Maryland* (Baltimore: Theo. Kroh and Sons, Printers, 1888), 9.

21. The *Third Annual Report of the Secretary of the Society for the History of the Germans in Maryland* (Baltimore: Theo. Kroh and Sons, Printers, 1889), 17-20.

22. Morris, *Life Reminiscences*, 88.

23. Morris, *Family Register*, Papers of Helen Berry.

24. Diary of Charles A. Hay, 10 May 1874, 17 July 1875.

25. Louise Morris Leisenring Reese, "Dr. J. G. Morris, Founder of the Maryland College," *Maryland Collegian*, February 1917, Papers of Helen Berry.

26. Morris, *Life Reminiscences*, 189-190.

27. John G. Morris, Circular on Lutherville Female Seminary, n.d., Papers of John G. Morris.

28. S. E. Furst, "Lutheran School for Lutheran Daughters," *Lutheran Observer*, 15 February 1884; J. H. Turner, "Lutherville Female Seminary," *Lutheran Observer*, 14 March 1884; J. H. Turner, "Baltimore, Easter, Lutherville," *Lutheran Observer*, 25 April 1884.

29. "Our Female Seminaries," *Lutheran Observer*, 18 April 1884; "Our Institutions: Their Future--Lutherville, etc.," *Lutheran Observer*, 9 May 1884.

30. Joel D. Swartz, "The New Lutherville, Its Specific Objects Considered," *Lutheran Observer*, 16 May 1884.

31. Mortgage Agreement, 7 April 1886, Mortgage Records of the Clerk of the Circuit Court, Baltimore County, Maryland, Vol. 119, Folio 526.

32. *31st Annual Report of the Managers of the House of Refuge* (Baltimore: Dowling and Co., 1882), 9-10.

Chapter 13: Finale

1. John G. Morris, "How Should A Pastor Know when His Usefulness Has Ended?," *Lutheran Observer*, 2 August 1895.

2. Ibid.

3. John G. Morris, "Should They Publish It?," *Lutheran Observer*, 17 July 1891.

4. John G. Morris, "Historical Society," *Lutheran Observer*, 21 June 1895.

5. Ibid.

6. John G. Morris, B. Sadtler, Wm. Dallman, "The Academy of Church History," *Lutheran Observer*, 5 April 1895; A. L. Graebner, "The Historical Academy," *Lutheran Observer*, 26 April 1895.

7. Peter Anstadt, "The Genuine Luther Relic," *Lutheran Observer*, 1 March 1895; Anstadt, "Dr. S. S. Schmucker as a Moralist," *Lutheran Observer*, 5 April 1895.

8. *The Eighth, Ninth, and Tenth Annual Reports of the Secretary of the Society for the History of the Germans in Maryland* (Baltimore: C. W. Schneidereith and Sons, 1894-1896), 3-4.

9. The *Fifth, Seventh, Eighth, Ninth and Tenth Annual Reports of the Secretary of the Society for the History of the Germans in Maryland* (Baltimore: C. W. Schneidereith and Sons, 1891, 1893, 1896), 4, 3-4, 11-19.

10. John G. Morris to John Gatchell, June 1893, Library Correspondence (MS 2008), Maryland Historical Society.

11. "Estate of Rev. Dr. Morris," *Gettysburg Star and Sentinel*, 29 October 189?; Last Will and Testament of John G. Morris, Papers of Helen Berry.

12. Morris, *Life Reminiscences*, 369; Maryland Historical Society, Minutes of Society Meetings, 11 November 1895.

Bibliographic Essay

The biographer of John Gottlieb Morris is blessed by the fact that much of Morris's personal correspondence and professional writings has survived. The richest sources of Morris material are in Gettysburg, Pennsylvania, at the Lutheran Theological Seminary and at Gettysburg College.

The Abdel Ross Wentz Library at the seminary has the largest collection of Morris correspondence: approximately a hundred letters dating from the 1830s to the 1880s that primarily document his activities as a Lutheran church leader and educator. These letters reveal Morris's perspective on the issues and personalities of his day. A partial manuscript diary composed by Morris is maintained in the Special Collections Department of Musselman Library at Gettysburg College. Its entries cover the late 1820s, the 1830s, and the 1880s. Of particular interest are the struggles Morris experienced as a new pastor and parent. The fate of the rest of the diary, which Morris referred to as the source for his *Life Reminiscences of an Old Lutheran Minister*, is unknown.

Another important source shedding light on Morris's career, personality, and family is the diary kept by his daughter Georgianna between 1853 and 1863. This diary is in the private collection of a Morris descendant, Helen Berry of Lutherville, Maryland. Among the other significant papers in the Berry collection are excerpts from the Morris family register of births and deaths and information concerning Dr. John Morris, the father of John Gottlieb.

Morris's correspondence documenting his scientific work is at the Smithsonian Institution and in the Special Collections Department of the Museum of Comparative Zoology Library at Harvard University. These collections of correspondence by no means equal the known output of the prolific Morris. It is hoped that over time other letters will be located.

Insights into Morris's career are found in the records of the major institutions with which he became involved. In Sources Consulted, following, I have identified specific series of records among the Maryland Historical Society, the Peabody Institute of The Johns Hopkins University, and the Lutheran Historical Society.

These archival materials, supplemented by the published proceedings of Lutheran church organizations (the Maryland Synod and the General Synod), document Morris's sustained contributions as a religious and cultural leader.

The extensive published writings of John Gottlieb Morris are key supplements to the manuscript and archival sources. The articles and books listed in Sources Consulted reveal Morris's views, often evolving over time, on religion, science, and history. Overall, the essential book is Morris's memoir *Life Reminiscences of an Old Lutheran Minister* (1896). Usually correct factually, this autobiography shows the different sides of Morris's personality and the passion, will, and intelligence he brought to his life's work. Another noteworthy source is the *Lutheran Observer*, which regularly published Morris's contributions from 1832 to 1895. There is one problem with the *Observer*—the lack of an index!

Several works proved especially useful in understanding the context of Morris's era and his wide-ranging intellectual activities. For deciphering the complicated nineteenth-century history of the Lutheran Church, E. Clifford Nelson's *The Lutherans in North America* is invaluable. Related useful works are Charles Glatfelter's 1987 history of Gettysburg College, *A Salutary Influence*, and Abdel Ross Wentz's centennial *History of the Gettysburg Theological Seminary*. Robert J. Brugger's *Maryland: A Middle Temperament* provides the background for understanding the state where Morris lived and worked for most of his adult life. The series of essays edited by David C. Lindberg and Ronald L. Numbers on *God and Nature* develops the theme of the nineteenth-century encounter between Christianity and science, a topic that strongly engaged Morris. Useful for understanding the historiography of Morris's era is David Levin's *History as Romantic Art*.

Sources Consulted

Primary Sources
Unpublished Records and Manuscripts

Baltimore, Maryland.
    Baltimore Archives.
    Records of the City Council.
    Maryland Historical Society. Library Correspondence (MS2008).
    _____. Minutes of Society Meetings, 1851-1895 (MS2008).
    Peabody Institute of the Johns Hopkins University. Record Group II. Records of
        the Board of Trustees. General Records, 1857-1967. Letterbooks, 1857-1905.
    _____. Records of the Library Committee, 1857-1936, 1966.
    _____. Minutes of Meetings, 1857-1976.
    _____. Record Group III. Office of the Provost, 1866-1911. Morris/Uhler
    Correspondence.
    _____. Record Group VI. Records of the Peabody Library, 1860-1966.
    _____. Papers of John Pendleton Kennedy.

Baltimore County, Maryland. (Towson) Clerk of the Circuit Court.
    Land Records.
    Baltimore County Historical Society. Louise Morris Leisenring Reese, "Memories
        of Oak Grove."

Cambridge, Massachusetts. Harvard University. Museum of Comparative Zoology
    Library.
    Special Collections-Catalogued Manuscripts and Publications. Correspondence of
        John G. Morris.

Gettysburg, Pennsylvania.
    Adams County Historical Society. Manuscript diary of Charles A. Hay,
        1859-1889.
    Gettysburg College Musselman Library. Special Collections—General Manu-
        scripts. Includes partially complete manuscript diary of John G. Morris.
    _____. Records of the Board of Trustees of Pennsylvania College. Correspondence
        to 1839.
    _____. Minutes of meetings of the Board of Trustees of Pennyslvania College.
    Lutheran Theological Seminary. A. R. Wentz Library. Papers of John G. Morris.
    _____. Papers of Samuel Simon Schmucker.
    _____. Records of the Alumni Association of the Seminary. Minutes of Meet-
        ings, 1841-1881.

_____. Records of the Board of Trustees of the Seminary. Minutes of Meetings.
_____. Records of the Lutheran Historical Society, 1843-1952.
Lutherville, Maryland.
  Papers of Helen Berry. Includes papers of Dr. John Morris, John G. Morris, and
    Georgianna Morris.
Washington, D.C. Smithsonian Institution Archives. Records Unit 52. Records of the
    Assistant Secretary. Incoming Correspondence, 1850-1877.
    _____. Records Unit 26. Records of the Secretary. Incoming Correspondence,
    1863-1869, MCA-OW.
    _____. Spencer F. Baird Collection. Incoming Correspondence, 1845-1887.
York, Pennsylvania.
Historical Society of York County. Files 1334 and 14153.

John G. Morris: Books

Morris, John G. An Address Delivered Before the Linnaean Association of Pennsylva-
  nia College, September 14, 1847. Gettysburg: H. C. Neinstedt, 1847.
_____. Bibliotheca Lutherana: A Complete List of the Publications of All Lutheran
  Ministers in the United States. Philadelphia: Lutheran Board of Publications, 1876.
_____. "Catalogue of the Described Lepidoptera of North America." Smithsonian
  Miscellaneous Publications, Vol. 3, no. 2. Washington, D.C.: Smithsonian
  Institution, 1860.
_____. *The Catechumen's and Communicant's Companion; Designed for the Use of Young
  Persons of the Lutheran Church, Receiving Instructions Preparatory to Confirmation
  and the Lord's Supper.* Baltimore: Lucas and Deaver, 1832.
_____. *Catherine De Bora*; or Social and Domestic Scenes in the Home of Luther.
  Philadelphia: Lindsay and Blackiston, 1858.
_____. *Fifty Years in the Lutheran Ministry.* Baltimore: James Young, 1878.
_____. "German Literature." *The Baltimore Book.* Edited by W. H. Carpenter and
  T. S. Arthur. Baltimore: Bayly and Burns, 1838.
_____. *The Life of John Arndt, Author of "True Christianity."* Baltimore: T. Newton
  Kurtz, 1853.
_____. *Life Reminiscences of an Old Lutheran Minister.* Philadelphia: Lutheran
  Publication Society, 1896.
_____. *The Lords Baltimore.* Fund Publication no. 8 of the Maryland Historical
  Society. Baltimore: John Murphy and Company, 1874.
_____. *Luther at the Wartburg: A Reformation Story of 1521.* Philadelphia: Lutheran
  Publication Society, 1882.
_____ and Benjamin Kurtz. *Lutherville and the Lutherville Female College.* Baltimore:
  John W. Woods, 1852.
_____. *Martin Behaim, the German Astronomer.* Pre-Fund Publications of the Maryland
  Historical Society, Vol. 2. Baltimore: The Maryland Historical Society, 1855.
_____. "Natural History as Applied to Farming and Gardening." Tenth Annual
  Report of the Board of Regents of the Smithsonian Institution. Washington, D.C.:
  A. O. P. Nicholson, 1846.

_____. "Necessities and Blessings of the Reformation." *The Year-Book of the Reformation*. Edited by Benjamin Kurtz and John G. Morris. Baltimore: Publication Rooms, 1844.
_____. *Register of the First English Lutheran Church From February 1857 to March 1859*. Baltimore: Frederick A. Hanzsche, 1859.
_____. *To Rome and Back Again; or the Two Proselytes*. Baltimore: T. Newton Kurtz, 1856.

John G. Morris: Articles and Periodicals

_____. "American Zoology No. 1: Entomology." *The Literary Record and Journal of the Linnaean Association of Pennsylvania College*, 1 (August 1845): 201-203.
_____. "The Asperity of Luther's Language.: *The Lutheran Quarterly*, 11 (January 1881): 1-13.
_____. "The Augsburg Confession and the Thirty-Nine Articles of the Anglican Church." *The Quarterly Review of the Evangelical Lutheran Church*, 8 (January 1878): 79-92.
_____. B. Sadtler, Wm. Dallman. "The Academy of Church History." *Lutheran Observer*, 5 (April 1895).
_____. "Biographical Sketch of Dr. John Morris, Surgeon of Armand's First Partisan Legion." *The Pennsylvania Magazine of History and Biography*, XVII (1883): 200-203.
_____. "Cabinet of the Linnaean Association." The Literary Record and Journal of the Linnaean Association of Pennsylvania College, 1 (March 1845): 102-103.
_____. "The Church." *The Quarterly Review of the Evangelical Lutheran Church*, 3 (October 1872): 481-494.
_____. "Collections of Natural History in Colleges." *The Literary Record and Journal of the Linnaean Association of Pennsylvania College*, 1 (November 1844): 3-52.
_____. "Geology and Revelation." *American Museum of Literature and the Arts*, 1 (November 1838): 277-283.
_____. "Historical Society." *Lutheran Observer*, 21 June 1895.
_____. "How Should A Pastor Know When His Usefulness Has Ended?" *Lutheran Observer*, 2 August 1895.
_____. "Letter From Gettysburg." *Lutheran Observer*, 9 April 1886.
_____. "The Lutheran Doctrine of the Real Presence of the Body and Blood of Christ in the Lord's Supper." *The Quarterly Review of the Evangelical Lutheran Church*, 13 (April 1883): 249-271.
_____. "Luther's Larger and Smaller Catechisms." *The Evangelical Review*, 1 (July 1849): 62-81.
_____. "The Maryland Academy of Science and Literature." *Maryland Historical Magazine*, 2 (1907): 263.
_____. "Paul Gerhard." *The Evangelical Review*, 6 (October 1850): 281-291.
_____. "Regeneration." *Lutheran Observer*, 2 April 1832.
_____. "Should They Publish It?" *Lutheran Observer*, 17 July 1891.
_____. "To Our Readers." *Lutheran Observer*, 31 August 1831.
_____. "The Translated Portions of Luther's Writings." *The Quarterly Review of the Evangelical Lutheran Church*, 12 (April 1882): 195-196.
_____. "The Young and German Luther." *The Lutheran Quarterly*, 12 (January 1882): 7-12.

American Association for the Advancement of Science. Proceedings of the American Association for the Advancement of Science, August 1859. Cambridge, Massachusetts: Joseph Lovering, 1860.

Evangelical Lutheran Synod of Maryland. Proceedings of the Annual Session, (1827). The Evangelical Lutheran Intelligencer, (1827-1828): 215.

_____. Proceedings of the Annual Session, (1828). The Evangelical Lutheran Intelligencer, (1828-1829): 212.

_____. Proceedings of the Annual Session, (1832). Lutheran Observer, 2 (1832-1833): 74.

_____. Proceedings of the Annual Session, (1833). Baltimore: Cloud and Pauter, 1833.

_____. Proceedings of the Annual Session, (1834). Baltimore: J. H. Dieger and Son, 1834.

_____. Proceedings of the Annual Session, (1835). Baltimore: Jas. Lucas and E. K. Deaver, 1835.

_____. Proceedings of the Annual Session, (1836). Baltimore: John W. Woods, 1836.

_____. Proceedings of the Annual Session, (1837). Baltimore: John W. Woods, 1837.

_____. Proceedings of the Twentieth Annual Session. Baltimore: John Murphy, 1839.

_____. Proceedings of the Twenty-Third Annual Session. Baltimore: Publication Rooms, 1841.

_____. Proceedings of the Twenty-Fourth Annual Session. Baltimore: Publication Rooms, 1842.

_____. Proceedings of the Twenty-Fifth Annual Session. Baltimore: Publication Rooms, 1843.

_____. Proceedings of the Twenty-Seventh Annual Session. Baltimore: Publication Rooms, 1845.

_____. Proceedings of the Thirty-Seventh Annual Session. Gettysburg: H. C. Neinstedt, 1855.

_____. Proceedings of the Fortieth Annual Session. Gettysburg: H. C. Neinstedt, 1858.

_____. Proceedings of the Forty-Second Annual Session. Gettysburg: H. C. Neinstedt, 1860.

_____. Proceedings of the Forty-Third Annual Session. Gettysburg: H. C. Neinstedt, 1861.

_____. Proceedings of the Forth-Ninth Annual Session. Baltimore: Sherwood and Co., 1867.

General Synod of the Evangelical Lutheran Church in the United States. Proceedings of the Fifth Convention. Gettysburg: H. C. Neinstedt, 1829.

_____. Proceedings of the Seventh Convention. Albany: Hoffman and White, 1833.

_____. Proceedings of the Eighth Convention. Troy, New York: N. Tuttle, 1835.

_____. Proceedings of the Tenth Convention. Gettysburg: H. C. Neinstedt, 1839.

_____. Proceedings of the Eleventh Convention. Baltimore: Publication Rooms, 1841.

_____. Proceedings of the Twelfth Convention. Baltimore: Publication Rooms, 1843.

_____. Proceedings of the Thirteenth Convention. Baltimore: Publication Rooms, 1845.

_____. Proceedings of the Fifteenth Convention. Gettysburg: H. C. Neinstedt, 1850.

_____. Proceedings of the Twentieth Convention. Gettysburg: H. C. Neinstedt, 1862.

_____. Proceedings of the Twenty-First Convention. Gettysburg: H. C. Neinstedt, 1864.

_____.Proceedings of the Twenty-Third Convention. Philadelphia: Jas. B. Rodgers, Printer, 1868.

_____. Proceedings of the Twenty-Sixth Convention. Philadelphia: Lutheran Publication House, 1873.

_____. Proceedings of the Twenty-Seventh Convention. Philadelphia: Lutheran Publication House, 1875.

_____. Proceedings of the Thirty-Second Convention. Philadelphia: Lutheran Publication House, 1885.

_____. Proceedings of the Thirty-Seventh Convention. Philadelphia: Lutheran Publication House, 1895.

Maryland Historical Society. Annual Report of the Officers and Committees of the Maryland Historical Society for 1884-1885. Baltimore: John Murphy and Company, 1885.

Society for the History of the Germans in Maryland. First Annual Report of the Secretary. Baltimore: Isaac Friedenwald, Printer, 1887.

_____. Second Annual Report of the Secretary. Baltimore: Theo. Kroh and Sons, Printers, 1888.

_____. Third Annual Report of the Secretary. Baltimore: Theo. Kroh and Sons, Printers, 1889.

_____. Fifth Annual Report of the Secretary. Baltimore: C. W. Schneidereith and Sons, 1891.

_____. Seventh Annual Report of the Secretary. Baltimore: C. W. Schneidereith and Sons, 1893.

_____. Eighth, Ninth, and Tenth Annual Reports of the Secretary. Baltimore: C. W. Schneidereith and Sons, 1896.

Secondary Sources
Articles

Bost, Raymond M. "Catechism or Revival." _Lutheran Quarterly_, (Winter 1989): 413-421.

"Entomological Reminiscences of William H. Edwards" _Journal of the New York Entomological Society_, LIX (June 1951): 135-136.

Haney, John Lawton. "John George Schmucker and the Roots of His Spirituality." _Essays and Reports of the Lutheran Historical Conference_, XIV (1990): 67-95.

Hay, Charles A. "The Lutheran Historical Society." _Lutheran Quarterly_, 18 (April 1888): 183-184.

Hoffert, Sylvia D. "A Very Peculiar Sorrow: Attitudes Toward Infant Death in the Urban Northeast, 1800-1860." _American Quarterly_, 39 (Winter 1987): 601-605.

Morris, Mary Hay. "Reminiscences by an Old Pupil." _The Maryland Collegian_, 34 (February 1917): 4-5.

Nichol, Todd W. "Lutheran Revivalism: A Request for a Reappraisal." *Essays and Reports of the Lutheran Historical Conference*, XII (1986): 97-117.

Schultz, Charles R. "The Last Great Conclave of the Whigs." *Maryland Historical Magazine*, 63 (December 1968): 393.

Scott, Donald M. "The Popular Lecture and the Creation of a Public in Mid-Nineteenth Century America." *The Journal of American History*, 66 (March 1980): 791-795.

Sheets, Kevin B. "Saving History: The Maryland Historical Society and Its Founders." *Maryland Historical Magazine*, 89 (Summer 1994): 135-142.

Stange, Douglas C. "Benjamin Kurtz of the Lutheran Observer and the Slavery Crisis." *Maryland Historical Magazine*, 62 (September 1967): 287.

Vicchio, Stephen J. "Baltimore's Burial Practices." *Maryland Historical Magazine*, 81 (Summer 1986): 137-138.

Books

Ahlstrom, Sydney. *A Religious History of the American People*, Vol. 1. Garden City, New York: Image Books, 1975.

Anderson, H. George. "The Early National Period, 1790-1840." In *The Lutherans in North America*. Edited by E. Clifford Nelson. Philadelphia: Fortress Press, 1980.

Anstadt, Peter. *Life and Times of Rev. S. S. Schmucker, D.D.* York, Pennsylvania: P. A. Anstadt and Sons, 1896.

Billington, Ray Allen, comp. *Allan Nevins on History*. New York: Charles Scribner's Sons, 1975.

Brugger, Robert J. *Maryland: A Middle Temperament, 1634-1980.* Baltimore: The Johns Hopkins University Press, 1988.

Butler, J. G., ed. *The Luther Statue at the National Capital: History—Unveiling—Addresses.* Washington, D.C.: R. Beresford, 1886.

Cunz, Dieter. *The Maryland Germans.* Port Washington, New York: Kennikat Press, 1948.

Dunlop, Leslie W. *American Historical Societies, 1790-1860.* Madison, Wisconsin: Cantwell Publishing Co., 1944.

Ferm, Vergiluis A. *The Crisis in American Lutheran Theology.* New York: The Century Co., 1927.

Galtfelter, Charles H. *A Salutary Influence: Gettysburg College, 1832-1985.* Gettysburg, Pennsylvania: Gettysburg College, 1987.

Greene, Suzanne Ellery. *An Illustrated History: Baltimore.* Woodland Hills, California: Windsor Publications Inc., 1980.

Hay, Anna Margaret (Suppes). *Genealogical Sketches of the Hay, Suppes and Allied Families.* Johnstown, Pennsylvania: Wm. H. Raab and Son, 1923.

Hollowak, Thomas L. *A History of the Maryland Historical Society Library, 1844-1975.* Baltimore: Maryland Historical Society, 1982.

Horwitz, Jonathan. *A Defense of the Cosmogony of Moses.* Baltimore: Richard J. Matchett, 1838.

Hovenkamp, Herbert. *Religion in America, 1830-1860*. Harrisburg, Pennsylvania: University of Pennsylvania Press, 1978.

Kuenning, Paul P. *The Rise and Fall of American Lutheran Pietism: The Rejection of an Activist Heritage*. Macon, Georgia: Mercer University Press, 1988.

Levin, David. *History as Romantic Art: Bancroft, Prescott, Motley and Parkman*. Stanford: Stanford University Press, 1959.

Mallis, Arnold. *American Entomologists*. New Brunswick, New Jersey: Rutgers Press, 1971.

Marty, Martin E. *Righteous Empire: The Protestant Experience in America*. New York: The Dial Press, 1970.

Moore, James R. "Geologists and Interpreters of Genesis in the Nineteenth Century." In *God and Nature: Historical Essays on the Encounter Between Christianity and Science*. Edited by David C. Lindberg and Ronald L. Numbers. Berkeley and London: University of California Press, 1986.

Olson, Sherry H. *Baltimore: The Building of an American City*. Baltimore: The Johns Hopkins University Press, 1980.

Osborn, Herbert. *Fragments of Entomological History, Including Some Personal Recollections of Men and Events*. Columbus, Ohio: The Author, 1937.

Parker, Franklin. *George Peabody: A Biography*. Nashville: Vanderbilt University Press, 1971.

Schmucker, Luke. *The Schmucker Family and the Lutheran Church in America*. Published by the Author, 1937.

Spitz, Lewis W. "The Lutheran Reformation in American Historiography." In *The Maturing of American Lutheranism*. Edited by Herbert T. Neve and Benjamin A. Johnson. Minneapolis: Augsburg Press, 1968.

Sprague, William B., ed. *Annals of the American Pulpit*, Vol. IX. New York: Robert Carter and Brothers, 1869.

Suelflow, August R. and E. Clifford Nelson. "Following the Frontier." In *The Lutherans in North America* Edited by E. Clifford Nelson. Philadelphia: Fortress Press, 1980.

Walsh, Richard and William Fox, eds. *Maryland: A History*. Annapolis, Maryland: Hall of Records Commission, 1983.

Wentz, Abdel Ross. *A Basic History of Lutheranism in America*. Philadelphia: Muhlenberg Press, 1955.

_____. *History of the Gettysburg Theological Seminary of the General Synod of the Evangelical Lutheran Church in the United States and of the United Lutheran Church in America, Gettysburg, Pennsylvania, 1826-1926*. Philadelphia: The United Lutheran Publication House, 1926

_____. *History of the Evangelical Lutheran Synod of Maryland of the United Lutheran Church in America, 1820-1920*. Harrisburg, Pennsylvania: Evangelical Press, 1920.

_____. *Pioneer in Christian Unity: Samuel Simon Schmucker*. Philadelphia: Fortress Press, 1967.

Dissertations

Parker, Franklin. "An Abstract of George Peabody, Founder of Modern Philanthropy." Ph.D. dissertation, The George Peabody College for Teachers, Nashville, Tennessee, 1956.

Seilhamer, Frank H. "The New Measures Movement in the Lutheran Church in America, 1820-1860." Bachelor of Divinity Thesis, Lutheran Theological Seminary at Gettysburg, 1960.

Newspapers

Baltimore Morning Sun, 11 October 1895, "Obituary, Dr. John G. Morris."
_____. 12 October 1895, "The Late Dr. Morris."
_____. 18 October 1895, "Will of Rev. Dr. John G. Morris Filed at Towson."
Baltimore Sun, 10 June 1928, "Lutherville School 75 Years Old."
Gettysburg Star and Sentinel, 15 October 1895, "Deaths Doings."
_____. 29 October 1895, "Estate of Rev. Dr. Morris."
Lutheran Observer, 16 April 1832 "First Annual Report of the Sunday School of the English Lutheran Church."
_____. 4 March 1854, "Myrtle From our Fathers' Graves."
_____. 4 January 1856, "Inconsistency--Then and New."
_____. 25 October 1867, "Selinsgrove and Gettysburg."
_____. 15 February 1884, "Lutheran School for Lutheran Daughters."
_____. 14 March 1884, "Lutherville Female Seminary "
_____. 18 April 1884, "Our Female Seminaries."
_____. 25 April 1884, "Baltimore, Easter, Lutherville."
_____. 9 May 1884, "Our Institutions: Their Future -Lutherville."
_____. 16 May 1884, "The New Lutherville, Its Specific Objects Considered."
_____. 1 March 1895, "The Genuine Luther Relic."
_____. 5 April 1895, "Dr. S. S. Schmucker as a Moralist."
_____. 26 April 1895, "The Historical Academy."
_____. 18 October 1895, "Death of Dr. J. G. Morris."
_____. 25 October 1895, "The Rev. Dr. John G. Morris: A Tribute to His Character."
The Missionary, April 1851, "Church Intelligence."
Our Church Paper, 10 January 1878, "The Diet."
_____. 15 August 1878, "The Diet."

Index

Numbers in italics refer to the illustration sections; the first number is that of the text page preceding the section, the second is that of the page in the section

Designed by Gerard A. Valerio,
Bookmark Studio, Annapolis, Maryland

Composed in Goudy Old Style by
Sherri Armstrong, Typeline, Annapolis

Printed and bound by
Thomson-Shore, Dexter, Michigan
on Finch Opaque Vellum